The
Philosophy
of Revelation

The Philosophy of Revelation

Herman Bavinck

BAKER BOOK HOUSE
Grand Rapids, Michigan

Reprinted 1979 by
Baker Book House Company
from the edition published in 1909 by
Longmans, Green, and Co.
ISBN: 0-8010-0767-4

PHOTOLITHOPRINTED BY CUSHING - MALLOY, INC.
ANN ARBOR, MICHIGAN, UNITED STATES OF AMERICA
1979

PREFACE

THE following lectures were prepared in response to an invitation from the faculty of Princeton Theological Seminary to deliver the L. P. Stone Lectures for the academic year of 1908 and 1909. Only six of them were actually delivered, however, at Princeton. These are represented by the first seven lectures as here printed. The author desires to express his thanks to Drs. Geerhardus Vos of Princeton, Nicholas M. Steffens of Holland, Mich., and Henry E. Dosker of Louisville for kindly rendering these lectures for him into English.

Some of the lectures have been delivered also at Grand Rapids and Holland, Mich.; Chicago; Louisville; New Brunswick and Paterson, N. J.; and New York.

Drs. G. Vos and B. B. Warfield have been good enough to prepare the manuscript for the printer and to see the book through the press.

The occasionally occurring superior numerals in the text refer to notes which will be found at the end of the volume. These notes are almost entirely of a bibliographical character.

It may be proper to mention that these lectures are published in Dutch and in German simultaneously with their publication in English.

CONTENTS

CONTENTS

PHILOSOPHY OF REVELATION

I

THE IDEA OF A PHILOSOPHY OF REVELATION

THE well-known Assyrian scholar, Hugo Winckler, some years ago boldly declared that "in the whole of the historical evolution of mankind there are only two general world-views to be distinguished, — the ancient Babylonian and the modern empirico-scientific"; "the latter of which," he added, "is still only in process of development."[1] The implication was that the religion and civilization of all peoples have had their origin in the land of Sumer and Akkad, and more particularly that the Biblical religion, in its New Testament no less than in its Old Testament form, has derived its material from that source. This pan-Babylonian construction of history has, because of its syncretistic and levelling character, justly met with much serious opposition. But there is undoubtedly an element of truth in the declaration, if it may be taken in this wider sense, — that the religious supranaturalistic world-view has universally prevailed among all peoples and in all ages down to our own day, and only in the last hundred and fifty years has given way in some circles to the empirico-scientific.

Humanity as a whole has been at all times supranaturalistic to the core. Neither in thought nor in life have men been able to satisfy themselves with the things of this world; they have always assumed a heaven above

1

the earth, and behind what is visible a higher and holier
order of invisible powers and blessings. This means that
God and the world while sharply distinguished have at
the same time stood in the closest connection; religion
and civilization have not appeared as contradictory and
opposing principles, but religion has been the source of
all civilization, the basis of all orderly life in the family,
the state, and society. Nor has this religious view of the
world been confined to the East, so that it might properly
be designated the oriental or old-oriental conception. We
find it in all lands and among all nations. Moreover, men
have not felt it a yoke or a burden pressing heavily
upon them; on the contrary, they have lived in the conviction that this is the normal state of things, that which
should be and could not be otherwise. Of a conflict between religion and civilization, generally speaking, no
trace can be discovered. The ancient view of the world
was thoroughly religious, and in consequence of this bore
a unified, harmonious character, so as to impart to the
whole of earthly life a higher inspiration and sacredness.[2]
Christianity introduced no change in this respect.
Towards the pagan world it assumed, to be sure, a negative and hostile attitude, because it could not take over
its corrupt civilization without radical cleansing. But
this was precisely the task it set for itself, namely, to
subject and adjust the whole of earthly existence to the
kingdom of heaven. It succeeded in conquering the old
world and leavening it with its own spirit. In the Middle
Ages there remained in the practical conduct of life elements enough which came into conflict with a system of
Christianity that had been externally imposed and not
inwardly assimilated; yet even here we meet with a unified view of the world which set its stamp upon every

part of life. Whether the mediæval Christian strove to control the world or to escape it, in either case he was guided by the conviction that mind is destined to gain the victory over matter, heaven to conquer earth.

The Reformation brought a change in so far as it endeavored to transform the mechanical relation between nature and grace of Rome into a dynamical and ethical one. The image of God not being a supranatural addition but an integral part of the nature of man, grace could no longer be considered a quantitative and material possession, preserved by the church, deposited in the sacrament, and communicated through the priest. According to the Reformers grace consisted above all in the gift of forgiveness of sins, in restoration to divine favor, in God's disposition towards man, so that it cannot be won by any works, but is given by God and apprehended in childlike faith. Over against the objective materializing of the benefits of salvation, the Reformers laid the stress on the religious subject; they gave due recognition, certainly, to the freedom of man; not, of course, to the freedom of sinful, natural man, but to the freedom of the Christian man, the spiritual man, who, having been made free by Christ, strives to fulfil the demands of the law in walking after the Spirit.

Great as was the importance of this religious-ethical movement of the sixteenth century, it was after all a reformation, not a new erection from the foundation. No assault was made upon the system of the old religious world-view; it was rather reinforced than weakened. Within the Church of Rome itself the Reformation in fact contributed in no small measure towards stemming the tide of religious indifference, and setting in motion an earnest effort towards improvement in life and morals on

the basis of Rome's own principles. This positive effect
of the Reformation is persistently ignored in Romanist
and liberal circles, and the Reformation movement systematically represented as the origin and source of the
Revolution. Cousin and Guizot agree in this judgment
with De Bonald and De Maistre.[3] French Protestantism
finds it acceptable, and puts forward and praises the
" Declaration of the Rights of Man " as a blessed fruit
of the labors of Luther and Calvin. And in Germany, by
men like Paulsen and Julius Kaftan, Kant is glorified as
a second Luther, the true philosopher of Protestantism.[4]

No doubt between these two mighty movements of
modern history certain lines of resemblance may be
traced. But formal resemblance is not the same as real
likeness, analogy as identity. Between the freedom of
the Christian man, on behalf of which Luther entered the
lists, and the liberty, equality, fraternity, which the
Revolution inscribed on its banner, the difference is fundamental. Luther and Voltaire are not men of the same
spirit; Calvin and Rousseau should not be named in the
same breath ; and Kant, with his epistemological and moral
autonomy, was not the exponent of the Reformation, but
the philosopher of Rationalism. This is implicitly acknowledged by all who accord the honor of emancipating
the mind of man in the sixteenth century to Erasmus
rather than to Luther, and who rank the Renascence in
importance and value above the Reformation.[5] According to this view Erasmus and his like-minded fellow-
workers attempted a regeneration of Christianity, but
sought this not, like Luther, in a repristination of the
teaching of Paul, but in a return to the Sermon on the
Mount. He is to be thanked, then, that supranaturalism
has slowly given way to materialism, transcendence to im-

manence, Paulinism to the religion of Jesus, dogmatics to the science of religion. Luther remains the father of the old Protestantism; to Erasmus belongs the glory of having been the first exponent of modern Protestantism.

In this historical judgment there undoubtedly lies an element of truth. Erasmus and his kindred spirits, no less than the Reformers, aimed at a simpler and more interior type of religion to be attained through contact with the Person of Christ. But the fact is lost sight of that all these men, in their conception of the essence of religion, remained entangled in mediæval dualism, and were thus in no position to effect a fundamental reformation of the doctrine and worship of the Church of Rome. The whole mental attitude of humanism was such as to render it, above everything, afraid of tumult, and bent upon preserving the "amabilis ecclesiæ concordia." "Summa nostræ religionis pax est et unanimitas," said Erasmus. But altogether apart from this, humanism was and remained one of the many "Aufklärungsbewegungen" which have periodically emerged in the Roman Church, and will not fail to reappear in the future. The experience of sin and grace which came to Luther in the monastery of Erfurt fixed itself in these two conceptions; the humanists felt no need of the liberty and joy which flow from the sinner's justification in the sight of God through faith alone and without the works of the law. Humanism, therefore, was nothing more nor less than the Reformed-Catholicism of the sixteenth century; in the end it not only broke with Luther, but came to the help of Rome and the Counter-Reformation.[6]

Nevertheless, there is this much of truth in the view in question, — that Luther and Erasmus were two different men, and the old and the new Protestantism are in

principle distinct. Confirmation of this has recently come
from an unprejudiced quarter, namely, from Professor
Troeltsch, of Heidelberg, in an important study of Protestantism contributed by him to *Die Kultur der Gegenwart*.[7] He acknowledges, of course, that the ancient
world-view was modified by the Reformation, and enriched with a new conception of religion; but he none
the less maintains that its general structure was preserved intact. In their view of the world and life, sin
and grace, heaven and earth, church and state, faith and
knowledge, Luther, Zwingli, and Calvin were children of
the Middle Ages, and revealed this fact at every point of
their activity as Reformers. The supranaturalism which
finds expression in the Gospel, and more particularly in
the theology of Paul, received the fullest consent of their
hearts. They, no doubt, moderated and softened the
eschatological and mystic-ascetic elements which characterized primitive Christianity; but, in Troeltsch's view,
they utterly failed to perceive the great differences which
exist within the New Testament itself between the Synoptics and the Apostolic Epistles, between Jesus and
Paul. The Christianity of the Bible, the Christianity of
the first four centuries was, to their naïve conception, an
undifferentiated whole, a system of faith and practice
which they believed themselves to have received unmodi-
fied, and which they meant to set as the pure expression
of the Christian religion over against the caricature that
the Roman Church had later made of it.

On the other hand, Professor Troeltsch thinks that
the modern, anti-supranaturalistic type of Protestantism
gained no hearing until the eighteenth century. For this
form of Protestantism is not to be understood as a logically or historically consistent development of the prin-

ciples of the Reformation, but as the product of "a great and radical revolution." In the so-called "Enlightenment" it presented the world with a new form of culture which differed in principle from the culture-ideal of the Reformation. Consequently not the sixteenth but the eighteenth century, not the Reformation but the "Enlightenment," is the source of that world-view which, turning its back on all supranaturalism, thinks to find in this world all that science and religion, thought and life, can ask.

In point of fact, before the eighteenth century the existence of a supranatural world, and the necessity, possibility, and reality of a special revelation, had never been seriously called into question. But Deism, springing up in England, emancipated the world from God, reason from revelation, the will from grace.[8] In its first exponents, Herbert, Locke, Toland, Collins, and their fellows, as also later in Kant, Fichte, and Lessing, it is true, it did not yet deny in principle the possibility and reality of revelation. But in the first place, from a formal point of view, it subjected the authenticity of revelation, especially of " traditional revelation," in distinction from " original revelation," to the critical test of reason, as may be seen in such writers as Herbert, Hobbes, and Locke. And, secondly, with respect to the content of revelation, it laid down the canon, that since we have no power to assimilate anything else, it can comprise nothing beyond truths of reason, that is, such truths as would, no doubt, sooner or later have been discovered by reason, but have been made known earlier and more readily by revelation. This concession, however, was deprived of all real value by adding that God had commonly given the earlier revealed truth in such a symbolical form that its essential rational content was not understood until the present age of enlightenment.[9] All deistic thought tended towards making revelation superfluous, and all action of God in the world unnecessary.[10] While the fact of creation was still commonly admitted, it served with the original Deists no other purpose than with Kant, and later with Darwin, namely, to give the world an independent existence. The world had in creation been so abundantly supplied with all manners of powers and gifts that it could dispense with God altogether, and could save itself without any outside aid and with completeness.

This principle of autonomy, transplanted into France, first sought to gain supremacy for itself by way of revolution. The French Revolution of 1789 furnished the first typical example of this. This was not a revolt like that of the Netherlands against Spain, or of the Puritans against the Stuarts, or of the American Colonies against Britain, for all these upheavals left untouched the political system, the fundamental principle of government, the *droit divin* of the magistracy. The Revolution in France sprang from a definite deistical theory, and bore from the outset a doctrinaire, specifically dogmatic character. Attaching itself to the fiction of the *contrat social*, it endeavored to subvert the entire existing social order, and to replace it by a newly conceived and self-manufactured order of things. It was a violent effort to establish the principle of popular sovereignty, and was hailed everywhere, even by men like Kant and Schiller, as the dawn of popular enfranchisement.[11]

But, although this Revolution was launched under the most favorable circumstances, enjoyed the advantage of international sympathies, and found imitation on a smaller or larger scale in all countries on the continent of Europe and in South America, it nevertheless passed beyond the experimental stage in none of these movements, but in them all, sooner or later, issued in failure. So far from realizing the ideal, they overwhelmed their fanatical adherents with grievous disappointment and a deep feeling of shame.[12] In the leading thought of the world the idea of revolution gradually gave way to that of evolution. The eighteenth century principle of autonomy was not abandoned, but its application and development were sought by a different method.

It is hardly necessary to say that the term evolution has not in itself, any more than revolution, an objectionable connotation. The idea of development is not a production of modern times; it was already familiar to Greek philosophy. More particularly Aristotle raised it to the rank of the leading principle of his entire system by his significant distinction between "potentia" and "actus." The true reality he did not place with Plato outside of and behind and above phenomenal things, but conceived of it rather as their immanent essence, not, however, as from the outset fully actualized in them, but as finding gradual realization in the form of a process. According to Aristotle, therefore, becoming and change are not to be explained by mechanical impact or pressure, nor by chemical combination or separation of atoms. On the contrary, he derived his theory of becoming from the facts of organic life, seeing in it a self-actualizing of the essential being in the phenomena, of the form in the matter. The essence, the idea of a thing, is not simply a quiescent archetype, but at the same time an immanent power propelling the thing and moving it on to its development in a definite direction. Evolution, as conceived by Aristotle, bears thus an organic and teleological character; the γένεσις exists for the sake of the οὐσία; *becoming* takes place because there is *being*.[13]

This idea of development aroused no objection whatever in Christian theology and philosophy. On the contrary, it received extension and enrichment by being linked with the principle of theism. For the essence of it, it appears also in modern philosophy, in Lessing, Herder and Goethe, Schelling and Hegel, and in many historians of distinction. Some of these, it is true, have severed the idea of development from the theistic basis on which it rests in Christianity, and by so doing have reverted to the ancient pre-Christian naturalism. Nevertheless, even so, their naturalism retains a specific character, clearly enough distinguishable from the later materialism. Whatever terms Goethe and Herder, Schelling and Hegel might employ to designate the core and essence of things, they never regarded nature as a dead mechanism, but as an eternally formative power, a creative artist. The notion that all higher forms of being have sprung through the action of purely mechanical and chemical forces from lower ones is entirely foreign to them. The ascending forms in the world of nature and spirit appear to them rather evidence of the inexhaustible fulness of life and the infinite creative power present in the universe.[14] With Hegel the entire world becomes one mighty process of thought, which in each of its moments and in each of its stages is rational, so far as it is real; but which at the same time, by the principle of immanent antithesis, to which it remains subject, is forced ever forward and upward. Whatever exists is therefore pure becoming, not being; it exists for no other purpose but to pass away; in pursuance of the law of the dialectic process the old continually gives way to the new. Hence we should draw back from all violent revolutions and futile experiments; the eternal spirit itself is unceasingly occupied in breaking down while building up, and in building up while breaking down. Process, evolution, endless and restless becoming, is the principle which governs the Hegelian system to a much higher degree, and much more one-sidedly, than those of Aristotle and Leibnitz.[15]

This doctrine of evolution, however, was too rationalistic, too aprioristic, too romantic in construction to withstand the onset of the natural science which was now growing up. It soon gave way before the mechanical and anti-teleological principles of the theory of descent. Darwin was led to his agnostic naturalism as much by the misery which he observed in the world as by the facts which scientific investigation brought under his notice. There was too much strife and injustice in the world for him to believe in providence and a predetermined goal. A world so full of cruelty and pain he could not reconcile with the omniscience, the omnipotence, the goodness of God. An innocent and good man stands under a tree and is struck by lightning. "Do you believe," asks Darwin of his friend Gray, "that God slew this man on purpose? Many or most people believe this; I cannot and will not believe it." The discovery of the so-called law of "natural selection" brought him accordingly a real feeling of relief, for by it he escaped the necessity of assuming a conscious plan and purpose in creation. Whether God existed or not, in either case he was blameless. The immutable laws of nature, imperfect in all their operations, bore the blame for everything, while at the same time guaranteeing that the world is not a product of chance and is progressing as a whole towards a better condition.[16]

Just as Darwin discovered the misery in nature, so Karl Marx discovered the misery in society. In the same year in which Darwin's *Origin of Species* was published, Marx's *Political Economy* also appeared. At the grave of Marx, on the 17th of March, in the year 1883, Friedrich Engels declared that, as Darwin had found the law of the development of organic nature, so Marx had discovered that of the development of human society. Darwin believed that his natural selection, with its adjuncts, had once for all disposed of teleology, miracles, and all supranaturalism; Marx was convinced that he had freed Socialism from all utopianism and established it on a firm scientific foundation. Both Darwin and Marx were thorough believers in the inviolability of the laws of nature and the necessary sequence of events; both were deeply moved by the fact that this necessary process of development has both in the past and present brought into existence terrible conditions; and both cherished the fixed hope that development means progress, and carries with it the promise of a better world, a better race, and a better society.

It goes without saying that this mechanical and anti-teleological conception of evolution left no room for miracles, for a world of the supranatural, for the existence and activity of God. Darwin, while at first adhering to the deistic belief in creation, afterwards declined more and more to agnosticism. It was his custom to dismiss religious problems by saying that he had not sufficiently reflected upon them and could not lay claim to a strong religious feeling.[17] And Marx was of the opinion that religion, "that opiate of the people," was destined to die a natural death in the perfect society of the future.[18] The belief that modern natural science, with its doctrine of evolution, had made an end of mediæval dualism with its conception of two worlds, and the principle of naturalism had permanently triumphed, found an echo in the widest circles. Revelation could no longer be considered a possibility. Renan declared apodictically; " Il n'y a pas de surnaturel." According to Haeckel, all revelations to which religions appeal are pure figments of human phantasy; the one true revelation is nature itself. And Strauss, not quite so sure that the victory had been gained and the enemy slain, called to battle with the summons: "The last enemy to be conquered is the conception of another world." The term evolution embodies in itself a harmless conception, and the principle expressed by it is certainly operative within well-defined limits throughout the universe. But the trend of thought by which it has been monopolized, and the system. built on it, in many cases at least, avail themselves of the word in order to explain the entire world, including man and religion and morality, without the aid of any supranatural factor, purely from immanent forces, and according to unvarying laws of nature.

Nevertheless, the transition from the nineteenth to the twentieth century has witnessed an important change in this respect. The foremost investigators in the field of science have abandoned the attempt to explain all phenomena and events by mechanico-chemical causes. Everywhere there is manifesting itself an effort to take up and incorporate Darwin's scheme of a nature subject to law into an idealistic world-view. In fact Darwin himself, through his agnosticism, left room for different conceptions of the Absolute, nay repeatedly and emphatically gave voice to a conviction that the world is not the product of accident, brute force, or blind necessity, but in its entirety has been intended for progressive improvement.[19]   By way of Darwin, and enriched by a mass of valuable scientific material, the doctrine of evolution has returned to the fundamental idea of Hegel's philosophy. The mechanical conception of nature has been once more replaced by the dynamical; materialism has reverted to pantheism; evolution has become again the unfolding, the revealing of absolute spirit. And the concept of revelation has held anew its triumphant entry into the realm of philosophy and even of natural science.[20]

Such generous concessions have not failed to meet with response from the side of theology. It is true the exponents of the "new theology" which has made its appearance in recent years, differ greatly among themselves as to the significance which should be accorded in revelation to nature or history, to individualism or collectivism, to the intellect or the heart. Nevertheless, the movement as a whole is clearly inspired and controlled by the desire to identify revelation and evolution, and for this purpose to shift the centre of gravity from the transcendence of God to his immanence. To it God is " that which is implied in all being, the reality behind all phenomena, the sum of the forces of the universe."   It is admitted that this idea of the immanence of God was not unknown in former ages; but never until the present has it been made the lever of a " moral and spiritual movement," such as may now be witnessed through the whole of Christendom, a movement which aims at the perfect reconciliation of religion and science and finds its highest expression in " the gospel of the humanity of God and the divinity of man."

It needs no pointing out that on this principle, as with Hegel, the divine revelation must be co-extensive with all that exists, with nature and history, with all nations and religions. Everything is a manifestation of God. The finite in all its parts is an essential element of the infinite. It *is* the infinite itself, as become finite in the creature. But there is a definite course and gradation in the self-realizing of God. From the inorganic it ascends to the organic, from the physical to the psychical, from nature to spirit, reaching its culminating point in man. " We are a part of the universe, and the universe is a part of God ; there is no real difference between humanity and deity ; every soul is a sparkle of the divine spirit." Humanity ever increasingly reveals God to us, in the same proportion that it develops and progresses. For everything is subject to the law of progress. Everything is continually in the making. Man has sprung from the animals, and has in the civilized portion of the race risen far superior to his ancestors; but still he has before him an endless vista of development. He is not " simply what he is, but all he yet may be." He is, and becomes ever more and more, an organ of the eternal consciousness. He was an animal, he became a man, and after humanizing comes deifying. By way of anticipation the Christian religion illustrates this principle in the person of its founder; in Christ humanity and divinity are one. According to Sir Oliver Lodge, Christ is the glorification of human effort, the upward development of manhood, the highest point of human striving, the supreme flower of our race. All men are potential Christs, all moving on by the development of the forces of our own nature into that Christhood[2f].

Although the New Theology likes to represent this conception as a new movement, it is at bottom nothing but a repetition of the pantheistic world-view which has been embodied in the systems of Erigena, Spinoza, and especially Hegel. And in all probability no greater success than was attained by these philosophers will attend the present attempt to harmonize after this fashion faith and science, the revelation of the Scriptures, and a materialistically or pantheistically conceived doctrine of evolution. There is cause for rejoicing that the intellectualism of the last century has been succeeded by a feeling for religion and mysticism, for metaphysics and philosophy; and that in religion itself there is now recognized a reality and a revelation of God. But joy over this change in the attitude of the leading minds of the age should not blind us to the danger to which it exposes us. The religious craving at present asserting itself bears a pronouncedly egoistic character; it reveals a longing rather for self-satisfaction than for knowledge and service of the living God; it seeks God not above but in the world, and regards his essence as identical with that of the creature. All of which goes to show that the world-view, which formerly offered itself under the name of "the scientific," has not essentially changed, but has simply, owing to various influences, assumed now a religious form, and taken up its position as a new faith over against the old faith.[22] The difference consists merely in the doctrine of evolution no longer contenting itself with standing as "science" by the side of or over against Christianity, but pressing on determinedly to usurp the place of Christianity as dogma and religion. Monism lays claim through the mouth of Haeckel and the monistic alliance not only to the title of the true science, but likewise to that of the one true religion.[23]

As a form of religion, however, monism hardly deserves serious consideration. A religion which has nothing to offer but an immanent God, identical with the world, may for a while æsthetically affect and warm man ; it can never satisfy man's religious and ethical needs. It fails to raise us above the actual, and supplies no power stronger than the world ; it brings no peace, and offers no rest on the Father-heart of God. This, after all, is what man seeks in religion, — strength, life, a personal power, that can pardon sin, receive us into favor, and cause us to triumph joyfully over a world of sin and death. The true religion which shall satisfy our mind and heart, our conscience and our will, must be one that does not shut us up in, but lifts us up high above, the world ; in the midst of time it must impart to us eternity ; in the midst of death give us life ; in the midst of the stream of change place us on the immovable rock of salvation. This is the reason why transcendence, supranaturalism, revelation, are essential to all religion.

Thus also is explained why humanity, no less than formerly, continues to think and live after a supranaturalistic fashion. As regards the heathen and Mohammedan nations, this needs no pointing out. As to Christendom, here also the Greek Church continues to occupy the orthodox position. The Roman Church, contrary to the expectation of many, has during the nineteenth century almost everywhere increased in power and influence, and yet in the encyclical letter of July 3, 1907, it repudiated without hesitation the notion that revelation involves nothing more than man's becoming conscious of his relation to God. And while Protestantism is divided within itself even more thoroughly than Romanism, yet to a large extent, among all classes in all lands, it too still holds to the fundamental elements of the Christian confession. Thus, notwithstanding all the criticism that has been brought to bear upon the Scriptures, the Bible retains its unique place in the church, — in the sermon, in the worship, in catechetical instruction. More than this, all our modern civilization, art, science, literature, ethics, jurisprudence, society, state, politics, are leavened by religious, Christian, supranaturalistic elements, and still rest on the foundation of the old world-view. "The stamp of this education," says Troeltsch, "Europe bears deep in its soul up to to-day." [24]   Much, therefore, will have to be done before the modern, pantheistic or materialistic, world-view shall have conquered the old theistic one. Nay, in view of the past history of mankind, it may safely be added that this will never happen.

Nor is there any warrant for ascribing this loyalty to the Christian supranatural world-view, to stubborn conservatism or incorrigible lack of understanding. It requires little discernment to perceive that the revelation which every religion, and more particularly Christianity, claims for itself is something essentially different from that which the new theology and philosophy would commend to us. This was frankly acknowledged not long ago by Friedrich Delitzsch. In his first address on *Babel and Bible*, he had affirmed that the Old Testament idea of revelation, like many other Old Testament ideas, was in perfect accord with that found in the Babylonian religion. This identification having been contradicted, he reverted to the point in his fourth lecture entitled *Rückblick und Ausblick*. Here he points out that the conception of revelation is no doubt modified by many to-day so as to make of it a humanly mediated, gradual process of historical evolution. But he immediately adds that such a conception, while quite acceptable to him personally, is, after all, only a weak dilution of the Biblical and theological conception of revelation.[25]   And there can hardly be two opinions on this point.   Not only does Scripture draw a sharp distinction between that revelation which God continues to give to the heathen through nature and the false religion to which the heathen have abandoned themselves (Rom. i. 19–23), as well as between that special revelation which he has granted to his people Israel and the idolatry and image-worship by which the people of God were constantly led away; but it also most emphatically proclaims as a fundamental truth, that Jehovah, who revealed himself to Moses and the prophets, is the true living God, and that all the gods of the heathen are idols and things of naught.

If this be so, it must be contrary to the plain intent of Scripture to identify revelation and development, divine law and human conduct, or to consider these as two sides of one and the same process.   When Hegel says of the infinite and the finite: "The truth is the inseparable union of both,"[26] we recognize in this not the *primum verum* but the πρῶτον ψεῦδος of his philosophy.   As in science one must distinguish between the ideas which God has deposited in his works, and the errors which constantly are being drawn from them as truth, even so revelation and religion are not two manifestations of the same thing, but differ as God differs from man, the Creator from the creature.   Although Gwatkin some times so widens the idea as to make revelation and discovery the same process viewed from different standpoints, he quite correctly explains that not every thought of man, but only true thought, echoes God's thought, and that religions can be viewed as divine revelations only so far as they are true.[27]

This distinction between revelation and religion, and

consequently the good right of supranaturalism, begins
slowly to dawn once more on people. Titius declared
some time ago that it is the common conviction of all
theologians from Kähler to Troeltsch that supranaturalism and Christianity stand or fall together. Certainly
Troeltsch insists over against Fr. R. Lipsius upon a certain supranaturalism. Loofs maintains, no doubt, that
the supranaturalism of the sixteenth and seventeenth centuries was of too clumsy construction for the science of
nature and history seriously to reckon with it. But he
propounds at the same time the pertinent question,
whether it is really an immutable axiom of all modern
culture that natural science has made belief impossible
in any kind of revelation except one that can be fully
explained on the principle of evolution, and in any kind
of redemption except one worked out by purely immanent
forces. And returning the answer to the question himself,
he declares : " The decisive battle between the ' diesseits-
religion,' based on pantheistic ideas of immanence, and
the traditions of a more robust theism has not yet been
fought out." Titius, adverting to this, gives his opinion
to the effect that a more exact investigation of the problem
of supranaturalism forms the chief task of the Dogmatics
of the future, and is of supreme importance for the absolute character of Christianity.[28]

With the reality of revelation, therefore, Christianity
stands or falls. But our insight into the mode and
content of revelation admits of being clarified ; and, in
consequence, our conception of this act of divine grace
is capable of being modified. As a matter of fact, this
has taken place in modern theology. In the first place,
the transcendence of God has assumed for us a meaning
different from what it had for our fathers. The deistic

belief that God worked but a single moment, and thereafter granted to the world its own independent existence, can no longer be ours. Through the extraordinary advance of science our world-view has undergone a great change. The world has become immeasurably large for us; forwards and backwards, in length and breadth and depth and height, it has extended itself into immensity. In this world we find everywhere second causes operating both in organic and inorganic creation, in nature and history, in physical and psychical phenomena. If God's dwelling lies somewhere far away, outside the world, and his transcendence is to be understood in the sense that he has withdrawn from creation and now stands outside of the actuality of this world, then we lose him and are unable to maintain communication with him. His existence cannot become truly real to us unless we are permitted to conceive of him as not only above the world, but in his very self in the world, and thus as indwelling in all his works.[29]

Thus the divine transcendence was understood by the Apostle Paul, who declared that God is not far from any one of us, but that "in him we live and move and have our being." The transcendence which is inseparable from the being of God is not meant in a spacial or a quantitative sense. It is true Scripture distinguishes between heaven and earth and repeatedly affirms that God has heaven especially for his dwelling-place, and specifically reveals there his perfections in glory. But Scripture itself teaches that heaven is part of the created universe. When, therefore, God is represented as dwelling in heaven, he is not thereby placed outside but in the world, and is not removed by a spacial transcendence from his creatures. His exaltation above all that is finite, temporal, and subject to space-limitation is upheld. Although God is immanent in every part and sphere of creation with all his perfections and all his being, nevertheless, even in that most intimate union he remains transcendent. His being is of a different and higher kind than that of the world. As little as eternity and time, omnipresence and space, infinitude and finiteness can be reduced to one or conceived as reverse sides of the same reality, can God and the world, the Creator and the creature, be identified qualitatively and essentially. Not first in our time, nor by way of concession to science or philosophy, but in all ages, the great theologians have taught the transcendence of God in this Scriptural sense.

Since, however, we take this idea more seriously at present, because of the great enrichment our world-view has received from science, this needs must give rise to a somewhat modified conception of revelation. The old theology construed revelation after a quite external and mechanical fashion, and too readily identified it with Scripture. Our eyes are nowadays being more and more opened to the fact that revelation in many ways is historically and psychologically "mediated." Not only is special revelation founded on general revelation, but it has taken over numerous elements from it. The Old and the New Testaments are no longer kept isolated from their *milieu;* and the affinity between them and the religious representatations and customs of other peoples is recognized. Israel stands in connection with the Semites, the Bible with Babel. And although the revelation in Israel and in Christ loses nothing of its specific nature, nevertheless even it came into being not all at once but progressively, in conjunction with the progress of history and the individuality of the prophets, πολυμερῶς καὶ πολυτρόπως. Even as Christ the Son of God is from above, and yet his birth from Mary was in preparation for centuries, so every word of God in special revelation is both spoken from above and yet brought to us along the pathway of history. Scripture gives succinct expression to this double fact when it describes the divine word as ῥηθὲν ὑπὸ τοῦ θεοῦ διὰ τῶν προφητῶν.

One of the results of the trend of present-day science is that theology is just now largely occupied with the second of these two elements, that of the historical and psychological " mediation." Its present interest centres rather in the problem *how* revelation has come about, than in the question *what* the content of revelation is. There is connected with this investigation the disadvantage that often the woods are not seen for the trees; that the striking analogies in other religions have dulled perception of what is peculiar to the religion of Israel; and that the discovery elsewhere of some trait more or less closely parallel is hastily given out as a solution of the problem of origin. But, apart from this, these historical and psychological investigations are in themselves an excellent thing. They must and will contribute towards a better understanding of the content of revelation; the ῥηθὲν διὰ τῶν προφητῶν will, in proportion as it is more profoundly understood, lead to a truer appreciation of the ῥηθὲν ὑπὸ τοῦ θεοῦ. For, since all historical and psychological research into the origin and essence of the religion of Israel and Christianity must leave their peculiarity untouched, what else will remain, but either to reject them 'on account of their alleged foolishness or to accept them in faith as divine wisdom?

Belief in such a special revelation is the starting-point

and the foundation-stone of Christian theology. As science never precedes life, but always follows it and flows from it, so the science of the knowledge of God rests on the reality of his revelation. If God does not exist, or if he has not revealed himself, and hence is unknowable, then all religion is an illusion and all theology a phantasm. But, built on the basis of revelation, theology undertakes a glorious task, — the task of unfolding the science of the revelation of God and of our knowledge concerning him. It engages in this task when seeking to ascertain by means of exegesis the content of revelation, when endeavoring to reduce to unity of thought this ascertained content, when striving to maintain its truth whether by way of aggression or defence, or to commend it to the consciences of men. But side by side with all these branches there is room also for a *philosophy of revelation* which will trace the idea of revelation, both in its form and in its content, and correlate it with the rest of our knowledge and life.

Theological thought has always felt the need of such a science. Not only Origen and the Gnostics, but also Augustine and the Scholastics, made it their conscious aim both to maintain Christianity in its specific character and to vindicate for it a central place in the conception of the world as a whole. And after Rationalism had set historical Christianity aside as a mass of fables, the desire has reasserted itself in modern theology and philosophy to do justice to this central fact of universal history, and to trace on all sides the lines of connection established by God himself between revelation and the several spheres of the created universe.[30]

It must be acknowledged that the attempt to outline a philosophy of revelation exposes one to losing himself in idle speculation. But, besides appealing to the general principle that the abuse of a thing cannot forbid its proper use, we may remind ourselves that this danger is just now reduced to a minimum, because philosophy itself has become thoroughly convinced of the futility of its aprioristic constructions, and looks to the empirical reality for the subject matter of its thought. A philosophy which, neglecting the real world, takes its start from reason, will necessarily do violence to the reality of life and resolve nature and history into a network of abstractions. This also applies to the philosophy of the Christian religion. If this be unwilling to take revelation as it offers itself, it will detach it from history and end by retaining nothing but a dry skeleton of abstract ideas. The philosophy of Hegel has supplied a deterring example of this, as is well illustrated by the *Leben Jesu* and the *Glaubenslehre* of Strauss. Speculative rationalism, to borrow a striking word of Hamann, forgot that God is a genius who does not ask whether we find his word rational or irrational. Precisely because Christianity rests on revelation, it has a content which, while not in conflict with reason, yet greatly transcends reason; even a divine wisdom, which appears to the world foolishness. If revelation did not furnish such a content, and comprised nothing but what reason itself could sooner or later have discovered, it would not be worthy of its name. Revelation is a disclosure of the μυστήριον τοῦ θεοῦ. What neither nature nor history, neither mind nor heart, neither science nor art can teach us, it makes known to us, — the fixed, unalterable *will* of God to rescue the world and save sinners, a will at variance with well-nigh the whole appearance of things. This will is the secret of revelation. In creation God manifests the power of his mind; in revelation, which has redemption for its centre, he discloses to us the greatness of his heart.[31]

The philosophy of revelation, just like that of history, art, and the rest, must take its start from its object, from revelation. Even its idea cannot be construed apriori. There is but one alternative: either there is no revelation, and then all speculation is idle; or else there comes to us out of history such a revelation, shining by its own light; and then it tells us, not only what its content is, but also how it comes into existence. The philosophy of revelation does not so much make this fit in with its system as rather so broadens itself that it can embrace revelation too in itself. And doing this, it brings to light the divine wisdom which lies concealed in it. For though the cross of Christ is to the Jews a stumbling-block and to the Greeks foolishness, it is in itself the power of God and the wisdom of God. No philosophy of revelation, any more than any other philosophy, whether of religion or art, of morals or law, shall ever be able to exhaust its subject, or thoroughly to master its material. All knowledge here on earth remains partial; it walks by faith and attains not to sight. But nevertheless it lives and works in the assurance that the ground of all things is not blind will or incalculable accident, but mind, intelligence, wisdom.

In the next place this philosophy of revelation seeks to correlate the wisdom which it finds in revelation with that which is furnished by the world at large. In former times Christian theology drew the distinction between special and general revelation. But it never wholly thought through this distinction, nor fully made clear its rich significance for the whole of human life. When modern science arose and claimed to have found a key to the solution of all mysteries in the principle of evolution, the attempt was made to withdraw successively nature, history, man, and his entire psychical life, from the control of the existence, the inworking, the revelation of God. Not a few theologians have yielded to this trend and with more or less hesitation abandoned the entire world to modern science, provided only somewhere, in the Person of Christ, or in the inner soul of man, a place might be reserved for divine revelation. Such a retreat, however, betrays weakness and is in direct opposition to the idea of special revelation. Revelation, while having its centre in the Person of Christ, in its periphery extends to the uttermost ends of creation. It does not stand isolated in nature and history, does not resemble an island in the ocean, nor a drop of oil upon water. With the whole of nature, with the whole of history, with the whole of humanity, with the family and society, with science and art it is intimately connected.

The world itself rests on revelation; revelation is the presupposition, the foundation, the secret of all that exists in all its forms. The deeper science pushes its investigations, the more clearly will it discover that revelation underlies all created being. In every moment of time beats the pulse of eternity; every point in space is filled with the omnipresence of God; the finite is supported by the infinite, all becoming is rooted in being. Together with all created things, that special revelation which comes to us in the Person of Christ is built on these presuppositions. The foundations of creation and redemption are the same. The Logos who became flesh is the same by whom all things were made. The first-born from the dead is also the first-born of every creature. The Son, whom the Father made heir of all things, is the same by whom he also made the worlds. Notwithstanding the separation wrought by sin, there is a progressive approach of God to his creatures. The transcendence does not cease to exist, but becomes an ever deeper immanence. But as a disclosure of the greatness of God's heart, special revelation far surpasses general revelation, which makes known to us the power of his mind. General revelation leads to special, special revelation points back to general. The one calls for the other, and without it remains imperfect and unintelligible. Together they proclaim the manifold wisdom which God has displayed in creation and redemption.

It will be impossible in the following lectures to develop a system of the philosophy of revelation, both formally and materially considered. I shall have to confine myself to setting forth the principal ideas that enter into the structure of such a system.

II

REVELATION AND PHILOSOPHY

IN entering upon our task we may derive encourage-
ment from the position accorded at present to philosophical thought. There is reason for rejoicing in the
reflection that from an object of contempt it has come to
inspire the warmest interest. When in the last century
the natural sciences began their triumphal progress, and
the enthusiasm Hegel had aroused gave way to sober dis-
enchantment, people turned their backs on all metaphysics
and for a while cherished the delusion that exact science
would sometime give a satisfactory solution to all the
problems of life. This was the so-called "period of
Renan," in which physics was satisfied with itself and
professed to have no need of metaphysics.[1]

But this period now belongs to the past. Natural
science, it is true, has by no means become insolvent, as
Brunetière asserted. On the contrary, it has gone on year
after year adding one great discovery to another. But
many have been disappointed in the foolish expectations
they had cherished regarding it: the *ignoramus et ignor-
abimus* has rudely awakened them out of their dreams.
Thus toward the close of the last century a great change
gradually took place in the prevailing mental attitude.
With the return to mysticism in literature and art, the
need of philosophy and metaphysics and religion reasserted
itself. This remarkable reaction has extended into the
very camp of natural science. Not only has Ostwald

published his "Lectures on Natural Philosophy," his
"Annals of Natural Philosophy," and Reinke his "Philosophy of Botany," but natural scientists have eagerly
discussed philosophical and especially epistemological
problems — witness such names as W. K. Clifford, Poincaré, Kleinpeter, Ostwald, Verworn. Haeckel, no doubt,
professes to base his conclusions wholly on facts, but even
he, none the less, recognizes that, in order to reach a monistic world-view, thought must be called to the aid of
perception, philosophy of science, faith of knowledge.[2]

Nor is this return to philosophy and religion the result
of arbitrary caprice. It has all the characteristics of a
universal and necessary phenomenon. It is not confined
to one people or one stratum of society, but appears in
many countries and among men of all ranks. It is not
peculiar to this or that particular branch of learning, but
manifests itself in the spheres of history, jurisprudence,
and medicine, as well as in that of natural science; its
influence is no less strong in literature and art than in
religion and theology themselves. Verlaine and Maeter-
linck, Sudermann and Hauptmann, Ibsen and Tolstoi and
Nietzsche are all equally dissatisfied with present-day
culture, and all seek something different and higher. They
endeavor to penetrate beneath the appearance of things to
the essence, beneath the conscious to the unconscious,
beneath the outward forms to the inner mystery of infinite life, of silent power, of hidden will. From every
quarter comes the demand for a new dogma, a new religion,
a new faith, a new art, a new science, a new school, a new
education, a new social order, a new world, and a new God.
The things offered under this label are too varied, and
often also too silly, to enumerate. Buddhism and Mohammedanism and the religion of Wodan are commended

to us, theosophy, occultism, magic and astrology, daemon-
ism and satan-worship, race- and hero-worship, ethical
culture and the pursuit of ideals, the cult of humanity
and of Jesus.   Reform movements are the order of the
day.   Modernism is in the air everywhere.[3]

Divergent as these tendencies may be, they all have
two characteristics in common.   In the first place, the
principle of autonomy, expressing itself on the one hand in
anarchism of thought, on the other hand in the auto-
soterism of the will.[4]   Each individual regards himself as
independent and self-governing, and shapes his own course
and pursues his own way.   Having nothing to start with
except a vague sense of need, men seek satisfaction in
every possible quarter, in India and Arabia, among the
civilized and uncivilized nations, in nature and art, in
state and society.   Religion is treated as a matter of purely
personal invention and individual construction, as a mere
product and element of culture.   Everybody has his own
religion, — not merely every nation and every church,
but every person.   Thus we hear of a religion of the modern
man, a religion of the layman, a religion of the artist, a
religion of the scientist, a religion of the physician.   It
has become a vogue to study and expound the religion
of Goethe and Lessing, of Kant and Schleiermacher, of
Bismarck and Tolstoi.

But in the second place these modern movements are all
alike seeking after religion, after the supreme good, abiding happiness, true being, absolute worth.   Even though
the word " religion " be avoided and the new-fashioned
term " world-view " preferred, in point of fact the satisfaction of no other need is aimed at than that which used to
be supplied by religion.   As to the proper definition of
such a world-view, there exists considerable divergence of

opinion.   But whether with Windelband we define philosophy as the theory of "the determination of values," as the science of "normal consciousness," or conceive of it with Paulsen as a mode of viewing the world and life "which shall satisfy both the demands of reason and the needs of the heart," in any case it is plain that philosophy is not content with a scientific explanation of reality, but seeks to vindicate the higher ideals of humanity, to satisfy its deepest needs.   Philosophy wishes itself to serve as religion, and from an attitude of contempt for all theology has veered round to a profession of being itself at bottom a search after God.[5]

The agreement between these various movements of reform extends, however, still farther than this.   The ways in which satisfaction is sought for the ineradicable "metaphysical need" appear to be many and divergent. But appearances are deceitful.   Some youthful enthusiast discovers an idea, which takes him by surprise, and he forthwith claims for it the importance of a new religion, or a new philosophy.   But historical study and scientific reflection will, as a rule, convince him in short order that the thing he regarded as new was, in point of fact, quite old, having in the past repeatedly emerged and passed away.   That which has been is that which shall be, and there is no new thing under the sun.   The new fashions in theology are as much like the old Arianism and Socinianism and Gnosticism and Sabellianism as one drop of water is like another.   The new roads in philosophy have all been travelled by the thinkers of ancient Greece.   It is difficult to square this fact with the theory of evolution and its boast of the wonderful progress of our times.   But in reality the limitations of the human intellect soon become apparent, the originality of human thought is readily

exhausted. Troeltsch strikingly observes that " the number of those who have had something really new to tell
the world has always been remarkably small, and it is as-
tonishing to observe on how few ideas humanity has actually subsisted." [6] The directions in which it is possible for
our thinking to move are not nearly so numerous as we
suppose or imagine. We are all determined in our thought
and action by the peculiarity of our human nature, and
then again by each one's own past and present, his character and environment. And it is not rare that those who
seem to lead others are rather themselves led by them.[7]

If, then, we attend to details, to words and forms of expression, to outward considerations and modes of presen-
tation, we seem in the presence of a chaotic mass of
religions and world-views among which choice is difficult. But when we penetrate to the centre of things
and consider principles, all this mass reduces itself to a
few types. " The epochs of human life," as Goethe's
saying has it, " traverse in typical development a series of
world-views." [8] And as every world-view moves between
the three poles of God, the world, and man, and seeks to
determine their reciprocal relations, it follows that in
principle only three types of world-view are distinguishable,—the theistic (religious, theological), the naturalistic
(either in its pantheistic or materialistic form), and the
humanistic. These three do not succeed one another in
history as Comte imagined his *trois états* to do. They
rather recur in rhythmical waves, more or less intermingle, and subsist side by side. Thus Greek philosophy
was born out of the Orphic theology, passed over into the
naturalism of the old nature-philosophy, and became
humanistic in the Sophists and the wisdom-philosophy
of Socrates. Plato in his doctrine of ideas went back to

the old theology and to Pythagoras; but, after Aristotle, his philosophy gave way to the naturalistic systems of Epicurus and the Stoa; and these in turn, by way of reaction, gave birth to the teachings of the sceptical and mystical schools. Christianity gave theism the ascendancy for many centuries; but modern philosophy, which began with Descartes and Bacon, assumed in ever increasing measure a naturalistic character till Kant and Fichte in the ego once more took their starting-point from man. After a brief period of the supremacy of the theistic philosophy in the nineteenth century, naturalism in its materialistic or pantheistic form resumed its sway, only to induce during these recent years a new return to Kant and the principles of humanism.

At present the materialistic form of naturalism has been generally discredited among all thinkers of repute. Practically it still survives and counts many adherents, but it has lost all hold upon the leaders of thought. Three causes have chiefly contributed to this.

In the first place, the criticism to which Darwinism in the narrower sense of this term has been subjected. It should be remembered that Darwin was not the father of the idea of evolution. This existed long before him. Bodin and Hobbes, Montesquieu, Voltaire and Rousseau, Kant and Schiller, had already taught that the original state of man was merely animal. Hegel had changed Spinoza's substance into a principle of active force, and made out of immutable being a restless becoming. But all these earlier thinkers held the idea of evolution in a purely philosophical form. Darwin, on the other hand, endeavored to supply it with a scientific basis in facts, just as Marx tried to detach the socialistic hopes from all utopianism and raise them to the rank of a scientific theory. But no sooner had Darwin succeeded in laying such a scientific foundation in his " struggle for existence " with its correlates of " natural selection " and " survival of the fittest," than the attack on his work and its demolition began. In rapid succession the principles of struggle for existence, of unlimited variability, of gradual accumulation of minute changes during vast periods of time, of the heredity of acquired qualities, of the purely mechanical explanation of all phenomena, of the exclusion of all teleology, were subjected to sharp criticism and in wide circles pronounced untenable. The prophecy of Wigand that this attempt to solve the riddle of life would not survive until the close of the century has been literally fulfilled. And the declaration of J. B. Meyer has met with wide assent that Darwin's doctrine of descent was not so much an hypothesis proposed to explain facts as rather an invention of facts for the support of an hypothesis.[9]

In the second place, natural science itself has undergone considerable modification in its fundamental conceptions. Physics and chemistry for a long time proceeded on the assumption of atoms, which, however minute, yet had the property of extension and were capable of filling space. With sober scientists this atomism never took the place of a scientific theory, but served simply as a working hypothesis within defined limits. Materialism, however, elevated this hypothesis into a theory capable of explaining the world, regarded the atoms as the ultimate and sole elements of the universe, and viewed all change and variation in the world as due in the last analysis to mechanical combination and separation of these primitive elements. Not merely was protest raised against this by philosophical thought as represented in Kant, Schelling, and Schopenhauer, on the ground that atoms possessing extension and filling space cannot at the same time be conceived as indivisible; but modern physics and chemistry themselves through their study of the phenomena of light, and their discovery of the Roentgen and Becquerel rays, and their insight into the endless divisibility of matter, came more and more to the conviction that *actio in distans* is absurd, that empty space between the atoms is inconceivable, that the atom itself is a mere figment, and that the existence of a world-æther filling all is highly plausible.[10]

To this must be added, in the third place, the effect of the criticism which has been brought to bear upon the naturalistic hypothesis from the epistemological point of view. Materialism made pretence to being monistic, but could furnish no support for this claim, seeing that in its atoms it continued to place matter and force side by side and had nothing to say about the relation between these two, and so remained obviously dualistic. Hence, in the name of monism materialism was condemned. Ostwald dispensed entirely with the conceptions of atom, matter, substance, "thing-in-itself," and substituted for them the idea of energy. What the vulgar notion regards as matter is a pure product of thought, and in itself nothing else but "a group of various energies arranged in space." These energies are the only reality. All our knowledge of the outside world can be subsumed under the form of representation of existing energy.[11]

But even this "energetic monism," which Ostwald sought to substitute for "material monism," did not prove a permanent resting-place. On further reflection it appeared that none of the outside world, including ourselves, is directly present to our ego, but comes to us through the medium of consciousness only. The ultimate elements, therefore, which are positively given and form the foundation of science, appear to be not matter and force, æther and energy, but sensations and perceptions. The phenomena of consciousness are the only fixed reality. Hence it becomes the task of all genuine, empirical, and exact science, taking its start from these phenomena of consciousness, to strip them of all accretions, and then to proceed to the construction of a system on the basis of these ultimate elements of "pure experience" only.[12]

These considerations, drawn from the philosophy of "pure experience," as advocated chiefly by Mach and Avenarius, led the Göttingen physiologist, Max Verworn, to a new form of monism, to "psychical monism." In the opinion of this scientist, materialism, while capable of rendering some service as a working hypothesis, is altogether without value as an explanation of the world. Mind cannot be explained from matter, nor phenomena of consciousness from the movement of atoms. Even the "parallelistic monism" of Spinoza, advocated of late chiefly by Paulsen, does not satisfy, because it is neither monism nor parallelism. Nor is the "energetic monism" of Ostwald more satisfactory, because it continues to distinguish between physical and psychical energy, thus falling back into dualism. There is no way of saving monism except by abandoning materialism and energeticism alike, rejecting altogether the distinction between soul and body as a delusion inherited from primitive man, and deliberately reducing reality in its whole extent to a "content of the soul."[13]

In view of the fact, however, that such "psychical monism" may easily lead to solipsism and scepticism, others have concerned themselves with establishing the objective reality of the phenomena of consciousness. The Marburg school, represented by Cohen, Natorp, Cassirer, and their colleagues, seeks to secure this end by finding the subject of experience, not like Protagoras, in the consciousness of the individual as such, but in this as rooted in and supported by a universal, objective, transcendental consciousness, which, although incapable of individual states of experience, yet bears in itself aprioristic forms and so offers to our representation a basis and a norm.[14]

Others, however, while equally intent upon maintaining the objectivity of knowledge, regard such a " transcendental psychical monism " as unwarranted and unnecessary. They believe an " epistemological or logical monism " sufficient to meet the requirements of the case. Especially Rickert, but also Schuppe, Leclair, Rehmke, Schubert-Soldern and their supporters, are convinced indeed that in order to escape from solipsism a universal consciousness must needs be assumed. But they do not understand by this a concrete, objective, real consciousness, carrying the individual consciousness in itself, like a sort of deity, something as Malebranche said that man sees all things in God. Their view rather is that a nameless, general, impersonal consciousness suffices, a consciousness which forms the abstract, logical presupposition of all human consciousness, but can never itself become the content of conscious experience, which therefore as a matter of fact amounts to the presence in the world of a universal potency attaining to consciousness in man.[15]

The unprejudiced mind, passing in review these several attempts to save monism, can scarcely fail to reach the conclusion that the history of this monistic movement provides to a remarkable degree its sufficient criticism. Its development is a rapid process of dissolution. The very name with which the philosophy of the preceding century loves to describe itself is open to objection. It is difficult to find in the history of science another such instance of the wanton abuse of a word. It is of comparatively recent origin, and came into vogue especially as an attractive designation of pantheism, which in its turn, if we may believe Schopenhauer, is but another name for atheism, although it takes leave of God after a somewhat more polite fashion. But while the name "pantheism" still bears some definite meaning, the term "monism" is so vague and meaningless as to make it impossible to attach to it any clear conception. All possible or impossible systems may be so designated. We hear of a materialistic, pantheistic, parallelistic, energetic, psychic, epistemological, logical, and still further of an empirical, a critical, an idealistic, a naturalistic, a metaphysical, a concrete, an immanent, a positive, and of several other kinds of monism.[16]

The name is particularly affected by the pantheistic materialism of Haeckel, who wishes by its use to brand every system differing from his own as dualism, and so to bar it out as unscientific. By his own " pure monism " he understands that there exists but a single substance which is at one and the same time God and world, spirit and body, matter and force. And in his opinion this monism is the world-view to which modern natural science stands committed. He agrees with Schopenhauer in declaring it equivalent to atheism, at least if God is to be conceived as a personal being. In the name of this monism he condemns as unscientific all who recognize in nature, in the soul, in consciousness, in the freedom of the will, I do not say a supernatural factor, but even any force different from and higher than that at work in the mechanism of natural science. That men of high standing, like Kant, von Baer,

Dubois-Reymond, Virchow, have kept aloof from this mechanical monism, is due, declares the President of the German Monistic Alliance, to inconsistency in thought or some decay of mental powers.

Such an act of scientific excommunication in itself betrays an arrogance little calculated to commend a theory. No one who has proofs to rely on need resort to "energetic language" like this. In the realm of science there is no pope to proclaim dogmas, no emperor to promulgate laws. All investigations here stand on equal ground, and truth alone is lord. But least of all is such a lofty tone in place when one's own system utterly fails to meet the scientific requirements laid down. Haeckel himself oscillates between materialism and pantheism, conceives of his substance as both God and world, ascribes to his atoms a principle of life and consciousness, and appears to be naïvely unconscious of the involved antinomies. And the same is true of all systems which offer themselves under this name of "monism." The name is a mere disguise under which are concealed the distinctions between God and world, mind and matter, thought and extension, being and becoming, physical and psychical energy, as with Ostwald, or consciousness and the content of consciousness, as with Verworn.

But even more serious is the objection that no one can tell us what this straining after monism in science and philosophy exactly means. Does it mean that there shall be recognized in the last analysis only one single and simple substance or force or law? But to lay down such an axiom apriori amounts to a palpable *petitio principii*, and applies to the world perchance a standard by which it neither can nor will be measured. The universe is doubtless much richer and more complex than we are able to imagine. Reinke very properly says : " I regard monism as an abortive attempt to understand the world. . . . The desire for unity, natural though it be, should never be given decisive weight in determining our world-view. The supreme question is not what would please us, but what is true." [17] No doubt science properly strives to reduce the phenomena as much as possible to simple principles and to subsume them under general laws. And in accordance with this our thoughts refuse to rest in a sort of eternal Manichaeism, which assumes two powers antithetically related to each other. But Sir Oliver Lodge truly observes that in this sense the striving after monism is proper to all science : " the only question at issue is, what sort of monism are you aiming at? " [18] When the use of this name is intended to imply that all multiformity in the world must be merely the manifestation of one substance, we must reject the demand as unwarranted, as the offspring of an aprioristic philosophical system, and as directly opposed to the results of all unprejudiced investigation of the phenomena.

The demand in question appears even more unjustified when we consider how the monists attain the desired unity. The actual world presents to us an infinite variety of things and phenomena, and by no empirical research do we discover that unity of matter and force out of which monism seeks to explain the world. If such a unity be assumed, it can be reached only by way of abstraction. Greek philosophy was the first to conceive the idea of a principle of things, wherein it found both the temporal beginning and the efficient cause of all phenomena. Such a principle always necessarily bears this characteristic, — that all the peculiarities which actuality presents to our view have been eliminated, and nothing is left except the notion of universal, abstract being, which is not capable of any further definition. Even if we suppose that thought can without logical fallacy reason from the full actuality to such an ἄπειρον, this would by no means prove that the world really had sprung from and been formed out of this ἀρχή. Pantheistic philosophy, to be sure, proceeds on this assumption, identifying as it does thought and being. But this is to forget that logical analysis is something totally different from real decomposition or regression. In geometry points are conceived as occupying no space, but it does not follow that such points can exist anywhere objectively in the real world. Real space and real time are always finite, but this does not prevent the attribution to them in thought of infinite extension and duration. Similarly the conception of ultimate being reached by abstraction is a mere product of thought, upon which nothing can be posited in the real world; nothing can come out of it because it is itself nothing.

The proof of this lies in the fact that the relation between the absolute and the world is described by pantheism only by the aid of varying images and similes. It speaks of *natura naturans* and *natura naturata*, of *substantia* and *modi*, of the idea and its objectivation, of reality and appearance, of the whole and its parts, of the species and the individuals, of the ocean and the waves. But it utterly fails to form a distinct idea or clear conception of this relation. Closely looked at, the relation assumed appears in each case to be either that of emanation or that of evolution. In former times, when thought was more accustomed to the category of substantiality, the former was in vogue. The absolute was represented as a fulness of being out of which the world flowed as water from a fountain. After criticism had attacked this conception of substance, thinking reverted to the category of actuality, and, under the influence of Hegel, substance was changed into a subject, being into an absolute becoming, and thus the idea of evolution was made supreme.

The term "evolution," in point of fact, has become a magic formula. Says L. Reinhardt: "The idea of evolution was like the kindling of a torch which suddenly cast a brilliant light upon the mysterious processes of nature, the dark recesses of creation, and gave us the simple, nay, the only possible explanation of them; evolution is the magic formula through which we learn the secret of the apparently insoluble riddle of the origin and development of the infinite variety of terrestrial creatures." [19] To all questions concerning the origin and the essence of things, of heaven and of earth, of minerals and of plants, of animals and of men, of marriage and of family, of the state and of society, of religion and of ethics, the same answer is invariably given: evolution is the key to the origin and existence of all things.

It is a pity that a conception which is to explain everything should itself so much need explaining.[20] The definitions that are given of it vary immensely. A widely different sense attaches to it in Heraclitus and Aristotle, in Spinoza and Leibnitz, in Goethe and Schelling, in Hegel and von Hartmann, in Darwin and Spencer, in Huxley and Tylor, in Haeckel and Wundt. And no single definition covers all the phenomena that are subsumed under the conception. In the several realms of nature, and in the various stages of historical process, the element of becoming that is met everywhere bears widely different characters. The transformation observed in the inorganic world is of a different kind from that seen in living beings. And among the latter, again, consciousness and will, science and art, the family and society, the individual and the body collective, have each its own nature and its own law. There is unity, no doubt, but this unity does not justify our dissolving the variety into a mere semblance. There is no formula which will fit the universe with all its wealth of matter and force and life. "Do not think it likely," says Lodge, repeating with slight modification a saying of Ruskin, — "do not think it likely that you hold in your hand a treatise in which the ultimate and final verity of the universe is at length beautifully proclaimed and in which pure truth has been sifted from the error of the preceding ages. Do not think it, friend; it is not so." [21]

The most striking proof of the pertinence of this criticism of monism has been furnished in a practical way by the rise of that new form of philosophical thought which introduces itself as pragmatism (activism, humanism), and already numbers conspicuous adherents in various lands. Though it has taken many by surprise, its appearance is easily explicable. When naturalism passes over from pure materialism to pantheism, this is tantamount to the return of philosophy to the ideas of life, mind, and soul. If, having recovered these, philosophy be unwilling to refer them to their origin in a personal God, it can find no foothold except in man. Hence, taking pragmatism as a general type of philosophical thought (as James himself describes rationalism and empiricism [22]) apart from all individual modifications, as these appear in James or Schiller, Pierce or Panini, Höffding or Eucken, we find in it a reaction of the ego from monism in its several forms, a self-assertion of the science of mind against the science of nature, of the one against the many, of man against the world. Very properly James calls pragmatism "a new name for some old ways of thinking." Wherever monism makes of the absolute a Saturn devouring his own children, wherever the substance is permitted to resolve the *modi*, the *natura naturans* the *natura naturata*, being the becoming, reality the appearance, into a mere semblance, there humanity, personality with its consciousness and will, with its sense of religious and ethical values, with its scientific and aesthetic ideals will never fail to enter an emphatic protest.

Thus Socrates brought philosophy back from heaven to earth. Thus in the Renascence and the Reformation the human mind shook off the shackles of scholasticism. Thus over against the dogmatism of the rationalists the philosopher of Königsberg asserted the autonomy of human knowledge and action. And when in the nineteenth century monism had waxed powerful, and had found in socialism an ally in the sphere of civil and practical life, the birthhour of a new sense of personality could no longer be delayed. Of this movement Carlyle was the first, the mighty, the paradoxical prophet. During the years 1833 and 1834 he lifted up his voice against the intellectualism of the school of Bentham and Mill, and pleaded the cause of faith, of personal conviction, of the experience of the soul. All of his ego rose in him and set over against the *no* of the world its strong, triumphant *yea*. I am greater than thou, O nature; I stand above thee, for I know and have power; in the life of my spirit, in my religion and ethics, in my science and art, I furnish proofs of my imperishable superiority. And this cry, born from distress of soul, found an echo everywhere. It was the same impulse that led a Sören Kierkegaard to revolt against the Christianity and Church of his time; that induced a

Ritschl to break as a church-historian with the Tübingen school; that made a Höffding range "values" above "facts"; that determined an Eucken, in the mental life of man, to choose his standpoint above the empirical reality; that in the Netherlands filled the poet de Génestet with horror at the web which Scholten's monism threatened to spin around him; that impelled a Tolstoi, an Ibsen, a Nietzsche to hurl their anathemas against the corruption of society; that caused the men of art to draw back from naturalism to symbolism and mysticism, and everywhere procured for the principle of "voluntarism" an open door and a sympathetic reception.[23]

While formerly the attempt was made to explain man from nature, thus doing violence to his personality, at present it is proposed to pursue the opposite method and seek in man the solution of the riddle of the world. Heretofore thinkers have looked backward, and investigated the past in order to discover the origin of man and how he became what he is; now the effort is to look forward, to inspire man to work for his future, with the watchword, "make life, the life thou knowest, as valuable as possible."[24]   Hitherto man has learned to know himself only as a product of the past : let him now learn to regard himself as "creator of the universe."[25]   For is it not evident that in man evolution has reached its culminating point?   Having after endless ages of strife and labor, after innumerable failures and disappointments of every sort, produced man, evolution now continues its task in and through man exclusively, with his co-operation and under his guidance.   Personality is the most precious product, the most valuable quintessence of the process of the development of nature.   Goethe's words, "Höchstes Glück der Erdenkinder ist nur die Persönlichkeit," are being quoted with universal delight and approval.

We see, therefore, that pragmatism as a philosophical theory stands by no means isolated, but is connected with a mighty, ever recurrent mental movement. None the less it has a shade and color of its own. True, at first sight it seems to be nothing more than the recommendation of a new method differing from that usually applied in philosophy; and sometimes it introduces itself with an amiable modesty befitting this humble claim. It disclaims every desire to advocate any dogma, and maintains no preconceived theories. Discouraged by the outcome of the philosophical systems, and sceptical as to the fruitfulness of philosophic thinking, it turns, we are told, its back upon all " verbal solutions, apriori reasons, fixed principles, and closed systems," and applies itself to "concreteness and adequacy, to facts, to action, and to power." Still this is nothing more than the old demand which we have become accustomed to hear from varying quarters, that science must not start from preconceived opinions, but with strict impartiality build on the simple naked facts. Empiricism through the ages has harped on this, and positivism has simply played again the same tune in a slightly higher and shriller tone.

In making this demand these schools of thought have acted under the naïve impression that they themselves stand outside of the pale of philosophy and are absolutely free from all preconceptions. Pragmatism also cherishes this conviction, and, through the mouth of Schiller, compares itself to a corridor or passage in a hotel through which all the guests from the different rooms must pass in order to reach the open air. This is, however, nothing but a well-meant delusion. Empiricism is as much a guest in

the great hotel of science, and as truly occupies a separate
room, as all other inmates of the building. All engaged in
the pursuit of knowledge recognize that thought must be
based on experience, and that no other foundation can
be laid on which to build science than that of the facts of
nature or history. The scientific investigator does not
resemble the spider or the ant, but the bee; he gathers the
honey of knowledge from the flowers of experience. In
order to see one has to open his eyes; in order to hear, his
ears. Even mediæval scholasticism, which, owing to various causes held the writings of antiquity, especially of
Aristotle, in excessive reverence, never failed to recognize
the principle that "omnis cognitio intellectualis incipit a
sensu." But there is and always has been difference of
opinion with regard to the influence which is exercised or
which should be exercised by the personality of the investigator in the discovering, observing, arranging, and sys-
tematizing of the facts. No difference exists as regards
the formal canon that science must proceed on the basis
of the facts. Pragmatism, in exhorting us to obey this
canon, does no more than reiterate a well-known and well-
nigh universally acknowledged principle. The difference
begins when the question *what* are the facts is reached,
how they are to be found and observed, to be classified and
elaborated.

The case of pragmatism itself furnishes the best illustration of this. While offering itself as a mere method, it
soon appears to be a theory and a system. It brings to the
investigation of things a preconceived judgment of its own,
both as to reality and as to truth.

As regards reality, pragmatism not only declares the
philosophy of materialism and pantheism aprioristic and
dogmatic, but passes the same judgment on all philosophy

which would recognize the reality of ideas and would count ideas among the facts to which consciousness bears witness. Appealing to the well-known words of Goethe, "In the beginning was not the word but the deed," it rejects all realism in the mediæval sense of this term, to take its stand consciously and unequivocally on the side of nominalism. All generic conceptions, such as God, the absolute, the world, the soul, matter, force, time, space, truth, substance, causation, language, religion, morality, and the like are considered, therefore, not designations of objective realities, but terms by means of which we put together for the sake of convenience certain groups of phenomena, mere "helps to thought," which have to prove their serviceableness and value in the using; by no means invested capital, but current coin, subject to fluctuation. To the pragmatist the world is in itself no unity, no organism, no kosmos, but an avowed multiplicity of phenomena, an infinite mass of facts, a ὕλη, a chaos.

Pragmatism adduces in favor of this nominalistic worldview the consideration already urged by Aristotle against Plato's doctrine of ideas, namely, that otherwise the world exists in duplicate, or even in triplicate. For, as James observes, to the rationalist the world exists either from the outset complete in the idea, or, at any rate, finished and ready in its objective reality exterior to us, in which case it once more appears in the form of a more or less imperfect copy in our minds. To the pragmatist, on the other hand, the unity of the world is not a given fact, but a growing thing, ever in process of becoming and improvement. In itself the world is essentially unformed matter, ὕλη, but "it is still in the making, and awaits part of its completion from the future." Or, better still, the world becomes what we cause it to be; "it is plastic, it is what

we make it." For this reason it is a matter of comparative
indifference how we conceive that it in the past became
what it now is, whether we explain it materialistically or
theistically. For, after all, the world is that which it is.
And the main question is not, What has it been? but
What is it becoming? What are we doing with it and
making of it? [26]

From this peculiar outlook upon reality pragmatism
reaps the advantage of being able to accord unstinted and
honest recognition to many facts which rationalism has to
ignore or explain away. The world is a chaos, full of pa-
thetic facts of sin and misery and sorrow, facts which the
philosophy of the absolute seeks in vain to justify or to
reconcile with the harmony of the universe. It also gives
due consideration to a great number of the most diversified
phenomena and experiences of religious and moral life,
and, without in connection with these raising the question
of truth and right, seeks to respect and appreciate them
from a psychological and sociological point of view. Since
it does not take its start from any idea of the absolute, not
even of absolute goodness or justice or ominipotence, it
does not feel called upon to furnish a theodicy. It does
not sacrifice reality to any theological or philosophical theory nor force it into the procrustean bed of any apriori
system. The world *is* a miserable world and in itself
cannot be anything else.

But while judging thus pessimistically of the past and
the present, pragmatism cherishes quite optimistic expectations with regard to the future. And in connection
with this it holds a peculiar conception of *truth*. Behind
and around about us, no doubt, gloom and darkness reign,
but ahead of us the dawn is breaking. For evolution has
now so far advanced as to produce man, and has com-

mitted to him the further improvement of the world. On man it depends what the world is to become. True, this renders the future more or less uncertain; the world is not saved, necessarily, by its own inherent powers; if to be saved, it must be saved by man. Still this salvation is possible, and in part even probable. Pragmatism is not wholly pessimistic nor wholly optimistic; its frame of mind might be described as melioristic. Although the world be wretched in itself, the power and the duty of saving it belong to us.

Man possesses such power because through a long series of ages he has come to be a knowing, and especially a willing and acting, being; his intellect and his will constitute him, in the midst of the sad, ugly reality, "a creative power." He has raised himself gradually to this plane. He was not endowed with such intellect and will at the start; he has slowly acquired them. Nor is he by nature endowed with a so-called "common sense," with innate knowledge of apriori forms, as even Kant from his rationalistic standpoint still imagined. The intellect itself, with all its content of conceptions, categories, laws of thought, etc., has been evolved in the struggle for existence, because it proved practically useful and valuable for life. And this consequently is the only criterion of truth.

Truth does not exist before or outside or independent of man. It has no more objective existence than the unity, the goodness, or the happiness of the world. It is nowhere to be found in its completeness, as though man could receive it after a purely passive fashion into his consciousness. Nor does its criterion lie in the agreement of our representations with the external reality, for it exists only *in* and not *outside* of man. It *is* not, but *becomes;* as the world in general, so truth is "in the making." Truth is that which in the experience of the life of knowledge and volition approves itself as useful. Its changeableness and relativity are necessarily given with this. There is no single truth that is settled absolutely, above all possibility of doubt; all truth remains subject to revision. Every truth is to be measured by its value for life, and for this reason may change any day. Science itself gives no knowledge of the objective reality. All it can do is to provide us with instruments for using the reality. It furnishes no absolute, but only relative, practical truth. It teaches no necessary, but only contingent, laws. That system is most true which is most useful. Truth, religion, morality, civilization in its whole extent, are all subject and subservient to life. The reality may be hard and chaotic; it is for us to make it true and good.[27]

III

TO pragmatism belongs the great merit of having freed us from the bane of monism and of having exposed the barrenness of its abstract conceptions. It deserves appreciation and praise so far as it turns its back upon "fixed habits, pure abstractions, and verbal solutions," calls us back to the facts, and places emphasis afresh on the practical element in all knowledge and science.

But if it may be justly demanded of every world-view that it shall satisfy both the requirements of the intellect and the needs of the heart, it will be seen that pragmatism also is unsatisfactory. It is itself not pragmatic enough. While professing to have no dogmas, and rejecting alike the philosophy of Plato and Aristotle, of Spinoza and Hegel, of Bradley and Taylor, in point of fact it aligns itself with the humanism of Socrates, links its thinking to that of Locke, Berkeley, Hume, and Kant, and simply replaces the philosophy of rationalism by that of empiricism. When it not only throws overboard the abstract conception of the absolute and its self-realization in the world-process, but also refuses to acknowledge as realities "upon which it can rest" God and his attributes, mind and matter, reason and conscience, and finds in all these names merely "a programme for more work, only with a practical value"; when it discards the idea of substance and resolves the thing into its properties; when it regards religion and philosophy as "largely a

matter of temperament, even of physical condition," and
places the criterion of all truth in "satisfactoriness"
alone; pragmatism proves that it is far from merely a
new method, but is to all intents a new philosophy, and
comes therewith into conflict with its own point of de-
parture and its own fundamental principle. No wonder
James declares that it cannot be refuted by pointing out
in it a few contradictions, but that the only way to learn
to understand and accept it is by becoming thoroughly
"inductive-minded" one's self through "a real change of
heart," "a break with absolutistic hopes."[1] Here we
touch the real core of pragmatism: it has abandoned all
hope of knowing anything that bears any absolute character, — not only God, but all ideas and names. It is
born from a sceptical frame of mind, and for this reason
as a last resort clings to what it considers ultimate.
incontrovertible facts.

It follows from this that pragmatism is not correctly
defined by saying that it "represents the empiricist attitude." Almost every school in science and philosophy
professes in the last analysis to set out from facts. Pragmatism carries with it a peculiar conception of the facts,
a peculiar judgment as to reality. Between rationalism
and empiricism, intellectualism and voluntarism, there is
a difference not merely in regard to "the value of facts,"
but in regard to the facts themselves. Pragmatism takes
a different view of things; its idea of the world is different
from that of the idealistic philosophy. According to the
latter the world is the embodiment of thought, rests in
mind and is governed by reason. In presenting this view
idealistic philosophy is not merely toying with abstract
conceptions or idle ratiocinations, but takes its start from
reality, — reality, to be sure, as seen by it. Even Hegel,

who certainly of all philosophers has most sinned by apriori constructions, had far more knowledge of the facts of nature and history than his opponents have given him credit for. But, if we may believe the pragmatists, the history of philosophy has been a long process of shelving all absolute metaphysical conceptions : first, the secondary properties ; next, substance and causality, matter and force, law and norm, truth and language. There are no apriori ideas or principles that govern the world. The world in itself is a chaos, a *rudis indigestaque moles*, which only through the knowledge and activity of man has been gradually transformed into a cosmos. True, pragmatism does not always consistently adhere to this bold assertion. James says in one place that space and time, number and order, consciousness and causality, are categories which are difficult to be rid of.[2] But, judging from its principle and tendency, pragmatism is opposed to all general conceptions, in which it recognizes not fixed, apriori categories, but only abstract names for the results of human thinking.[3]

Against such pragmatism the objection must be urged, not that it strives to be empirical, but that it is not nearly sufficiently so; inasmuch as it excludes from its horizon the most important and principal facts. Reality, the whole, rich reality is something different from what this new type of philosophy sets before us; it contains more elements, more "facts," than pragmatism takes into account. The only possible way of demonstrating this is by briefly inquiring how we approach reality and in what way we discover its content. From this it will appear that neither materialism nor humanism, but only theism, that neither emanation nor evolution, but revelation alone, is capable of solving the problem.

The only path by which we are able to attain reality is that of self-consciousness. The truth of idealism lies in this, that the mind of man, in other words, sensation and representation, is the basis and principle of all knowledge. If there be an objective reality, a world of matter and force, existing in the forms of space and time, then it follows from the nature of the case that the knowledge of it can reach me through my consciousness only. In this sense it is quite proper to affirm that the object exists for the subject alone, and that the world is our representation. Apart from consciousness I know nothing, whether of myself or of any other province of reality. In the defence of this truth idealism holds strong ground over against that naïve naturalism which thinks it possesses in atoms and æther, in matter and energy, a directly given reality, and which loses sight of the influence exerted by the subject in every perception of an object.

But idealism is wrong when from this incontrovertible fact, that reality can be approached only through the medium of consciousness, it draws the conclusion that perception is a purely immanent act, and that therefore the object perceived must itself be immanent in the mind. It is quite true that nobody can see himself pass before the window, or can lift himself by his own hair; in other words, that no one can know reality except through his consciousness, since it is obviously impossible to know without knowing. Perception on the part of the subject renders a double service; it is at once the condition and the instrument of the perception of the object. None the less there is a great difference between the view that subjective perception is the means and organ, and the other view that it is the principle and source of the knowledge of the object. The mistake of idealism lies

in confounding the act with its content, the function
with the object, the psychological with the logical nature
of perception. Perception is an act of the subject, and
sensation and representation, as truly as concepts and
conclusions, have a purely ideal, immanent existence.
But perception as such terminates upon an object, and
sensation and representation, logically considered, by
their very nature are related to a reality distinct from
themselves. Hence psychology and logic differ in character. It is one thing to consider the representations as
they lie in consciousness and another thing in and through
them to apprehend the reality. To ignore this difference
means to remain entangled in a sort of psychologism, im-
prisoned in one's self and doomed never to reach reality.

This is seen most clearly from the efforts which, in
spite of its fundamental error, idealism has ever been
making to escape from the logic of illusionism and to
maintain the objectivity of knowledge. Two methods
chiefly have been adopted for this purpose.

The one method is that of those who on the principle of
causality reason back from the representation as an effect
to an objective reality as its cause. The other method is
pursued by those who admit that we cannot infer reality
from the representation, but nevertheless think that by
way of the will the desired goal can be attained. They
reason that man is not exclusively nor primarily consciousness and representation, but force, impulse, and
will; he is himself a substance, a reality; his essence
consists not in the *cogitare* but in the *movere*. Not
by his thought, but by his willing, which continually
meets resistance and finds its freedom opposed, man is
led to assume behind his representation a corresponding
reality.

Against this whole manner of reasoning the objection must be urged at the outset, that it does not appear with what right idealism believes in the law of causality and makes use of it in bridging over the gulf between thought and being. But, even neglecting this objection, we find that neither of the two methods leads to the goal contemplated. For previously to all reasoning about representation and will, all men, the unlearned as well as the learned, and even children and indeed animals, are convinced of the reality of an objective world. Not even the thinker, who by scientific reflection has reached the position of idealism, can divest himself of his belief in this reality. Eduard von Hartmann even declares that without this belief it is impossible for man to live. " Without this faith in the reality and continuity of what we perceive," says he, " we should be unable to live for a moment, and hence this naïvely-realistic faith, coälescing with the perception itself, by way of intuition, into an indivisible act, forms an indispensable, practically inalienable ingredient of our mental equipment."[4] As though idealism had become frightened by its own practical consequences, Paulsen and Verworn hasten to assure us, that, whether one's philosophy be idealism or realism, everything in life remains the same, and science retains its truth and value.[5] But, in addition to this, the facts directly contradict the assumption that reality is reached only through a process of reasoning from representation or will. It is by no means in every case that we posit reality behind our representations. Difficult as it may be to point out the difference theoretically, practically we all draw a distinction between the waking and dreaming states, between the representation of reality and hallucination. And in the same manner we ascribe reality to many things with which our will has no concern whatever, and from which it experiences no resistance whatever. The sun and the moon and the stars possess no less reality for us than the stone against which we strike our foot or the wall which shuts off our view.

Now, since we are not in the least conscious of any such process of reasoning or inference, some have thought that these activities take place in the subconscious region of our mind.[6] This, however, entirely fails to make the matter more plausible. For either an unconscious inference of this kind must be the precipitate of long years and ages of experience, in which case it would presuppose the very thing to be established by it; or the human mind must by its very nature be under the necessity of connecting its representations with reality, in which case the procedure can neither be unconscious nor consist of an act of syllogistic reasoning; or, as von Hartmann actually represents it, it is something accomplished in us by the great Unconscious, in which case it is no conclusion of ours, and all self-activity of man in thinking and acting disappears. When idealism has begun by severing the representation in its origin and essence from reality, it has lost the power to reinstitute the inward connection between them. The mind, having once shut itself up in the circle of representations, is unable to free itself from this self-constructed prison. Whithersoever it may turn, it perceives nothing but representations, products of its own consciousness; its will is a representation; the resistance that will encounters is a representation; the ego is a representation. Representations gird it about on all sides, and nowhere is access open to reality; for no inference can be drawn from thinking to being; from the representations there is no bridge to reality. Just as little as Satan can be cast out by Satan is there escape from representations by means of representations.[7] Idealistic philosophy is like the she-bear which draws all her nourishment from her own breasts, and thus eats herself up, *ipsa alimenta sibi*.[8]

The case becomes entirely different if we take our starting-point not from the representations as such, but from self-consciousness; if for the act of *cogitare* we substitute the fact *cogito*. But modern psychology seeks to obstruct also this last road to reality. It bids us remark that we do not observe in ourselves any ego, any soul, any substance, but only a continuous succession of phenomenal states of consciousness, and that we lack warrant to infer from these the existence of a bearer or substrate. This obstruction, however, is easily removed, because the same mistake is made here that before was found to vitiate the reasoning with regard to the reality of the outside world. As our perception does not have for its object the representations, but in and through these the things themselves, so in the phenomena of consciousness our own ego always presents itself to us. In neither case is there involved any process of reasoning or inference. As the external perception, of itself and immediately, convinces of the reality of the perceived object, so the perception of self in the phenomena of consciousness assures us spontaneously and immediately of the existence of ourselves.

Of course a distinction must be made here between the psychological investigation to which the man of science subjects the phenomena of consciousness, and by means of which he may abstract these from the self-consciousness, and the state of self-consciousness experienced in daily life by every man, the scientist not excluded. But in the latter case the self is always and immediately given in self-consciousness. If this were not so, we should indeed be shut up to the proposition, advocated no doubt by idealism, but none the less paradoxical, which is formulated by Max Verworn as follows: " There is no such thing as a soul *dwelling* in the human body, nor as a man which is the *seat* of sensations, but a man *is* a complex of sensations, and to others as well as to himself he *consists* of sensations." [9] That this is a paradox is recognized even by John Stuart Mill, for in spite of his actualistic standpoint, he declares that here a dilemma confronts us: we must either believe that the ego is distinct from the phenomena of consciousness belonging to it, or accept the paradox that a series of sensations can become conscious of itself as a series. [10] Here, as little as in the case of outward perception, does monism suffice. There is a distinction, an irremovable distinction, between the representation and the thing of which it is a representation, and there is an equally sharp and equally indelible distinction between the phenomena of consciousness and the subject that manifests itself in them. How else could unity and continuity of psychical life, how could memory and imagination, thinking and judging, comparison and inference, be possible ? The ego is not an aggregate of parts, not a mass of phenomena of consciousness, afterwards grouped together by man under one name. It is a synthesis, which in every man precedes all scientific reflection, an organic whole possessing members. It is complex but not compound. [11]

In self-consciousness, therefore, we have to deal not with a mere phenomenon, but with a noumenon, with a reality that is immediately given us, antecedently to all reasoning and inference. Self-consciousness is the unity of real and ideal being; the *self* is here *consciousness*, not scientific knowledge, but experience, conviction, consciousness of self as a reality. In self-consciousness our own being is *revealed* to us, directly, immediately,

before all thinking and independently of all willing. We
do not approach it through any reasoning or exertion of
our own; we do not demonstrate its existence, we do
not understand its essence. But it is given to us in
self-consciousness, given gratis, and is received on our
part spontaneously, in unshaken confidence, with immediate assurance. In self-consciousness the light dawns
for us on our own being, even as nature emerges from
darkness and stands revealed in the rays of the sun.
To ignore this fact of self-consciousness, this primary
fact, this foundation of all knowledge and activity, to
make it dependent on our own affirmation, to undermine it by doubt, is to commit against ourselves and
against others not merely a logical but also an ethical
sin. It is to shake not only the foundation of science,
but also the indispensable basis of all human conduct;
to weaken all confidence, spontaneity, volitional energy,
and courage. And no effort of the will can repair afterwards the injury which has been wrought by thought.
The will lacks the authority and the power to become
the foundation of faith and knowledge, of religion and
morality. " Practical reason " cannot bear the weight
which " theoretical reason " has cast off of itself, and
" theoretical reason " is not in a position to demonstrate
that which is the presupposition of all demonstration.
The " will to believe " may be indispensable to faith,
but it can never become the ground of faith; and every
demonstration of the intellect must rest on the intuitive
certainty of self-consciousness.

In self-consciousness, however, there is revealed something different from and more than our own self.
Or rather, the ego that is revealed to us in self-
consciousness is no cold, bald unity, no dead mathe-

matical point, no quiescent, unvarying substance but is rich in content, full of life and power and activity. It is no monad without windows, no insensible " Reale " lying beneath the psychical phenomena and bearing them as the stage bears the players. On the contrary, it is itself immanent in the psychical phenomena and develops itself in and through and with them ; it is capable of working out its own salvation with fear and trembling, but also of working its own destruction and ruin. It *is*, but at the same time it *becomes* and grows ; it is a fulness of life, a totality of gifts and powers, which do not play their rôles behind the curtain, but reveal themselves and find development in the multiform activities of psychical life, in the whole man with all his works. Augustine was the first who so understood self-consciousness. Socrates did not comprehend this ; for although he brought philosophy back from nature to man, he was interested exclusively in gaining true conceptions of knowledge and conduct. And later Descartes took, it is true, his starting-point from thought, but thought meant for him the essence of the soul. Augustine went deeper and found more ; he discovered reality within himself. The scepticism into which Greek philosophy had issued had lost, together with God and the world, also the self-certainty of man. But when the Christian religion revealed to us the greatness of God's heart, and in the day-spring from on high visited us with his tender mercy, it at the same time cast its light on man and on the riches and value of his soul. It imparted to him a new certainty, the certainty of faith ; it restored to him his confidence in God, and therewith his confidence in himself. And by this light of revelation Augustine descended deep into his own inner life ; forgetting nature, he desired to know

naught else but God and himself. There he found
thought, to be sure, but not thought alone; beneath
thought he penetrated to the essence of the soul, for in
himself always life preceded thought; faith, knowledge;
self-consciousness, reflection; experience, science; he first
lived through the things which later he thought and
wrote. Thus Augustine went back behind thought
to the essence of the soul, and found in it not a simple
unity, but a marvellously rich totality; he found there
the ideas, the norms, the laws of the true and the good,
the solution of the problem of the certainty of knowledge, of the cause of all things, of the supreme good;
he found there the seeds and germs of all knowledge
and science and art; he found there even, in the triad
of *memoria*, *intellectus*, and *voluntas*, a reflection of the
triune being of God. Augustine was the philosopher
of self-examination, and in self-consciousness he discovered the starting-point of a new metaphysics.[12]

The mind of man is indeed no *tabula rasa*, no empty
form, but a totality of life from the very first moment of
its existence. And when it becomes conscious of itself,
this self-consciousness is not a mere formal apprehen-
sion of existence, but always includes in it an appre-
hension of a peculiar nature, a particular quality of
mind. It is never a consciousness of pure being, but
always a consciousness of a specific being, of a definite
something. This is acknowledged even by those who
follow Herbert Spencer in assuming that the rational,
moral mind of man has been slowly evolved out of an
animal state and has acquired in the struggle for existence a set of general conceptions, a common sense, to
which attaches, up to the present day, great practical
value, and which is transmitted as a *habitus* from parents

to children.[13] By this evolutionary explanation the difficulty is simply pushed back into the past, into the life of
our ancestors. In actual life we never see mere sensation
developing into thought, and it is highly improbable
that such a transition will ever be witnessed, as, for example, in the case of apes. But such an evolution is no
easier to understand in the past than in the present;
between perception and intellect, representation and conceptions, association of representations and conceptual
thinking, there is a fundamental difference. Association
combines representations according to accidental, external points of resemblance; thought combines conceptions
according to the laws of identity and contradiction, cause
and effect, means and end. Causation, for example, is
something wholly different from habitual association, because it has its essence in an internal and necessary connection of phenomena. Unless the thinking mind be
introduced into the explanation from the outset, every
effort to make it emerge out of the faculty of perception
by way of evolution must remain futile. Very properly
Mr. R. W. B. Joseph, in his criticism of James, observes,
that in order to acquire a " common sense," man must
needs be possessed antecedently of mind. " A mind which
had no fundamental categories and whose experience was
purely chaotic would not be a mind at all." The nature
of mind consists just in " the fundamental modes of its
thinking." [14] But, be this as it may, the evolutionists
themselves will have to acknowledge that to the mind of
man, as at present constituted, this " common sense " is
an integral possession which belongs to it from the start.

When we endeavor to determine more closely the
nature of this mind and descend for this purpose into
the depths of self-consciousness, we find at its very root

the sense of dependence. In our self-consciousness we
are not only conscious of being, but also of being something definite, of being the very thing we are. And this
definite mode of being, most generally described, consists in
a dependent, limited, finite, created being. Before all
thinking and willing, before all reasoning and action,
we are and exist, exist in a definite way, and inseparable
therefrom have a consciousness of our being and of its
specific mode. The core of our self-consciousness is, as
Schleiermacher perceived much more clearly than Kant,
not autonomy, but a sense of dependence. In the act of
becoming conscious of ourselves we become conscious of
ourselves as creatures.

This dependence is brought to our knowledge in a twofold way. We feel ourselves dependent on everything
around us; we are not alone. Solipsism, although the
inevitable outcome of idealism, is in itself an impossible
theory. According to the philosopher Wolf, there lived
in his day in Paris a pupil of Malebranche, who advocated solipsism, and still found adherents, *quod*, Wolf
observes, *mirum videri poterat.* Even Fichte felt compelled, chiefly by moral considerations, not to regard
himself as the only existent being.[15] Every man knows
that he does not exist alone, that he is not able to do
what he pleases, that on every side he is curbed and
hedged in, and encounters resistance. But in the second
place we feel ourselves, together with all creatures, wholly
dependent on some absolute power which is the one infinite being. How this power is defined does not matter
for the present; the main point is that all men feel themselves dependent on a being which is the cause and ground
of all being. This sense of dependence, with its twofold reference, is not a philosophical conception, not an

abstract category, not "a verbal solution," but a fact
which in point of certainty is equal to the best established
fact of natural science. It is something genuinely empirical, universally human, immediate, the very core of
self-consciousness, and involves the existence of both the
world and God.

True, from the standpoint of idealism this last-named
conclusion will be rejected. Still, two things need to be
sharply distinguished in connection with this. That the
belief in the existence of an objective world (and likewise
of God) is a fact nobody can deny. The most thoroughgoing idealist cannot ignore the fact that all men without
distinction, and antecedently to all reasoning, are convinced
of the reality of the world, and that he himself in daily
life shares this conviction, nay, finds it indispensable for
knowledge and activity. Nor did Kant himself deny this
fact. The problem which Kant set himself to solve was not
how the world of our perception, the *Wahrnehmungswirk-
lichkeit*, is produced, for it is self-evident that we obtain
this from perception, and that from the first we conceive
of it as existing in space and time. But, starting from
this world of perception and presupposing it, Kant sought
to answer this other question, — how we can obtain
scientific knowledge of this empirical world. And for
this problem he offered the solution, that such knowledge
cannot come through sense-perception, because the latter
discovers nothing but an orderless mass of phenomena ;
that scientific knowledge is possible and attainable only
when the human mind introduces order into this chaos
of phenomena and subjects it to its own law. According
to Kant the mind has such a law of its own : it carries
in itself all sorts of apriori forms, which are not called
apriori because in point of time they precede perception,

or because they lie ready-made in our minds, but because they are independent of perception and are produced and applied by the mind in the very act of working on the representations.[16]

From this activity of the mind in acquiring scientific knowledge, idealism (whether rightly or wrongly appealing to Kant cannot and need not be here investigated) has drawn the conclusion that the world of perception is either in part or in whole a product of the perceiving subject. But in doing this it confounds two questions which Kant kept distinct. The world of perception is given to us in our consciousness, not as dream or hallucination, but as phenomenon and representation, involving, according to universal belief, the existence of an objective world. This empirical and undeniable fact is recognized, and to some degree explained, only when self-consciousness is conceived in the sense above defined as the unity of real and ideal being; when it is recognized as a matter of intuitive certainty that in self-consciousness both the existence and the specific mode of existence of the self, the ego, are revealed. For in that case the gulf between the reality and the representation, between being and thinking, is bridged over. And with the selfsame certainty with which we assume the existence of our own ego, the existence of the world is recognized. For the representation is connected with reality by the same inner tie that binds self-consciousness to the self. It is the same sense of dependence that inheres in the mind as a whole which also inheres in all its representations and activities; the ego does not exist in a quiescent state, nor lie insensible outside of and behind the psychical phenomena, but is immanently active in them, and attains in them its revelation and development; and self-consciousness does not exist apart from the representations, but lives and realizes itself in them; it imparts its own certainty to these representations; it in them feels assured of itself. To undermine belief in the external world, therefore, always carries with it the undermining of self-confidence and of volitional energy, of the faith the mind has in itself, and hence of the superiority of the mind to nature, of religion and morality. Not evolution, but revelation, is the secret of the mind; in our self-consciousness, independently of our co-operation and apart from our will, the reality of our ego and of the world is revealed to us. Whosoever here does not believe shall not be established.

In seeking to obtain knowledge of this world of perception science must needs set out from this fact of inner consciousness. It can and must endeavor to understand this; but the reality of the fact should not be made dependent on our ability to explain it. We do not know how the world can exist, or how, in this world, consciousness is possible, yet no one doubts the reality of either. It is imperative, both logically and ethically, that science shall respect the reality of the soul's inner consciousness, for if it refuses belief here, it undermines its own foundation. Epistemological idealism furnishes the most forcible demonstration of this. For according to this theory reality is itself a ὕλη, a chaos, and order is first introduced into it by the knowledge and activity of the human mind. The world in itself is neither true nor good; it is we who slowly make it true and good. No doubt in this proposition, even when thus paradoxically expressed, there is always contained this much of truth, that the world apart from man is imperfect and unfinished. In the Pentateuchal account of creation the preparation of the earth

is described from this very point of view; in man the
world finds its head and its lord. Hence man is given a
vocation with reference to this world. Though good, yet
it is not "finished." It exists in order to be replenished,
subjected, made the object of knowledge, and ruled over
by man. To this extent it would be proper to say that it
was man's task to make the world true and good.

But the idealistic philosophy understands all this in
quite a different sense. It takes its position in the second verse of the first chapter of Genesis, placing itself
not *after* but *before* the preparation of the earth by God's
omnipotent hand. The earth in itself, apart from man, is
a waste and empty chaos, unformed, without ordinances
and laws, without light and color. Now right here a
difficulty emerges of so serious a nature that it divides
the idealists into two camps, which we may, perhaps, call
the "thoroughgoing" and the "half-hearted" idealists.
The thoroughgoing idealists dispense even with the ὕλη,
and regard the entire world as a product of the human
mind, and man not merely as the orderer, but also as the
creator of the world. It was in this sense that Fichte
affirmed that the ego posits the non-ego, and Paulsen,
along with many kindred spirits in our own day, declares
that the objects of the external world are "a creation of
the subject." [17] Most idealists, however, draw back from
this phenomenalism, which would seem bound to issue
into solipsism; they, therefore, with Locke, draw a distinction between the primary and the secondary qualities
of things, and, while ascribing to the latter a purely subjective origin, uphold the objective reality of the former
as something that belongs to them independently of man.
If this latter position, however, be correct, and the
primary qualities, such as impenetrability, extension, num-

ber, motion, can lay claim to independent existence, then the assertion that the world in itself is nothing but chaos seems overbold; for on such a view there must be in it substance and causality, law and government, order and measure, and man appears to be not the creator, but merely the orderer of the world. And in his ordering of the world he is dependent on these primary qualities; he is not absolutely free, or autonomous, but determined in his knowledge and activity by the objective world. But in that case his activity cannot, even with regard to secondary qualities, be held to be an autonomous, creative one. It is true, idealism considers the subjective nature of these secondary qualities the impregnable fortress of its position, and believes that both epistemologically and physiologically the correctness of its view in this respect has been irrefutably demonstrated.

Epistemology, however, teaches the very opposite of what idealism asserts. The perceptive and cognitive activity of man is only in a psychological, and not in a logical, sense a purely immanent act of the mind. Both perception and representation would cease to be what they are if nothing existed that was perceived and represented. On both the character of logical transcendence is indelibly impressed; by their very nature they point to an objective reality, detached from which they would become equivalent to hallucinations and illusions. As self-consciousness presupposes the self not outside but in the content of consciousness, so by the same law and with the same certainty the representation, which does not operate outside of self-consciousness but is the product and content of it, points back to an object. This explanation of the character of perception has not been modified in the least by the physiology of sensation. Physiology has clarified to a very important degree our insight into the conditions under which, the ways by which, and the means through which, perception takes place, but the act of perception itself remains precisely what it was before. We now know that the sensations of sight and of hearing cannot originate except under the condition of some millions of aether-vibrations per second, that the sensation of seeing is attended by an image thrown inverted on the retina of the eye, that smell and taste depend on a chemical dissolution of the constituents of the object, that nervous stimuli are transmitted from our sense organs to the centre of the brain. But the nexus that exists between all these intermediate processes and the perception itself utterly eludes us. What, for example, has the sensation of color as such to do with 437 billions of vibrations per second?   What has the sensation of hardness or softness to do with stimulation of the nerves?   The distinction between the cause and the condition, between the mediation and the object of the perception, for all this, retains its full validity.   Just as writing and reading, telegraphy and telephony avail themselves of all sorts of mechanical movements of hand and tongue or of all kinds of visible signs and audible sounds, and nevertheless presuppose at each end of the process a thinking subject which by means of the signs understands the thought, so the sense-organs, together with all further intermediaries, are only the conditions under which, the ways in which, the subject sees and hears, tastes and smells, but in no wise the cause, and hence not in any way the explanation, of these perceptions. After all physiological investigation the mental act of perception remains as mysterious as before. Before and after there remains unshaken and unreduced the distinction between subject and object, between the act of perception and the object of perception, between sight, hearing, smell, taste, touch, on the one hand, and being seen, heard, smelled, tasted, touched, on the other hand. Both grammatically and logically the distinction between the active and the passive voice remains in force.

The moderate idealists, therefore, were wrong in conceding the subjectivity of the secondary qualities. Of course, continued observation and reflection may improve and render more accurate our perceptions of color and sound, of smell and taste, as well as those of space and time, of size and distance; both soul and body, the mental faculties and the senses, need teaching and training. But this does not affect the fundamental character that should be ascribed to the perceptions of the secondary qualities or the maintenance of their objectivity. It is already noteworthy that a number of such thinkers as Berkeley and Hume, Paulsen and Wundt, Eucken and Stumpf, consider the distinction between primary and secondary qualities unfounded and arbitrary.[18] In regard to space- and time-relations errors are no more excluded than in regard to perceptions of color and sound. Apart from secondary qualities, space, extension, form are incapable of becoming objects of perception. The objective validity of the secondary qualities in no respect falls behind that of the primary qualities. If it be given up with respect to the former, it will be impossible to maintain it with respect to the latter; semi-idealism arbitrarily stops short half-way. But, apart from this, if such a great difference exists between the two groups of qualities, it is hard to understand that ordinary observation, in the learned and the unlearned alike, has remained entirely unaware of this. And yet ordinary observation in other cases draws all kinds of distinctions. It knows quite well that an hallucination is different from a representation; if a person hurts his foot on a stone, it predicates the pain, not of the stone, but of the subject. It knows that food can be called healthy in a figurative sense only, because it promotes health (which is the attribute of a human being). And it is likewise aware that the senses of smell and taste are much more subjective than the others, so as to lie outside the region of disputation. Yet, notwithstanding all this, ordinary observation adheres to the conviction that the representations are no more light or dark, green or red, sweet or bitter, than they are high or low, round or square, near or distant, but that all these qualities belong to the object, and that the subject does not produce, but only perceives and takes knowledge of them.

It is impossible, therefore, to remove or separate these qualities — and the secondary no less truly than the primary ones — from the object. It will not do to say with Verworn, The stone is hard — a sensation; it is heavy — a sensation; it is cold — a sensation; it is gray — a sensation, etc., and thence to conclude that what I call a stone is nothing but a specific combination of sensations. Or rather, it is possible to talk in this way, but it is not feasible to practise it in actual life. We may proceed after this fashion in abstract thinking and come to maintain that nothing objective remains; but such an abstract procedure is no proof that we can act on it in practical life. The important point is precisely that the stone is a specific combination, or rather a complex, of qualities, which occur in combination with one another, and which are not held together subjectively in my consciousness, but objectively in the thing itself.[19] And so it is with every object we perceive and with the entire world spread out before our eyes. The world is not a group of perceptions formed by

us for economic reasons, for the sake of the practical necessities of life, but a complex of qualities which exist
objectively and are mutually bound together, a totality
which cannot be reduced to any representation of ours.
As little as subjectively the ego, the personality, admits of
being resolved into a series of sensations, can the world of
our external perception be reduced to a group of representations. In both cases we are face to face with one and
the same fact. In consciousness our own being, and the
being of the world, are disclosed to us antecedently to our
thought or volition; that is, they are *revealed* to us in the
strictest sense of the word.[20]

In man's self-consciousness, however, still more is implied. Unless there were more, the result obtained could
not satisfy us. For without more we should not be warranted in speaking of revelation, and could not maintain
our confidence in the testimony of our self-consciousness.
A true unity would be unattainable for us; naturalism
and humanism, materialism and idealism, monism and
pluralism, would continue to stand in irreconcilable
opposition to each other. We should in that case
have to call in doubt even the possibility of objective
knowledge, and not be able to answer the objection that
all our knowledge is pure delusion and imagination.
Idealism has felt the seriousness of this objection, and has
been led by it to seek in some way or other in the absolute
the ground for the objectivity and the reality of our
knowledge. In regard to the nature of this absolute
there is difference of opinion. Malebranche conceived
of it as a personal God in whom we see all things. Green
speaks of an eternal consciousness. The Marburg
school assumes a transcendental consciousness, which
bears in itself the apriori forms. Rickert believes that

an abstract impersonal consciousness will suffice. Paulsen and von Hartmann think of an absolute substance which is the only true being and of which all real things are unsubstantial accidents.

That idealism has come to such a belief in the absolute cannot cause surprise. For it set out by breaking down the bridge between thinking and being, and thus created a chasm which, afterwards, no reasoning of the intellect could fill up nor any act of the will overleap. Thinking lost hold upon being. If, therefore, it was not to lose itself in subjective dreaming, but actually to issue in knowledge of the truth, it was necessary to re-establish, either high in the air or deep underground in the absolute, some connection between thought and being, between subject and object. The absolute thus serves to guarantee the truth of human thought. According to some it is not even necessary that this absolute shall restore the reality of the objective world or shall itself know all things according to truth; it suffices if it be no more than the objective norm of thinking or that as unconscious force it attain to consciousness in man.

Although the attempt to recover after this fashion the lost unity of thought and being deserves appreciation, it is impossible to regard it as the true solution of the problem. Here again it is the testimony of self-consciousness that enters a protest. It has already been observed that Schleiermacher apprehended better than Kant the essence of self-consciousness when he defined it as an absolute sense of dependence. It now remains to add that in this sense of dependence self-consciousness at the same time posits the independence and freedom of man. Apparently this is an irreconcilable antinomy, but it will be shown presently that these two testimonies of self-consciousness are not mutually exclusive, but inclusive, of each other. Even Schleiermacher himself overlooked this, and Kant was so far justified in affirming the autonomy of human knowledge and action. For no matter whether learned or unlearned, all of us without distinction are conscious that we ourselves perceive, we ourselves think, we ourselves reason, we ourselves draw conclusions, and in the same manner that we ourselves deliberate, will, and act. Religion and morality, responsibility and accountability, science and art, all the labor and culture of humanity are built on this basic assumption. Hence the absolute cannot be conceived as an unconscious and involuntary force. No doubt from time to time the deity has been so conceived by a few "intellectuals," but pantheism has never been the creed of any people, the confession of any church. Men have, it is true, often broken up, along with the unity of the world and the unity of the human race, the unity of God also; but the personality of God has remained firmly established, always and everywhere, among every nation and in every religion. Just as confidently as man is convinced in his self-consciousness of his own existence and of the reality of the world, does he believe also in the reality and personality of God.

This belief is interwoven with his self-consciousness, more particularly with its double testimony to dependence and freedom. These are not antagonistic, but rather postulate each the other. The sense of dependence is the core of self-consciousness and the essence of religion, but it is not a mere *de facto* dependence, as the unconscious and the irrational creation is dependent on God; in man it is a *sense* of dependence; the dependence in him attains to a cognizance, to a testimony of his self-consciousness, and thus certainly does not cease to exist, but yet assumes a different form. It becomes a felt, conscious, voluntary dependence, a dependence of man as a rational and moral being, and for this very reason it becomes a sense of absolute, *schlechthinnige* dependence. If the sense of dependence did not include this element, if it did not know itself as a conscious and voluntary dependence, it would cease to be absolute, because the most important factors in man, consciousness and will, would fall outside of it, or stand opposed to it. Consequently, if man repudiates his dependence, withdraws from it, he does not thereby become independent, but his dependence changes in nature. It loses its rational and moral character and becomes the subservience of a mere means to an end. Man, in becoming a sinner, does not rise, but falls; does not become like God, but like the animals. Therefore the feeling, the sense of dependence, conscious and voluntary dependence, includes the freedom of man: *Deo parere libertas; Libertas ex veritate.*

This testimony of self-consciousness, combining dependence and freedom in one, is further the basis of religion, and likewise of morality. It leads man everywhere and always, and that quite freely and spontaneously, to belief in and service of a personal God. In view of the universality and the spontaneity of religion many have assumed an innate idea of God. But this representation is scarcely well conceived, and the name is somewhat unfortunately chosen. Of course, in the strict sense of the term innate ideas do not exist. They savor rather of rationalism and of a mysticism which separates man from the world, than of a Christian theism which finds God's eternal power and divinity revealed in the works of his hands. It is the mind of man, with all of its peculiar nature

and organization, its intellect and reason, heart and conscience, desire and will, and with the ineradicable consciousness of its dependence and freedom, that is innate, brought
into the world in principle and germ at birth, not acquired
later phylogenetically or ontogenetically.   Thus, when
man grows up and develops in accordance with the nature
implanted in him, not in detachment from the world and
the social organism, but in the environment in which a place
was assigned to him at birth, he attains as freely and as
inevitably to the knowledge and service of a personal God
as he believes in his own existence and that of the world.
He does not invent the idea of God nor produce it ; it is
given to him and he receives it.   Atheism is not proper
to man by nature, but develops at a later stage of life,
on the ground of philosophic reflection ; like scepticism,
it is an intellectual and ethical abnormality, which only
confirms the rule.   By nature, in virtue of his nature,
every man believes in God.   And this is due in the last
analysis to the fact that God, the creator of all nature,
has not left himself without witness, but through all
nature, both that of man himself and that of the outside
world, speaks to him.   Not evolution, but revelation alone
accounts for this impressive and incontrovertible fact of
the worship of God.   In self-consciousness God makes
known to us man, the world, and himself.

Hence this revelation is of the utmost importance, not
only for religion, but also for philosophy, and particularly
for epistemology.   All cognition consists in a peculiar
relation of subject and object, and is built on the agreement of these two.   The reliability of perception and
thought is not assured unless the forms of thought and
the forms of being correspond, in virtue of their origin in
the same creative wisdom.   Philosophy itself has not failed

to perceive the necessity of this, but by taking a wrong start it has strayed either to the right or to the left. It either, with Hegel, has identified thought with being and raised logic to the rank of metaphysics ; or with Kant and humanism it has separated thought from being, leaving to logic a purely formalistic character. In either case the true relation between thought and being, and hence the correct principle of all cognition and knowledge, are imperfectly recognized. As even von Hartmann admits, there is no other way of doing justice to both subject and object except by recognizing that it is one and the same reason "which is active in consciousness as a principle introducing order into the sensations, and in the objective world as the principle of synthesis for the things in themselves." [21] The forms of being, the laws of thought, and — to add this here for the sake of completeness — the forms of conduct, have their common source in the divine wisdom. The three departments of philosophy, physics, logic and ethics, form a harmonious whole. What monism seeks in the wrong direction, and cannot attain unto, has here been reached, viz., the unity which does not exclude but includes the multiformity the σύστημα of philosophy.

On this firm theistic foundation, finally, there is room for belief in the progress of science and the realization of the ideal of truth. There is some degree of warrant for the assertion that the truth *is* not, but *becomes*. As a matter of fact, the truth nowhere meets us "cut and dried," ready, as it were, to be simply taken into our consciousness. On the contrary — and this is the difference between "revelation" and "discovery" — man has to conquer the truth in the sweat of his brow, with the exertion of all his strength, foot by foot and piece by

piece. The branches of knowledge have without exception "grown up in the practice of life itself "; [22] they
have all been born of necessity, and possess a practical,
economic value. Nor is the truth a mere copy, a portrait
of reality; it is something different from a *globus intellectualis*. No one, by the mere act of gathering into his
consciousness a complete account of Goethe's life and
labors, to their smallest details, will attain the truth concerning Goethe; such knowledge is a mere chronicle, not
science; a photograph, not a painting; a copy, not a living
reproduction. Science aims at something higher: it seeks
not the dead, but the living; not the transitory, but the
eternal; not the reality, but the truth. Only it does not
find the truth apart from the reality. Whosoever wants
to know Goethe must inform himself as to his person
and labors. Whosoever wants to know nature must open
his eyes. Whosoever desires to enter the kingdom of
truth, no less than he who wants to enter the kingdom
of heaven, must, to quote Bacon's words, become as a
little child which learns by obeying. We do not create
the truth, and we do not spin it out of our brain; but, in
order to find it, we must go back to the facts, to reality,
to the sources.

All science rests on the assumption that reality is not
co-extensive with the phenomena, but contains a kernel
of divine wisdom, being the realization of the decree of
God. In so far the truth is bound to reality, and finds
its criterion in correspondence with reality. But the
truth transcends the empirical reality, because and in
the same degree that scientific investigation descends
more deeply and penetrates more fully into its essence.
And the truth thus found by science is adapted to
consciousness, as it can be discovered and received by

consciousness alone.   It would, therefore, not be improper to say that for us the truth comes into being only by being made the object of our knowledge and an element of our consciousness.   For this purpose God has deposited the truth in nature and Scripture, that we might have it, and by knowing it might rule through it.   In the knowledge of the truth lies the end of its revelation ; reality is an instrument to enable us to find the truth ; reality is intended to become truth in our consciousness and in our experience.   Reality, therefore, does not offer us in the truth a mere copy of itself, so that the world, as pragmatism objects, would be duplicated.[28]   In the truth, reality rises to a higher mode of existence ; having first lain in darkness, it now walks in the light ; having once been a riddle, it now finds its solution ; not understood at the beginning, it now is " declared."

So the truth obtains an independent value of its own. Its standard does not lie in its usefulness for life, for, if usefulness were the criterion of truth, then perfect unanimity ought to prevail in regard to usefulness, and life itself ought to be a value not subject to fluctuation.   But in regard to life, what counts is not merely existence, or pleasure, or intensity, but first of all content and quality.   And it is precisely by truth that this content and quality are determined.   The truth is of more value than empirical life : Christ sacrificed his life for it.   None the less, by doing so he regained his life. Truth is worth more than reality ; it belongs to that higher order of things in which physis, and gnosis, and ethos are reconciled, and in which a true philosophy gives full satisfaction both to the demands of the intellect and to the needs of the heart.

IV

REVELATION AND NATURE

GOD, the world, and man are the three realities with which all science and all philosophy occupy themselves. The conception which we form of them, and the relation in which we place them to one another, determine the character of our view of the world and of life, the content of our religion, science, and morality.[1] But at the very outset there emerges a profound difference of opinion in regard to the sciences which are devoted to these important subjects. It is often represented as if only the special science of theology concerned itself with God and divine things, and as if all the other sciences, particularly the natural sciences, have nothing whatever to do with God; nay, as if they would even forfeit their scientific character and become disloyal to their task, should they refer to him or take account of him. A chasm is thus created, objectively, in the sphere of reality, between God and the world, and, subjectively, in man, between his intellect and heart, between his faith and knowledge; even if the very existence of God be not denied and all right of existence be refused to faith.

But such a dualism is impossible. God does not stand apart from the world, much less from man, and therefore the knowledge of him is not the peculiar domain of theology. It is true, theology especially occupies itself with his revelation, in order that its nature and contents may be, so far as possible, scientifically understood. But this

revelation addresses itself to all men; the religion which
is founded on it is the concern of every man, even of the
man of science and the investigator of nature; for all men,
without exception, the knowledge of God is the way to
eternal life.   Moreover, the man who devotes himself to
science cannot split himself into halves and separate his
faith from his knowledge; even in his scientific investigations he remains man,—not a purely intellectual being, but
a man with a heart, with affections and emotions, with
feeling and will.   Not only mankind, but also every individual, finds, as he grows to full consciousness, a view of
the world already prepared for him, to the formation of
which he has not consciously contributed.[2]   And the demand which truth and morality make on him is not, and
cannot be, that he shall denude himself of himself, but
that he shall be a man of God, furnished completely unto
every good work.   The thinker and philosopher, as well as
the common citizen and the day laborer, have to serve and
glorify God in their work.

This leads immediately to the conclusion that natural
science is not the only science, and cannot be.   The
French and English use of the word "science" might, unfortunately, lead us to think so,[3] and gives support to
the idea of Comte that humanity has successively traversed
the three stadia of theology, metaphysics, and positivism,
and only now has reached the standpoint of true science.
But history knows nothing of such a progression; the
sciences do not develop successively one after the other,
but more or less side by side and in connection with one
another.   By all sorts of interrelations they exercise an
influence on each other, and thus support and promote
each other.   Nor, in the development of science, do all
things move on as simply as is postulated in the easy and

aprioristic scheme of the doctrine of evolution. No universal formula, which endeavors to embrace the entire course of history, is true; and Comte's law also fails in the face of the criticism of life in its richness. Not uniformity, but differentiation and totality, are everywhere the distinctive marks of life.[4]

To the sciences of nature, therefore, there belongs in the circle of the sciences the same liberty of movement and work which is the right of every other science. They have their own object, and therefore their own method and aim. In their effort to know and to explain natural phenomena they have no need to call in the aid of a *Deus ex machina* and make of faith an *asylum ignorantiæ*. As a science, natural science busies itself not only with the succession, but also with the causes, of phenomena. In searching after these causes the conception of evolution, as a working hypothesis, has done eminent service. Analogies and relations have been traced out and discovered, which otherwise would not so easily have been found and investigated. But here the mistake has been made that evolution, which has proved, like, for instance, the physical atom, useful as a working hypothesis, has been elevated to the rank of a formula of world-explanation and elaborated into a system of world-conception. Thus natural science leaves her own domain and passes over to that of philosophy. It must acquiesce in the other sciences, of religion and ethics, of jurisprudence and æsthetics, coming also to their rights and incorporating the results of their investigations too into the structure of an all-embracing view of the world.

The representation is therefore wrong, that faith in the existence and providence of God finds its home exclusively in the chasms of our knowledge, so that as our investigations proceed, we must be continually filled with anxiety, and steadily lose the territory of our faith in proportion as more and more problems are solved.   For the world is itself grounded in God; witness its law and order.[5]   Faith naturally insists, — how could it fail to do so? — that it shall retain a place in the world.   It maintains its demand that natural science shall retain consciousness of its limitations and that it shall not form a conception, out of the narrow sphere in which it works, in which no room is left for the soul and immortality, for intelligence and design in the world, for the existence and providence of God, for religion and Christianity.   Natural science remains, therefore, perfectly free in its own sphere ; but it is not the only science, and must therefore cease striving to construe religious and ethical phenomena after the same physico-chemical and mathematico-mechanical fashion as is warranted and required in the case of numberless natural phenomena.   In principle what faith demands is that science shall itself maintain its ethical character, and shall not put itself at the service of the evil inclination of the human heart in its endeavor to explain the world without God and to erect itself into a self-supporting and self-sufficient divinity.

No barrier is thus erected around natural science which it cannot respect; but rather a boundary is assigned to its sphere of labor which is demanded by its own object and character.   For whereas formerly the concept "nature" frequently embraced all creation, and, as *naturata*, was distinguished from God as the *natura naturans*, it is nowadays usually limited to sensible objects and phenomena, so far as they are not produced by human art. In this sense nature stands, then, as the non-ego, in antithesis with the human psyche, as the observing and knowing subject. But because the mechanical view has a perfect right of existence in a part of the territory which history has gradually assigned to natural science, and has indeed led in it to various valuable results, many have drawn the conclusion that natural science is the only true science, and that the mechanical solution is the only true solution of all phenomena. Haeckel goes even so far as to claim that every one who still believes in a soul, or a principle of life, deserts the domain of science, and seeks refuge in miracles and supernaturalism.[6] On the other hand, von Hartmann justly maintains that whosoever, as a scientist, deems the mechanical explanation of the phenomena of life, for instance, insufficient, and endeavors to explain them in another way, namely, by a principle of life, deals with the matter just as scientifically as any other.[7] And Ostwald has even called the mechanical view of the world " a mere delusion," which cannot be utilized even as a working hypothesis.[8] In fact, the conception that the world as a whole and in all its parts is one vast machine is so absurd and self-contradictory that it is difficult to understand how it could even for one moment have satisfied and dominated the human mind. For aside from the fact that even a machine would postulate an intelligent maker,[9] the other fact remains that a machine which is eternally self-moving, and never has ceased to work and never will cease to do so, is in conflict with all our experiences and all our thinking. In point of fact the world, far from being intelligible as a machine, is "in no respect self-explaining, but in every respect mysterious." Its very existence is a riddle. The great miracle before which we stand is, that there is something which *is*, that there is an existence of which we are unable to point to the ground.[10] To the world, as a whole and in all its parts, we ascribe only a contingent existence, so that its explanation is not found in itself. Physics points back to and is founded in metaphysics.

This is already evident from the fact that the science of nature, although it has in many respects the advantage over the mental sciences, still utilizes, and is compelled to utilize, all sorts of ideas which are not derived from experience, but are present from the very start. Ideas like "thing" and "property," "matter" and "force," "æther" and "movement," "space" and "time," "cause" and "design," are indispensable to natural science; but they are derived from metaphysics. They serve as logical apparatus which precedes all observation; and yet they are so far from plain and clear that they, each in itself and all together, contain a world of mysteries. Naturally this does not satisfy the human mind. It endeavors, whether successfully or not makes no difference, to apprehend the meaning and the truth, the principle and the cause, of these ideas. Natural science may for a time despise philosophy; by and by it must return to it, because it has itself proceeded from it.[11] When the "thirst for facts" has been in a way satisfied, the "hunger for causes" will come to the surface.[12]

The proof of this is found herein, that no one is able to banish from his heart or to remove from his lips the question of the origin of things. Haeckel justly observes, however, that this question lies outside of the domain of natural science. If creation ever took place, "it lies entirely beyond the scope of human knowledge, and hence can never become the object of scientific investigation." But he does not stop there, but immediately proceeds: "Natural science regards matter as eternal and imperishable, because the origination or annihilation of the smallest of its particles has never yet been proved by experience." In announcing this dogma of the eternity of matter, however, it is not the student of nature but the philosopher, not science but faith, that speaks; for what he objects against faith is of force against himself: " where faith begins, there science ceases." [13] And this is all the more forcible because elsewhere he is compelled to admit: " We nowhere reach a knowledge of ultimate causes "; even if all the riddles of the world and of life were solved, the one great riddle of substance would confront us like a sphinx.[14] Physics, then, is not the only science solving all riddles, but before it and above it stands metaphysics. If, nevertheless, it wishes an explanation of the origin of all things, it commits itself to what, scientifically considered, as Lodge says, " must be viewed as guess-work, being an overpressing of known fact into an exaggerated and over-comprehensive form of statement." [15]

Not less great are the difficulties which confront natural science when it investigates the essence of things. Here we have to deal with three factors, — space, time, and a *quale*, howsoever we may further define it, which in space and time makes their mutual relations possible. These factors, too, the science of nature does not find by its own investigations, but rather postulates from the start. And these ideas again embrace a whole array of difficulties. We do not know what space and time are in themselves. We do not know the relation which they sustain to matter and force; and of their finiteness or infinity we can form not the slightest notion.[16] Kant points out in his antinomies of reason that with these ideas we confront difficulties which are

insoluble to our thought. The affirmation that the world
has had no beginning and has no limits, involves us in the
self-contradictions of an infinite time and an infinite
space, for the sum total of finite parts, however many
they may be, can never equal infinitude.[17]   Time and
space are therefore the existence-form of the world and
the conception-form of our consciousness; but they cannot
be identified with that which is the absolute ground and
cause of all existence.   In this sense they belong not to
" reality," but to " appearance," or rather, they appertain
only to creation, but not to the Creator.   And since an
eternal time and a boundless space are like a wooden iron,
our thinking forces us to distinguish the absolute from
the relative.   Monism does not exist here, and if it
nevertheless be sought here, it can bring us nothing but
confusion.   Eternity and time, immensity and space, do
not differ quantitatively but qualitatively.   And since the
words " absolute," " eternal," " immense," " infinite," are
predicates, and, when substantivized, form only empty
abstractions, they presuppose a transcendent subject,
differentiated from the world, to whom they belong.
That is to say, physical science, which thinks through
its own conceptions, and fathoms its own nature, issues
in metaphysics and rises straight to God.

Not less involved is the problem presented by the
third conception, of which the science of nature makes
use, namely, the idea of some sort of substance which
exists in the forms of time and space and makes their
interrelation possible.   In a formal sense natural science
is " the exhibition of the coherence of reality as a unified
system of regulated relations of dependence between
elements of space, time, and number." [18]   Its aim is —
whether rightly or wrongly — to comprehend all change

and movement in a mathematical formula and to reduce
all qualitative differences to quantity. So far as it strives
after this aim, it is a formal science. But it is self-
evident that reality is not comprehended in these formal
definitions. Reality is something else and something
more than a complex of quantitative relations. These
presuppose precisely a *quale*, which exists in those relations. Even if we knew all the laws of motion and
of change to which matter is subject, with all that its
essence would still remain a mystery. Astronomy may be
able to compute the movements of celestial bodies, but
this does not enlighten us in regard to their nature and
composition.

Now, ideas concerning the substance of things, even
among the votaries of natural science, diverge very
widely. But even the very first question, whether such a
substance exists, or whether the psychic sensations are
the ultimate elements of reality, falls entirely outside of
the bounds of physics and brings us again into the
domain of philosophy. When Max Verworn attacks
materialism and " energetism " in the name of monism,
he no longer speaks as a physiologist, but as a philosopher.
But even he, although he repels the antithesis of subject
and object, of spirit and matter, of soul and body, does
not find monism. For when he says that the entire
physical world is only " a content of the psyche," he
begins, without admitting it, with the reality of the
psyche, that is of substance, and differentiates between it
and its contents. As long, therefore, as science believes
in itself, it cannot escape the necessity of postulating in
and above experience a unity, a bond, a subject, which
tests and orders this experience.[19] And as the experience
subjectively presupposes a subject which experiences, it

also objectively points to a reality, which just as little
as the subject is exhausted in relations. In the subject there is a difference between a *Beziehendes* and a
Bezogenes; and in the object there is a difference
between the relations and the reality of which they are
predicated. Very truly Fechner says : " Not merely the
detailed phenomena, but also that which holds them
together, has reality ; nay, to the latter belongs the highest
reality." [20]   But whatever we may think of this, the
question of the reality of the soul and the world belongs
to metaphysics ; it is not answered by empirical investigations, but by metaphysics, that is to say, in other words,
by faith.

The same is true with reference to the problem of the
ultimate nature of that reality which must be accepted
unless we are willing to sink into solipsism. Whether we
take the theistic standpoint here, or accept some one of
the different forms of monism, we do not attain to our
conception of the nature of reality by the way of experience, but must permit ourselves to be led by metaphysical
reasoning on the basis of observation. And it is not exact
science, but faith and the character of our personality, which
decides the matter here. It is not presumable that physics
and chemistry, however far they may extend their researches, will ever change this state of affairs. Chemistry
still has some seventy elements, whose resolution or composition it cannot effect and which differ from one another
in qualities. And although physics reduces the phenomena
of light, heat, and electricity to vibrations, it has not yet
succeeded in reducing the qualitative differences, which
manifest themselves in these phenomena, to quantitative
relations. The nature of the ultimate element of things
is still utterly unknown. Whether these elements are

atoms, which differ only in size, form, and weight, or even
in quality, or whether these ultimate elements of existence are rather "monads" or "reales," matter or energy,
or both together — all this is a fit subject for philosophic
speculation, but must *per se* far transcend all observation.
In our day natural science, in order to explain the phenomena of light and electricity, assumes the existence of
an ether, which fills all space. But this ether has never
been observed, and its nature is unknown. A great effort
is being made to discover an original stuff, which lies at
the base of all matter, especially since Sir William Ram-
say's announcement that radium can be transmuted into
helium and lithium; and hypotheses have already been
constructed which see such an original stuff in hydrogen
or in the electron or in the ether. But for the time being
W. A. Shenstone is perfectly justified in saying, "that we
are still very far from knowing definitely that atoms are
composed entirely of electrons, or that electrons are nothing but electric changes; and though electrons have been
shown to exhibit electric inertia, it has not been proved
that the inertia of atoms is also electrical." [21]

And just as little as all matter has been reduced to one
original stuff, have the different forces been as yet shown
to be only forms of one original force. Force in itself is
a mysterious phenomenon. When Ostwald seeks to reduce all matter to energy, he can only hypostatize and per-
sonify a conception which has been derived from matter
by abstraction, and mistakenly imagines that he has thus
eliminated matter.[22] Similarly every specific force is an
unexplained mystery; the force of gravitation, for instance,
is not an explanation, but only the name of a phenomenon,
and it is even questionable whether the name is exact.[23]
Especially in regard to the vital force, differences of opin-

ion assert themselves.   Mechanism and vitalism here stand
in bitter opposition, and the neovitalists are at war among
themselves on the question whether the cause of life is
to be sought in a special force of the organism, or rather
in an idea or form dominating and governing this organism.   And thus the riddles increase step by step, as science
penetrates more deeply into the essence of things or rises
higher in the ascending scale of creation.   The cell is the
last and lowest form of life, but the cell-core and proto-
plasm, which form the cell, are not homogeneous, and point
to different compositions; the original *individua* of bio-
plasts are not of one kind; plants, animals, and man do
not yet form an uninterrupted ascending chain of creatures; even the animals have not been reduced to one
primordial type, and are nowadays usually divided into
eight classes.   Everywhere in creation we face an endless
differentation, an inconceivable multiformity of creatures,
an inexhaustible wealth of essence and life.

Beyond question it is the duty of science to reduce this
chaos of phenomena to order.   It has to give us the thread,
following which we may not lose our way in this labyrinth,
but find the right path.   But, as has already been said, it
is an aprioristic and wholly unjustified assumption that
this path through the labyrinth of the world must lead
to monism, — particularly when monism itself has been
erected on an utterly aprioristic view of the world; namely,
on the conception that this world must find its explanation
in itself.   But unity, true unity, a unity which does not
destroy differentiation, but rather includes and enfolds it,
may come, and can come, only when the entire world is
conceived as the product of the wisdom and power which
reveal God's eternal plan.   Only a personal God, who is
both will and intelligence, can call a world into existence,

which is one and yet differentiated ; just as man alone, who has been created in his image, is a knowing and willing being, a knowledge-making and tool-making animal.

But suppose for a moment that all matter and all force, all existence and all life, could be reduced in our thinking to one ultimate principle ; even so nothing is gained for the truth of monism or for the explanation of the world. For first of all the old logical rule is still in force — *a posse ad esse non valet consequentia.* The mere fact that in our thought we can form the conception of a world which has produced itself from one substance through the action of one force, would not prove at all that this conception is the true one and that reality corresponds to this conception. For instance, it is well known that the elements which constitute the bodies of living beings are, besides oxygen, carbon, hydrogen, nitrogen, and sulphur. But these four elements are never found in a free state, but always in combination with oxygen (oxidized), especially in the form of carbonic acid, water, sulphuric acid, and saltpetre. In order, therefore, that they may be serviceable for the formation of albumen and other organic compounds, they must first be separated from the oxygen (deoxidized). To the question whether, in earlier periods of this world's existence, free carbon, hydrogen and sulphur existed, an answer could be given by experience alone; but in the nature of the case this is not available. Logical analysis is thus something different from real decomposition. Even if chemistry should ultimately discover a single original element, even that would not at all prove that this original element existed in the beginning separately, and has slowly and gradually, through a variety of mechanical combinations, brought into being the several existing elements.[24] Physics never is empowered to conclude from the *posse* to the *esse*, from the conception to the reality; it is not limited by any extraneous power, but by its own character.

Still, for the sake of argument let us also admit that there was originally only one element and one force, from which by slow degrees everything has developed. Then natural science would be simplified, but the riddle of the multiformity of the world would continue undiminished.[25] It would be merely transferred and moved backwards; transferred to the one substance and moved back to an endless past. And by this it would even be increased in intensity. For the question thus becomes: how, from one single uniform original element, by any possibility, this world, with its endless differentiations, could have been produced. The answer to the atomists used to be that the Iliad could not have been produced by an accidental collocation of a font of type. But there is nothing here to compare to the difficulty of the monists in explaining the world. For an alphabet at least consists of different letters, and language may illustrate how the human mind can from a few sounds form tens of thousands of words. But the new monism lets the Iliad of the world arise out of the collocation of the same letter and the same sound. Such a process is possible only if the one world-substance is elevated to deity and invested with the attributes of omniscience and omnipotence, which, according to theism, belong to the personal God alone. Without metaphysics, without faith, without God, physics does not reach its mark. But the deity which is finally invoked is a *Deus ex machina;* the faith in which it hides itself is an *asylum ignorantiæ;* and the divinity which it conceives is one of its own making.

In the conflict which nowadays rages on all sides, and

which is frequently represented as a conflict between science and faith, physics and theology, the principal difference, therefore, does not concern the question, What is nature? but rather this other one, What is God? If possible, this will be still more clearly seen if we call attention finally to the problem of motion. Nothing proves more clearly that this problem cannot be solved than the fact that philosophy throughout the ages and among all nations and down to the present day divides itself into two tendencies. With Zeno, "becoming" is sacrificed to "being," or with Heraclitus, "being" to "becoming." In point of fact, we can spare neither, for "becoming" presupposes "being." There can be no question of change if there is no identity and continuity of the subject.[26] But monism cannot accept this differentiation, endeavors to reduce motion to rest or rest to motion, and thus once again sacrifices the facts of reality to a play of ideas. And by this endeavor it gets, at every subordinate point which is raised by the problem of motion, in an *impasse* which has no outlet.

For whether motion is reality or appearance, the questions of its cause and nature, its laws and aim, can never be suppressed. If now there is no *primum movens*, no "being" which gives existence to the "becoming," nothing is left but to think of motion as eternal. And Haeckel accordingly affirms that the substance of the universe, with its two attributes, matter and energy, fills infinite space and is in an eternal motion, and that this motion thus proceeds in an endless time.[27] But such words, though no doubt they endure to be set side by side on paper, form in thought an intolerable antinomy. Eternity and motion can be just as little correlated in one and the same subject as infinitude and space (or time), as the absolute and the relative, as God and the world. And this is all the less possible if the world, according to Haeckel's notion, is a vast machine. For a machine which keeps on working forever, without ever coming to a stop, is an inconceivable and impossible *perpetuum mobile.* If the world is eternal, it is no machine; if it is a machine, it cannot be eternal.

A similar difficulty arises with respect to the nature of motion. Man has always lived in the conviction that there is no effect without a cause. Even if in earlier times numerous phenomena or occurrences were explained by the operation of divinities, of spirits, or of mysterious powers, this is merely a proof that the law of causality is not an invention of modern times, but is a category of the human mind. Neither did men in early times ascribe all phenomena to supernatural operations, nor is this done to-day among the so-called "nature-peoples." For everywhere and always there has been quite an extended sphere in which things were referred to natural causes. From his origin man has worked in order to eat; has applied himself to fishing and to the chase, to agriculture and stockraising, and, in a primitive way, also to knowledge and art. By the aid of the means at hand he has obtained food and clothing and shelter. The conception of natural causes has never been wholly lacking in man. But no doubt this domain of natural causes was much more limited than at the present day. Science has gradually expanded the idea of nature and of the natural. And every reasonable man rejoices in this expansion of our knowledge, which is at the same time power and domination of spirit over matter.

But when science seeks to apply the law of causality in such sense as to permit only a mechanical relation between cause and effect, it not only passes beyond its competence, but also cuts itself off from explaining the phenomena. For just as motion presupposes no less continuity than change, causality implies both that cause and effect stand in relation to one another, and that the effect is something more than, or at least something different from, the cause. For if this were not so, everything would remain where it is, or at least at the same level; everything would revolve in a circle, and there could be no possible question of progress, ascent, or development. Now reality teaches us certainly to recognize such progress and development; there is a great differentation of being. And even in the sphere where we speak, and justly so, of mechanical causality, causality is not at all exhausted by mechanism. We call it by that name, no doubt, but this name does not cover the much richer reality.

Lodge has said very truly: " There is no necessary justification for assuming that a property exhibited by an aggregate of particles must be possessed by the ingredients of which it is composed; on the contrary, wholly new properties may make their appearance simply by aggregation." [28] The simplest combinations of elements already manifest properties different from those of the elements themselves. Water differs in nature from each of its two components, — oxygen and hydrogen; vitriol is different from any of its three components, — iron and sulphur and oxygen.[29] And in a much higher measure this is true of organic beings. Heredity has been for years the object of keen investigation, but no one will affirm that its secret has been disclosed and that its explanation has been accomplished. The variety of the theories which have been framed concerning it — those of Lamarck and Darwin, Erlsberg and Haeckel, Nägeli and de Vries, Weismann and Hertwig — is enough to show that not one of them is satisfactory. For the present we can only say that there is such a thing as heredity, and that there is such a thing as variability, as certainly we might very well have expected from the beginning. But of its cause and relations we thus far know nothing. All change seems, in varying degrees, to be a sort of generation which produces something newer and higher. Thus change, progress, and development are possible, but thus also it becomes manifest that the attempt to transmute all causality into mechanical relationship is doomed from the very start. In causality other forces are at work than those which can be expressed by figures.

This being so, the laws of nature also assume an aspect different from that which still is often ascribed to them. Really we can speak of natural laws only from the standpoint of theism. Natural laws exist only when there is a lawgiver, who stands above nature and who has decreed that seedtime and harvest, and cold and heat, and summer and winter, and day and night shall not cease while the earth remains. Abstracted from God as the law-giver, the laws of nature are nothing but a human and ever fallible description of the way in which things operate. Like substance and force and motion, these natural laws are frequently no doubt hypostatized and elevated to the rank of powers and rulers over things. But against this the words of von Hartmann are pertinent, that " Of all entities created by hypostatizing abstractions probably that of (natural) law as a power antedating the existence of things, hovering over them and controlling them, is the most fictitious." [30] Our natural laws are only a formula for the method of work and of motion of the things.

Therefore they are far from fixed, are anything but unchangeable; on the contrary they are changed, modified, restricted, enlarged, according as we learn to know the things better. Robert Mayer, for instance, the discoverer of the law of the conservation of energy, completely excluded from this law the entire domain of psychical life, and considered it a great error to identify things physical and psychical.[31] And although Wundt in the first edition of his *Lectures on the Human and Animal Soul*, published in 1863, applied this law in the psychical domain too, he expressly receded from this position in the second edition of his work, published in 1892, and has since defended the theory of psychophysical parallelism, — a change of opinion which brought upon him the gibe of Haeckel, that it was usual in old age for "a gradual degeneration to set in, in the brain as well as in the outer organs."[32] Similarly Lodge offers very serious objections to the laws of the constancy of matter and energy, since at best they are applicable only to the forces which we know at present and as we now know them. But in case that matter should prove the phenomenal form of a complex of ether, production and dissolution of matter would be possible. And in case that life should prove to be more than a physico-chemical force, we would have to modify the law of the constancy of energy, as some have already proposed to do, since the discovery of radium. So long, therefore, as matter in its essence is unknown, and the resident forces of creation are not exhausted by us, all formulation of laws is necessarily tentative, and a large degree of modesty is the proof of a scientific spirit.[33] For in the last analysis all laws of nature, whatever philosophical standpoint we may occupy, are determined by the nature of that being which is the ground and origin of all things and the force of all forces. Laws, ordinances they are, therefore, then only, and in so far only, as they may have a metaphysical character.

And, moreover, only in that case can there be any question, in the development of the world, of a meaning and an aim. Darwin rejoiced in the discovery of natural selection, because he thought that by its aid he could explain the adaptations of nature without a divine intelligence.[34] Helmholtz found the novelty of the doctrine of descent, in its exhibition how "adaptation in the formation of organisms can be produced by the blind reign of natural law without the interference of any intelligent factor."[35] And notwithstanding his mechanical view of the world, Haeckel continues to talk about means and aim, about egoistic and altruistic duties, about a "fundamental law of ethics," and about ethics as "the science of norms."[36] The attack of the evolutionary hypothesis is really not directed against adaptation in nature. On the contrary, although it proceeds from a mechanical causality, it lays all its stress on the tendency and aim of the development. It loves to pose as the theory of progress, and to tell us that evolution has successively originated life, consciousness, will, and all that is true, and good, and beautiful; that it has gradually ennobled the struggle for existence, and has made it a "battle of the spirit," for that which is noblest and best. Causality in the doctrine of evolution does not antagonize teleology, but is only a means and an element in the process of development. By the one it ascribes to nature *compulsion;* by the other, will and *fitness* (*sollen*).[37]

But as soon as this adaptation in the world is taken as a teleological proof of the existence and providence of an intelligent power, opposition is aroused, and all

monstrosities and rudimentary organs, all disasters and
mishaps are called to the witness-stand, to break down
the force of this proof. There may be an unconscious
and blind adaptation, but no conscious and intelligent
one. Haeckel once said that the eye and the ear are
so marvellously constructed that they might seduce us
into believing in a creation according to a definitely
thought-out plan of construction. But he steels himself
against the "seduction." And thus he betrays the fact
that the so-called conflict between science and faith lies
not in the realm of the physical, but in that of the metaphysical; concentres not in nature, but in God. What
nature is to us is determined by what we think of God
and who he is for us.

It is, therefore, by no means an indifferent matter for
science, and especially for physics, what ground we occupy
in metaphysics. We may not think as we please; even
scientific work has a moral character, and we have to
render an account of it as well as of every idle word.
When we sever nature from God, and do not consider
nature as a work and revelation of God, but look on it in
the completest sense as ἄθεος, this unbelief immediately
turns into superstition. Without God all things go wrong,
both in our living and in our thinking. The denial of the
existence of God includes, in the same moment, the ele-
vation of the creature into the place of God. This is manifested in the materialism of Haeckel, when he openly
avows his atheism, but at once invests his substance with
the predicates of eternity, omnipresence, omnipotence, etc.,
which belong to God alone. It comes even more clearly
into evidence in the energetic-psychical and logical monism.
For there is bound up with this the acknowledgment that
the world is no machine, which man can take apart and

put together again, but an unconscious, mysterious power, which produces and directs everything. The intelligibility of nature, which was so long believed in by science, is therefore more and more giving place to the confession of its unknowableness. Some years ago Fechner preached his hylozoism and, as many Greek philosophers had done, conceived of the universe literally as a living organism, and this conception has of late found acceptance with many. In 1889 Vogt ascribed to atoms a sense of pain. Haeckel not only sees in the attraction and repulsion of atoms the forces of love and pain, but he animates all plastidules and replaces the wood- and water-nymphs of the Greeks by countless elementary souls and spirits, which are the properties of cells.[38] The laws of nature — although they are only a defective formulation of the way in which forces, which are but imperfectly known, are working — are elevated to the rank of mythical beings, like the *abstracta* of the Romans.[39] All investigators of nature apply to nature the conceptions of power, force, industry, labor, resistance, tension, etc., without stopping to consider that all these things are borrowed from human personality, have a psychological content, and are therefore, when robbed of it, nothing but empty forms. In the essence of the thing, what is done is what is ascribed as a naïve error to primitive man: nature is explained by animistic or anthropomorphic conceptions.[40] The issue of science in our day, in a remarkable manner, reaches out the hand of fellowship to man, such as he existed, according to the common idea, in his infancy.[41]

Recent literature and art afford even more startling proof of this deification of nature than science. For without in the least belittling its value, it may be said, on good grounds, that recent art, as a whole, has as its aim

to represent man as powerless over against nature. Its
revival in the last century was a reversion to mysticism.
The essence of things did not exist in material atoms, but
it was life, infinitely deep life, eternally operative force.
From this principle advance could be made to symbolism,
which sees in art an attempt to give a suggestion, in sound
or color, in line or arabesque, of the inexpressible; and
then further to a glorification of the *mystici*, and an æsthetic prizing of religion, especially of the Romish worship, as happened with the "néo-Chrétiens" of France.
But from the pantheistic and agnostic conception of the
universe, the conclusion could just as well be drawn
that the everywhere operative force is a mysterious blind
fate, of which man is the plaything and against which
nothing can prevail. It is thus that in the art of the
present day nature is pictured. It is provided with secret
powers, dark operations, soft moods, and over against it
man is degraded to the point of a mere natural being,
which, borne down by heredity, is abandoned to the play
of his lusts and passions, stripped of his spontaneity, liberty, and personality, and left incapable of aught but
living himself out, like a plant in the field.[42] Thus the relation of man to nature, notwithstanding the victories of
science, becomes the very opposite of what it was before.
The Christian view of nature is gradually giving place
to that of the heathen peoples; and the widely spread
movements of theosophy and spiritism, of telepathy and
astrology, assist in this degradation of man under
nature. The un-deification of nature turns into deification of nature, the royal liberty of man into fatalistic
subjection.

Man can attain to a true, free relation to nature only
when he stands in his true relation to God. And this we

owe to Christianity alone. In the polytheistic religions of India and China, Babylon and Egypt, Greece and Rome, man cannot obtain his freedom over against nature, because all creatures, plants and animals, woods and trees, mountains and brooks, stars and suns, are conceived as inhabited by gods or spirits. Over against all this man is tortured by a continuous fear and unbroken anxiety. But this relation is utterly changed when we listen to Moses and the prophets, to Christ and the apostles. They are all free over against nature, because, through communion with God, they are elevated above nature. Deification of nature is here just as inconceivable as contempt of nature. "Paganism oscillates between overbearing abuse of the world and childish dread of its powers." But in Israel this is wholly different. " With sovereign self-consciousness the Hebrew faces the world and nature. Fear of the world is unknown to him ; nevertheless he meets it with a sense of the highest responsibility. As God's representative man rules the world, but in that capacity only. He may not obey his caprice, but only the revealed will of God." [43]

Man owes this free and royal relation to nature first of all to the fact that all the world is recognized as created by God. Here at once the truth is found for which monism seeks in vain. There must be a unity, which lies at the bottom of all diversity. But this unity cannot be found within the world, for matter and force, spirit and matter, the physical and the psychical, the psychical and the ethical, personality and association cannot be reduced to one another; they do not exist *after* each other, but each with its own concept and valuation, *side by side with* each other. Whosoever, within the world, tries to reduce unity to multiformity, being to becoming, spirit to

matter, man to nature, or the reverse, always plays false
with the other half of the distinction. Thus physics calls
for metaphysics; nature itself shows, in the core of its existence, that it does not exist of itself, has not been originated by evolution, but is grounded in *revelation*. And
revelation, by the word of prophets and apostles, confirms
this and gives us, in the wisdom and omnipotence of God,
in his sovereignty and counsel, that unity for which the
human spirit thirsts. So soon, therefore, as this theistic
monism is surrendered, after a brief and unsatisfactory
trial of materialism and pantheism, polytheism in different
forms returns.[44] The power of nature and the power of
the morally good fall asunder as in Manichaeism; to man
and nature, nations and religions, different origins are ascribed; and since the forces at work in the world cannot
be reduced to unity, each of them in its own sphere is
hypostatised, and first in the conception, but later also in
the imagination, they are made gods. But the revelation
which comes to us in Christ protects us from all this. It
joins itself to the revelation, which nature itself makes
known to us; it elevates this to its fullest right, and maintains it in its real value, and by its doctrine of creation
cuts all polytheism and all dualism up by the roots. Not
only mind but also matter, not only man but also nature, is
of divine origin, and has lain in the thought of God before
it came into being.

The doctrine of creation maintains the divinity, the
goodness and sacredness of all created things. In this
world man now receives his own independent place.
He is of kin to all the world, formed out of matter,
earthy of the earth; nothing natural is strange to him.
But in one respect he is different from all creatures; he
is the son, the image, the similitude of God, his offspring.

Thereby he is elevated above animal and angel, and destined and fitted for dominion over all the world. In this relation of man to God and to the world is the foundation laid and the origin given of all science and art. For how can it be explained that man through his senses can observe the world, and through his intelligence can know and understand it? Whence this wonderful correspondence of knowing and being? What is the basis of the belief that the conception and the thought in the human brain are no imagination and no hallucination, but correspond with the reality? What is the ground for the harmony between subject and object, the ego and the non-ego? What is the root from which springs the unity of the laws of existence, the ideas of our thinking, the norms of our actions? In what do physis, gnosis, and ethos find their common systema? What is the foundation of the symbolism of nature, not in the sense of an unfounded nature-theosophy, but in the sense in which Christ saw in the world a parable of the kingdom of heaven; in the sense in which Goethe said that "all transitory things are but a parable"; in the sense in which Drummond in "the natural law" detected an analogy of the law of the spirit? On what, in a word, are founded comparison, metaphor, poetry, art, and all science and all culture? On what else do they rest but on the confession that one word, one spirit, one divine intelligence lies at the foundation of all things and maintains their unity and mutual relations?

And thus finally place is found for the acknowledgment of the diversity of the world. Nothing is simpler than to allow, according to the scheme of emanation, all things gradually to descend from above; or, according to the scheme of evolution, all things gradually to ascend from

below. In a museum, and equally in the mind, it is a very
easy matter to place one creature by the side of another
and to fill in the missing links by some hypothesis or individual construction. It is just as easy as — to use a hu-
morous example — to explain the origin of the English
fox, from the Greek word ἀλώπηξ, by assuming that the
transitional forms, *lopex*, *pex*, *fex*, have disappeared.[45]
But reality laughs at this system just as it laughs at the
aprioristic world-construction in Hegel's philosophy. Creatures do not exist in succession to one another, in a straight
line of development, but side by side ; they thus live out
their lives and hold continually with one another a living,
organic, diversified, reciprocal relation. So it was throughout all the ages, and so it is yet, in our day. The constancy of the species is·an undeniable fact, in the face of
all variability of which we are cognizant in the historical
period which we know. The weaker specimens and species
do not die out, according to the law of "natural selection," but continue to exist, side by side with the stronger,
to this day. Existence is not simply and alone a battle of
all against all, but also a continuous mutual supporting and
aiding. There is much hatred, but there is also much love
in the world. The diversity of the world is a fact which,
taken in connection with its harmony, can find its explanation only transcendently in a personal God. For F. A.
Lange has said very correctly: "When after a free and
grand fashion we ascribe to the one God a unified plan of
operation on a large and comprehensive scale, then the
coherence of all things according to the principle of law
and effect, not only becomes conceivable, but even appears
a necessary consequence of this assumption."[46]
Against this organic view of the world only one
argument is advanced. But it is an argument which

is of very great weight, for it is drawn from the awful
misery of the world. And this misery, viewed both as
sin and suffering, is a touching and heart-breaking fact.
The whole creation is in travail. Anguish is the fundamental trait of all living things. A great secret pain
throbs through nature. Everywhere the lawless, the
chaotic, lies at the base of the orderly; there is an
inexplicable restlessness in all things. Vanity, change,
death are written on all existing things. Humanity
walks by the margin of an abyss of guilt. It perishes
under the anger of God and is troubled by his wrath.
How can such a world be reconciled with the wisdom,
the goodness, the omnipotence of God? Both philosophy
and theology have made many attempts to solve this
problem. It has been sought to find the explanation of
misery, metaphysically, in the finite, or to give it, æsthetically, a part in the harmony of the world as a whole,
or to interpret it, pædagogically, as a strengthening of
man's spiritual life. The infralapsarians have deduced
it from the justice of God. Others, with Lotze, have
despaired of finding any explanation, or have even taken
refuge in a limitation of God's omnipotence and wisdom,
and have found in matter or in the laws of nature a
limit to his working.[47]

But even if there is a measure of truth in each of
these various theories, the misery of the world is too
great and too diversified to be explained from any single
cause, or to be subsumed under any single formula.
And it is not lessened by it all. What profit is there,
for instance, in saying: "Who to-day thinks of the
San Francisco earthquake as an act of God and not as
a mechanical occurrence?"[48] Is God then no longer
the God whose providence extends over all? Pragma-

tism is so far within its right that it finds all these
explanations insufficient and misleading, and calls attention once more to realities. It breaks mere appearance,
it snatches the blindfolding from our eyes, and it avows
openly that this world is a chaos, which can become
good and true only through the hands of men.

But in so doing it forgets that, in its deepest sense,
the struggle lies not between man and nature, but is
fought out in the heart of man himself, between his
what is and his what ought to be. The struggle is
primarily of an ethical rather than of a physical nature.
This is proved first of all by the fact that all the
acquisitions of culture, however rich they may be, do
not quiet the restlessness of the heart and are unable to
silence the voice of conscience. Moreover, according to
the testimony of the heroes of our race, all the misery
of the world can be overcome by faith. And that is the
only way which revelation — that in nature already, but
far more plainly that in the Scriptures — points out to us
for the reconciliation of the discord. It makes no effort
to explain all the suffering of the world. It allows it to
remain where it is and accepts it: accepts it so fully
that no pessimistic literature can surpass the pathos of its
complaint. But revelation does not incite man to resistance and rebellion, but lays bare to his consciousness the
guilt in his own life. It casts him down in his littleness,
and says to him, Who art thou, O man, that repliest
against God? But then, also, it immediately raises him
from his humiliation; it preaches to him no stoical apathy
or fatalistic acquiescence in things, but it makes him
through the Word to know the will of God to save the
world notwithstanding all its misery, and it fills his
soul through the Spirit with the patience of faith, so

that weak man can endure all his pain, can glory in tribulation, and, with God, can overcome the world. If God is for us, who can be against us? And this is the only victory which overcomes the world, even our *faith.*

V

THE indispensability and significance of revelation appear in history in an even higher and richer measure than in nature. But so soon as we set foot on this domain, our attention is immediately attracted by an interesting controversy which for several years has been waged by historians among themselves.

When the natural sciences in the last century, attained all manner of brilliant results through the application of the inductive method, the wish arose in many breasts that history might be studied after the same method, and thus reach equally certain results. There was ultimately only one science, that of nature; whatever was reckoned to the so-called intellectual sciences must be reduced to and embodied in natural science if it were to retain its claim to the name of science. Thus historical investigation could be considered a true science only if its object — historical occurrences — were conceived as a mechanical process, dominated from the beginning to the end by the same laws as nature. But in the attempt to make of history an empirical, positive science there were developed from the very beginning different tendencies. All were at one in the conviction that the events of history were just as inevitable as the phenomena of nature, and that they should be observed and fixed just as unprejudicedly and objectively as the latter. But a great difference of opinion arose upon the question how these facts were to be understood and from what causes they were to be explained.

There are some who, like Buckle, de Greef, Mongeolle, seek the ultimate and principal causes of historic events in the physical environment of climate, soil, and food, and base history on anthropogeography. There are others who, like Taine, and especially Gobineau and H. St. Chamberlain, consider the race the principal factor in history and ask of ethnology the solution of historical problems. Men like Le Bon, Tarde, René Worms, Ratzenhofer, and Sighele try to find the explanation of historical facts in psychology and social circumstances; whilst many scholars like Hobbes, Rousseau, Comte, Spencer, von Hellwald, Schäffle, Durkheim, and others, cherish the idea that society itself is to be looked upon as an organism of a higher order, which, like all living things, stands under the dominion of biological laws, and is gradually developed and perfected in the struggle for existence by natural selection and heredity. The Socialists, Marx, Engels, Kautsky, and their fellows, look at everything from the viewpoint of the conflict between the classes, and defend the materialistic or economic view of history, according to which the consciousness of man does not determine his being, but reversely his social being his consciousness. And finally, in these last years, Karl Lamprecht has appeared as a defender of the culture-historical method, which discovers the deepest ground of historical events in the folk-soul, and therefore seeks after a social-psychological solution of the problem.[1]

This endeavor to bring, in these different ways, surety and certainty into the science of history, is easy to understand. For history differs from physics in this respect, that it does not have the object of its investigation immediately at hand so as to be able to experiment upon it, but can know it only by means of a testimony which others, either intentionally or unintentionally, directly or indirectly, have given. Even though this testimony is not accepted unconditionally, but is first subjected to a severe criticism, there must enter into the study of history, through the interposition of tradition, a certain personal element of trust which is not found, or at least not in such a degree, in the investigation of natural phenomena. This personal element in historical research is considerably augmented by the fact that we are unable to assume as objective and dispassionate an attitude to the persons and testimonies with which history brings us into contact as to natural phenomena. In history we are not disinterested observers, but live the lives of other men, are attracted or repelled by them, feel sympathy or antipathy towards them. And especially in the case of important persons or great events, such as, for instance, the origin of Christianity, the Reformation, the Revolution, etc., our convictions, our heart, and our emotions play an important part. From the very start personal interest makes itself felt in our criticism of the witnesses, and it continues to exercise its influence in the pragmatic description and judgment of events. A believer in and a denier of the divinity of Christ cannot judge the books and contents of the Old and New Testaments in the same way; and we cannot expect the same history of the Reformation from a Roman Catholic and from a Protestant.[2] In historical research the personality of the student is felt much more strongly, therefore, than in natural science; the science of history splits into tendencies and thus seems to lose its claim to the name of science. We can therefore perfectly understand the effort which is made to rescue history, as a science, from this subjectivity, and to make it just as objective and exact as the science of nature, which seems the same to all men, without distinction of religious convictions.

To this was added in the last century that the field of history was expanded in an extraordinary way, in no less degree indeed than that of natural science. What in the fifteenth century the travels of Vasco de Gama, Columbus, Magellan, Cook, etc., had been for our knowledge of the earth, the discoveries of Champollion, Rawlinson, Grotefend, Layard, W. Jones, Burnouf, and others, became for our knowledge of history. Whilst historical knowledge was formerly confined to a few countries and peoples, it has now widely extended itself to all sorts of peoples, and reaches back into the past to times far earlier than Moses. This extraordinary extension of the domain of investigation has, naturally, increased the material inconceivably, and made it necessary, in order to create order in this chaos, to conceive the events in their mutual relations and to discover the process and the law which is hidden in them. It was inevitable that the ideological view of history presented by Hegel and the Tübingen school should give place under the inspiration of natural science to a positive and nomological treatment of history. It was no longer permissible to construe the facts in accordance with a preconceived idea; but, inversely, from the facts the laws must be learned which controlled them in their development.

Apparently this positive treatment of history goes to work in an utterly unprejudiced manner, purely empirically and inductively. But actually it is just as much dominated by a preconceived idea as the ideological treatment of Hegel, and this idea is in both cases that of evolution, conceived in a mechanical or in a dynamic sense. It is silently presupposed that, in the last analysis, one and the same causality originates all events and causes them to succeed each other according to the law of progressive development, in a straight, upward line. Monism and evolution are the principia of the modern view of history, just as in the last lecture they proved to be such in the investigation of nature. But it deserves attention at the outset that the conception of evolution, when applied in history to a family or a tribe, to a people or to humanity, has an entirely different sense from that which it bears in individual organisms. In a remarkable study of the idea of development and its application to history Mr. Galloway says perfectly correctly that the idea of development is an *idolum fori*, "a stock phrase in the scientific marketplace."[3] We can conceive what must be understood by development in an organism. The germ, the egg, the embryo expands itself, through the working of the power of assimilation, and becomes bigger and stronger; the child grows up into a youth and a man. But when development is spoken of in a people or in humanity, we fall immediately into difficulty with the question of what is here the subject, the germ or the embryo of the development, and in what this development consists. We can no doubt speak of a unity in the case of a people or of humanity; but this unity is necessarily of a different kind from that of an individual organism. The comparison not only, — for this has to a certain extent the right of existence, — but the identification of society and of a people with an organism, led Spencer, Schäffle, and others, into all kinds of error and artificiality, which no one would now be willing to take responsibility for. Society is not a biological organism, but an organization, which no doubt is not exclusively established by the will of man, but certainly not without it. Before we can investigate the origin and the development of such an organization as a family, society, or people, other factors than merely biological ones must come into consideration; just as in an organism forces are at work which are not found in a machine. Monism overlooks the difference between a biological, a psychical, and an ethical organism, just as it does that between an organism and a mechanism; but nevertheless this differentation continues to exist in reality without any abatement.[4]

We might speak of evolution in families, nations, or humanity if men successively increased in height, in size and weight, in strength or length of life, or even in intellectual, moral, or religious capacity, in "capability of culture." But this is by no means the case. Years ago Buckle said that the child born in a civilized country probably does not excel that of barbarians; and when this remark is understood strictly as referring to the capacity and not to the *milieu* of the child, it is rather strengthened than weakened by ethnological investigation.[5] The capacities and gifts of the culture-people of to-day are, on the average, no greater than those of the Greeks and Romans, Babylonians or Assyrians; the seventy or eighty years of which the Scriptures speak are still the limitation of the life of the strong; the religious sensibility, moral capacity, adaptation to art, etc., by no means advance with the years; "everywhere," as Professor de Vries says, "the characteristics of individuals librate about an average, and everywhere they do it according to the same law."[6] We might cherish the hope of progress, however slow it might be, if it were established that characteristics, once attained, are transmitted by heredity. But on this there exists the greatest possible difference of opinion. Experience teaches us that numberless characteristics, both intellectual and moral, are not transmitted from parent to child. Learned men not rarely have stupid children; pious parents frequently bring up godless children; the gifts of grace prove to be no heirloom. Newly acquired variations do not always continue, but disappear after one or more generations. Every variety displays a tendency to return again to the original type, and nowhere, among plants, animals, or men, do we find an inclination to continue to vary in any one given direction. And yet, on the other hand, we see organisms appreciably modify themselves under the influence of climate, soil, food, and other circumstances, and transmit their variations to their descendants. Races and national types, the nose of the Bourbons and the lip of the Hapsburgs, the varieties among the descendants of the horse and the dog, prove this conclusively. But a straight line of development is nowhere indicated. Heredity is a dark region. We can do no more for the present than with Delage state the fact that modifications acquired under the influence of environment generally are not, but sometimes are, hereditary.[7]

Thus we can predicate with certainty only this of the idea of evolution in humanity, that later generations are more favorably situated than the earlier ones, by reason of the inheritance which has come to them, in money and goods, in science and art, in civilization and culture. But this inheritance can hardly be denominated by the name of evolution; for these several possessions of culture have not organically developed from a germ and have not evolved themselves, but are the product of the thought and will of man. The discovery of America, the discovery and application of steam power, the knowledge and use of electricity, did not come spontaneously, nor are they the necessary product of economic or social factors, but they presuppose thirst for knowledge and intense intellectual labor in man. It is true man is here subject to the influence of his environment, and is perhaps as much indebted to it as it is to him. But the influence certainly does not come exclusively from one side; discoveries and inventions frequently are due to extraordinary personalities, whose origin and existence remain a mystery, despite all biographical investigation. A genius like Goethe is far from explained when we know that he inherited his " stature " from his father and his " cheerful disposition " from his mother. Evolution is a great word, but it turns its back on difficulties and sums up a rich and complicated reality under a vague formula.[8]

This appears all the more clearly when we consider that the advantages of culture, handed down by progenitors, cannot be taken up, conserved, and increased by their descendants without some action on their part. Although every man is born from the community, and is formed by it, he has to begin again for himself at the very beginning. He has to begin with the exercise of his bodily members and senses, with learning to read and write and cipher. From his birth on he must strive to make the inheritance of the past his own; he must " labor for it in order to possess it." And there is the possibility and danger that he may squander, dissipate, and turn to his own destruction the treasures which fall in his lap at his birth. Individuals, but also families, tribes, and peoples, are exposed to this danger. Culture may be a blessing, but it can also be a curse; it does not always advance, it may degenerate and come to nothing; it can be augmented, but it can also be destroyed and annihilated through the decadence of nations, through calamities and wars.   And in the strifes between peoples it is not always the cultured peoples which are victorious, but as the history of the Babylonians and Assyrians, of the Greeks and Romans, of the Franks and Germans teaches us, very frequently those peoples who are poor in culture and well-nigh devoid of civilization.[9]   When they take over the culture of the conquered peoples afterwards, this does not happen on their part, except in the course of a long lapse of time and by the efforts of their own intellectual strength.

All these considerations show that history presents a character far too involved and complicated to be reduced to one common formula or to be explained from one cause.   Monism, no doubt, endeavors to do this with history as well as with nature.   But all efforts to comprehend historical personages and occurences exclusively from mechanical, physical, biological, psychological, social, or economic factors, have only succeeded in making evident the richness of life and the complication of conditions.

Lamprecht, for instance, goes back to the folk-soul, and finds in it the ultimate cause of history.   But questions multiply themselves as soon as we try to give to ourselves a somewhat clear account of this folk-soul.   What are we to understand by it, and where is it to be found?   How did it originate, and what factors influenced its formation?   And if it exists, what is its dominant element?   For no more than the soul of a man can it be a simple phenomenon.   If the folk-soul is really a soul, what plays the chief rôle in it?   Intelligence, the emotions, or the will; concepts or feelings, hunger or love?   And further, what is the connection between the folk-soul and the folk-body, and between it and all nature, climate and soil and nourishment? As many questions, so many enigmas.[10] Instead of attaining unity, we come to an infinite diversity. For the folk-soul is no unity; it lacks the unity of self-consciousness, which in man is expressed in his soul.[11] And it is a matter of great wonderment that, at a time in which psychology is endeavoring to dissolve the individual soul into a complex of experiences, historical science wishes to believe in the unity of the folk-soul. In point of fact, it thus walks in the same path which is followed by natural science when it just abstracts in thought the forces of nature, and then personifies them through the imagination. The conception of a folk-soul is just as useless for history as that of an organism. There may be analogy, there is no identity. In a much higher degree than is the case in nature, we stand in history before a complex of causes and operations which are utterly unknown to us in their essence and interrelations, and cannot be comprehended in one single word. "There is just as little such a final and simple word of history, which can express its true sense, as nature has such a word to offer."[12]

The same difficulty which erects itself against the monistic doctrine of causality returns when the attempt is made to distinguish in history an ascending series of periods, and to express each of those periods in a single name. Of course, we are compelled to speak of periods in history, and to characterize them by some trait or other. If that could not be done, it would be quite impossible to bring order into the chaos of events. We speak, therefore, without hesitation, of ancient, mediæval, and modern history; of the age of the Reformation and of the "Enlightenment." But we must not forget that we do not comprehend the totality of such a period, by any means, in such a formula. The age of the Reformation, for instance, was also that of the Renascence, of the revival of philosophy and of natural science, of the origin of world-communication and world-commerce. The eighteenth century was the golden period of the " Enlightenment," but it also witnessed the activity of Pietism, Moravianism, and Methodism; it also gave being to Winckelmann and Lessing, Goethe and Schiller, Rousseau and Kant. And when the children of the nineteenth century felt the need of characterizing their own age, they called it the age of historic sense and of the natural sciences, of commerce and communication, of steam and electricity, of autonomy and anarchy, of democracy and popular power, of reason and of mysticism, of cosmopolitanism and of the national consciousness; and all felt that no one of these names answers to the fulness of the reality.[13]

And we must further keep in view that all division of the world's history, however unprejudicedly it be studied, quietly assumes the unity of the race and a monistic-evolutionary conception of its history. The consequence is that only a narrow strip of peoples is taken into account and is abstracted from all other peoples. And at the same time events and conditions are deliberately placed in succession to one another which in reality occurred side by side. A distinction is made between the stone, bronze, and iron ages; between the chase, the pastoral life, agriculture, manufacture, and commerce; between an Asiatic-despotic, mediæval-feudal, and civil-capitalistic society; between a natural-, money-, and credit-system of commerce, a home-, city-, and national-organization, a form of economy based on the principle of need, and one based on the principle of acquisition; between symbolism, typism, conventionalism, individualism, and subjectivism in the history of the German people; between savagery, barbarism, and civilization; between matriarchy, patriarchy, polygamy, and monogamy; between fetichism, polytheism, and monotheism; between theological, metaphysical, and positivistic phases, etc. But in all these distinctions it is forgotten that the relations and conditions which are thus placed in a series one after another exist throughout the ages side by side in different peoples, and even within the same people in different strata of society. The excavations in Assyria and Babylon, in Egypt and Greece, have informed us that a high civilization existed even in antiquity; industry and technic, science and art, commerce and society had even then reached a h'gh degree of development.

It is therefore futile to attempt to divide the history of humanity into sharply defined periods, in accordance with the evolutionary hypothesis. Ranke saw better when he said that not every succeeding period stands above the preceding. A period precedent in time does not serve exclusively, as the system of Hegel demanded, to prepare for a succeeding one: it also occupies an individual, independent position, and represents an independent value. Even if a period is older in history, it is very possible that it may have something which it alone possesses and by which it excels all others. The classical period, the middle ages, and also every one of the succeeding ages, have each something peculiar to itself, a special gift and calling, and they add, each in its own way, to the capital of humanity. The same is true of the nations. They do not simply stand in regular order, the one after the other; but, whether isolated or in communion, they live on together. And all these periods and peoples have not only a horizontal significance for what succeeds, but each period and each people has also vertically its own significance for God, who created and guided it. " Each period stands immediately related to God, and its value does not at all depend on what proceeds from it, but on its very existence, on its very self." [14]

In the division into periods the monistic-evolutionary view of history comes into still greater difficulties. It may at best point out that the history of a people here or there has followed a certain course. It can never furnish the proof that this course is really necessarily and universally prescribed to all peoples. True, it makes this the starting-point of its monistic law of causality, and this is inevitable. But this starting-point is arbitrarily chosen and is contradicted by facts. Who dares to contend that every people has passed through or must pass through the periods of stone and copper and iron; of the chase, agriculture, and industry; of theology, metaphysics, and positivism, and the like? Even more than in nature, in history laws, if they exist at all, must bear an empirical character. They cannot be determined beforehand, but have to be derived from the facts. But this exposes us to the greatest difficulties. It is true, it is thoroughly justifiable to search in history also for the reign of law, for a connection between cause and effect, for an order and a plan. In the chaotic, in the arbitrary, in the accidental, we find no resting place, either for our intelligence or for our heart. But it is equally certain that this reign of law has not yet been found in history, and presumably never will be.

If we do not know, in one way or another, and to a

certain extent from elsewhere, it is impossible to determine in a purely empirical way from the facts, what
course history takes and must take, and to what end it
is advancing. We feel the need of this knowledge; in
our innermost soul we all believe in such a course and
such an aim in history. For if history is to be truly
history, something must be accomplished by it. It is
the very sense and value and meaning of history that
in it and by it something shall be realized which makes
it worth while for history to exist, with all its misery and
pain. But the positivistic method does not enable us to
find this order and this aim of history. In nature we
scarcely know as yet what laws really are; but, as is seen
and acknowledged more and more, in history we have as
yet got no farther than that we perceive a certain rhythm
in its events.[15]

And accordingly opinions about the meaning and aim
of history are widely divergent. There is difference of
opinion as regards the place which should be assigned to
the great men in history, and to each man and people in
particular. Are the individual men only thoroughfares
for the idea, phenomena of the Universal Being, expressions of the folk-soul, waves of the ocean; or have
they each a significance for eternity? There is difference
as regards the method by which a rule of judgment may
be found. We stand over against the persons and the
events not only as onlookers, but also as judges; we
cannot assume a neutral attitude with respect to them
as we may do in the case of nature. But where is the
standard which we have to apply to be found, and how
is it to be applied? And in the closest connection with
this there is a great difference about the true contents, the
moving-forces and the aim of history. Are these to be

found in the development of the understanding and in
the advance of science as Buckle thought; or in the idea
of liberty as Kant and Hegel imagined; in the establishment of an order of government as Breysig thinks; or
in production as Marx supposes? Are they to be found in
mind or in matter, in man or in culture, in the state or in
society? The history which is studied in an exclusively
empirical way gives no answer. And since every one
seeks an answer and cannot live without such an answer,
the science of history raises itself to philosophy of history;
for the cause and aim, the essence and development of history cannot be understood without metaphysics.

In recent years this conviction has reasserted itself in
the minds of many. A strong reaction has arisen against
the monistic-evolutionary view of history. In 1883 Dilthey already declared the need of a "criticism of the
historical reason;" in 1894 Windelband pronounced an
oration on "History and Natural Science," in which he
laid stress on the independence of the former; Heinrich
Rickert followed him in 1899, with an essay on "The
Science of Culture and the Science of Nature," and published in 1902 an important logical introduction to the
historical sciences, entitled, "The Limits of the Application of Conceptions framed by Natural Science." Since
then the scientific discussion of the character of the science of history has been unbrokenly prosecuted, and flows
out in a long series of orations and treatises, which apparently increases day by day.[16] And still further there
is also a difference among those who antagonize the nomological science of history. According to Windelband and
Rickert the sciences of nature and history are alike empirical and positive; but they are distinct in the aim with
which they are studied. The natural sciences take their

start, like the mathematical sciences, from general propositions, axioms, and postulates; or else search, like the empirical sciences, in the natural phenomena for the universal, the idea, the law; they are therefore nomothetic in character. On the other hand the historical sciences do not search out the universal, but the particular, *das Einmalige* ("the singular"), and they have their strength in the realizing power of conception; they have an ideographic character. But this is not all. For historical science by no means takes up everything which is particular and has occurred at some time or other, but it makes selection and treats only that which in a definite sense is important and possesses a real value. Just as the individual man retains in his memory only that which has been of importance for his life; so the history of a people or of humanity retains the memory of those persons and occurrences only which were significant for the universal progress, for the development of the whole. To accomplish this sifting of the material the historian must therefore be " a man of judgment." He must proceed from the belief that there are " universal values " and must derive these from ethics. Ethics is therefore the " epistemology of the historical sciences." According to the system of " values " which this science offers, the facts of history are sifted, ordered, estimated. History, in a word, is not a science of nature, but a science of culture.

Others, such as Dilthey, Wundt, Sigwart, go back one step farther still. They seek the difference between natural and historical science, not only logically in the aim with which they are cultivated, but also in the contents of each group. The character of the historical sciences is not sufficiently expressed by the name " sciences of culture," but receives full justice only when they are indicated as mental sciences over against the natural sciences. The historical sciences occupy themselves with their own distinct object; they come into touch with other factors than the natural sciences. They concern themselves with man, with his psychic faculties and functions, and therefore they follow a different method and have a different name from the natural sciences.[17]

This reaction against monism in the science of history is already remarkable, because it does not stand alone, but is connected with the entire movement which manifested itself toward the close of the last century, in many different countries and in various spheres, and which has in a previous lecture been characterized as a revolt of the will against the reason, of the heart against the understanding, of liberty against necessity, of man against nature.[18] But it is also remarkable on its own account, because it has once more clearly enunciated the difference in aim and contents between the natural and historical sciences and has demanded for the latter independence and liberty of movement. History is something else and something more than a process of nature which develops itself after a dialectic method, is independent of the consciousness, the will, and the aim of man, and is the necessary product of a power which works, as a whole, without consciousness and will.[19] But we cannot halt even at the conception of history as science of culture or mental science. For if history, in distinction from natural science, were to teach us really, in a definite sense, only the particular *das Einmalige* ("the singular"), it would cease to be science and would become art.

Rickert has the courage to draw this conclusion, and refuses to acknowledge any laws in this domain. The so-called "laws" in history are nothing but *Wert-*

formeln, formulas of valuation.[20] Now we admit
that *das Einmalige* ("the singular") has great significance in history.[21] But when this is postulated, in contradistinction to and to the exclusion of the "particular"
in nature, this position cannot be assumed without criticism. For if the natural sciences generalize and search
for laws which apply to a multiplicity of cases, this does
not permit us to conclude that these particular cases are
without value and have only served as illustrations of the
universal laws; we must hold, rather, that they all have
an historical significance in the process of the world, a
place and task of their own.[22] Moreover it is not true
that natural science, in its entirety, directs itself only to
the discovery of the universal; it is easy to say this, as is
explained by Professor Heymans, so long as one thinks
only of the abstract natural sciences, like physics and
chemistry; but it can by no means be applied when the
concrete natural sciences, like geology and astronomy,
are taken into consideration. For the student of geology
the physical and chemical laws are not ends, but means,
the means to account for the appearance of definite
phenomena in the earth-crust, which, as they appear
and are to be explained, mostly occur only once and
no more.[23]

On the other hand historical science cannot avoid all
abstraction and generalization. It is true, history does not,
like nature, make us acquainted with laws, although
even here more and more doubt arises whether, in any
sphere, we have really attained to the knowledge of the
laws of elementary phenomena.[24] But this does not in
the least hinder us from concluding that the historian
by no means fixes his attention on *das Einmalige* ("the
singular") alone, but connects every person and every

event with the past, searches out the connection of facts, and thus carries on his investigations under the guidance of an idea, a plan, a course in history.   He who would deny this would make history itself an impossibility and reduce it to the viewpoint of a chronicle.   From this point of view the historian would see trees but no forest; would retain facts but no history; would have bricks but no building; would have details but no living, organic whole.   It cannot be denied that historical investigation has at times lost itself in such details, and in that way has called into existence the danger of historicism and relativism.   And Nietzsche was fully justified when he broke out in wrath against such a treatment of history, for the overwhelming flood of details does not elevate us, but crushes us down; it robs us of our independence and freedom; it denies the superiority of mind over matter.[25] Troeltsch remarks, therefore, that " All history uses the study of details rather as a means and never views it as a final aim.   And in truth it is the means of understanding the great closed cycles of human civilization, of the leading nations, of the important circles of culture, of the great branches of culture." [26]   Without undervaluing the significance of details, history aims at the knowledge of the idea, of the sense of history.   Bare facts do not satisfy us; we want to see behind the facts the idea which combines and governs them.[27]

The newer view of history so far recognizes this that it makes the essence of history to lie in the realization of values.   If this is so, the historian must be " somewhat of a man of judgment," and must possess a standard by which he can judge of the values in history.   The danger is here far from imaginary that the historian, in determining these values, will permit ·his own interest to intrude itself and will test all facts by his own limited insight and his own selfish advantage. Rickert sees this danger, and discriminates therefore between practical and theoretical, personal (individual) and general valuations, demanding that the historian shall lay the former aside and thus be wholly objective.

But granting the practicability of this certainly very difficult discrimination proposed by Rickert, the question will nevertheless remain whence we must derive the standard of the general valuations. It is not to be supposed that history itself will furnish it. It would seem, no doubt, that Troeltsch is of this opinion when he says that history, notwithstanding that everything in it is relative, yet sets forth and maintains "norms, ideals of life, contents of life," which may be compared with one another by the historian. He therefore proposes wholly to lay aside the old historico-apologetic and speculative method, to replace it by that of the history of religions, and in this way to prove the (relative) truth and value of Christianity.[28] But if history, as Troeltsch says elsewhere, makes everything relative, occupies itself only with *das Einmalige* ("the singular") and the individual, and cannot "find a standard of universal application," it must be impossible for it to furnish us with the norms and ideals by which we may estimate facts and persons. In a fact, by itself, there is of course no qualitative difference; the crime "happens" just as well as the noblest act of self-sacrifice; to a purely objective view sin and virtue are in the same sense products as vitriol and sugar.[29] The expectation that history is to realize ideals of life and norms proceeds from the assumption that history is not a "play of endless variants," but forms a whole which is animated by a governing idea, by

the providence of God.[30] A comparison of persons and
facts in history is possible only, then, when the historian is from the start a "man of judgment" and brings
to his task a standard of judgment acquired elsewhere.
And the question remains, whence we must derive the
standard for measuring " universally valid values."

The outcome and the result, the use and the profit, —
culture, in a word, — can scarcely serve the purpose of such
a standard, although Rickert sometimes seems to incline
to this idea. For the standard would then be wholly
utilitarian, even if it be social-eudæmonistic in character;
and all truth and virtue would become subordinated to
utility. But, apart from this, such a standard would be
no standard at all, *i. e.* it would be no norm or rule,
which is fixed in itself, and therefore can serve for
impartial and fair judgment of phenomena and facts. If
their culture-value is to determine the truth and goodness
of things, this value itself ought to be fixed for all. But
this is so little the case that the greatest possible difference exists about the contents and the value of the products of culture. And this entirely without considering
the other question how we who have our place in its
midst can take the final issue of history for a standard.
The question, therefore, continues to clamor for an
answer, where the standard is to be found which can be
used in judging historical facts and personages. History
itself does not present it ; immanently, within the circle of
historical phenomena, it cannot be found. If history is
to be truly history, if it is to realize values, universally
valid values, we cannot know this from the facts in
themselves, but we borrrow this conviction from philosophy, from our view of life and of the world, — that is to
say, from our faith. Just as there is no physics with-

out metaphysics, there is no history without philosophy, without religion and ethics.

Very certainly there is no history without religion, without faith in a divine wisdom and power. For suppose that philosophy, especially ethics, could offer us an absolute standard, by which historical values may be judged — a possibility which is by no means unconditionally determined — still the final and most important question is not answered : What is the ground for the belief that such an absolute value has an objective existence and must be realized in history, notwithstanding all opposition? What right have we to expect that the good will ultimately be victorious? Rickert is of the opinion that the existence of such an absolute, transcendent value can be accepted and maintained without postulating a transcendent reality. But he himself does not entirely escape this postulate. For he has to assume that the idea of value, which, in accordance with the German idealism, he considers as the highest, namely, "development unto freedom," is "itself in some way inherent in the nature of the world." [31] This idea, then, has an objective reality, perhaps not in a personal, transcendent God, but immanently in the nature of the world. It is difficult, however, to attach a clear conception to these words. The ideas of freedom, of truth, of goodness, of beauty, have no existence in themselves, but are abstractions, which we have formed by our thinking. They are no transcendent powers or forces which realize themselves and can break down all opposition, but they are conceptions which we have derived from reality and have disassociated from it by our thinking. When later on we hypostatize these abstractions, and when we clothe them with divine wisdom and power, then we do in reality nothing but what natural science frequently does with its force and laws, and what the Roman of old did when he elevated justice and truth and peace and all sorts of possible and impossible abstractions to the rank of divinities. It is therefore in vain when we say that this idea is grounded in the nature of the world. For it passes comprehension how the idea of freedom, if it is no more than an idea, can be grounded in the nature of the world and can realize itself. And if it is indeed capable of so doing, then it must be more than an idea, and we cannot conceive of it in any other way than as an attribute and power of a personal God. In point of fact, goodness, justice, wisdom, etc., have no existence in this world but as personal attributes. And therefore not only the theology of all the ages, but also philosophy in a good number of its interpreters, has postulated the existence of a personal God. In the newer philosophy Kant here set the example, and at the present time he is followed in this respect by Eucken, Howison, and many others.[32] If history is to remain what it is and must be, it presupposes the existence and activity of an all-wise and omnipotent God, who works out his own councils in the course of the world. The more we penetrate in our thinking to the essence of history, as to that of nature, the more we grasp its idea and maintain it, the more it will manifest itself as rooted in revelation and as upborne by revelation; the more it will lift itself up to and approach that view of history which Christianity has presented and wherewith Christianity in its turn confirms and supports revelation in nature and in history.

Historians, it is true, to the detriment of their own science, sometimes assume an inimical or indifferent attitude towards Christianity. Rickert, for instance, will have none of it. He is of the opinion that the philosophy of history has done wholly away with it, that the image of the world has been totally changed, and that the idea of "a closed, explorable (*übersehbar*) cosmos" is utterly destroyed. The doctrine of Giordano Bruno about the infinitude of the world has caused shipwreck to all world-history in the strict sense.[33] Indirectly, however, this declaration is a confirmation of the importance of Christianity for history; for it is indeed the special revelation in the Scriptures which has made a world-history possible and without which it is threatened with destruction. The significance of Christianity for history is therefore universally acknowledged.[34]

In the first place the confession of the unity of God is the foundation of the true view of nature and also of history. If this be denied, we must either abide by the multiplicity of reality, by a pluralism of monads and souls, spirits or "selves," demons or Gods; or because man can never find satisfaction in such a multiplicity, we have to search in the world itself for a false unity, as is done by monism in its various forms, and then all differentiation is sacrificed to this false unity. The souls of men then become parts and phenomena of the one world-soul, and all created things become *modi* of the one substance. Only, then, when the unity of all creation is not sought in the things themselves, but transcendently (not in a spacial, but in a qualitative, essential sense) in a divine being, in his wisdom and power, in his will and counsel, can the world as a whole, and in it every creature, fully attain its rights. A *person* alone can be the root of unity in difference, of difference in unity. He alone can combine in a system a multiplicity of ideas into unity, and he alone can realize them by his will *ad extra*. Theism is the only true monism.

But to the unity of God the unity of humanity stands very closely related, and this also is of fundamental importance for history. The evolutionary hypothesis usually accepts this unity, although the right to do so from its own standpoint may well be doubted, and it considers man as the highest creature, as the crown of all creation. Thus Heinrich Schurtz, for instance, says that, whilst the question cannot be scientifically decided whether humanity originates from one couple or more, yet all investigation of the races must proceed from the fact that "humanity forms one great unity." [85] And not only this, but human nature also is considered one and unchangeable. The same historian of culture says elsewhere, that changes of bodily structure still proceed with animals, but that man, having attained the height at which he now stands, no longer reacts on his environment by unconscious bodily changes, but by weapons and instruments, by science and art. The development of the mind has put a stop to changes in bodily structure. And this mind itself is stationary in its structure. Years ago Virchow declared this; Ammon has proved it; and Hugo de Vries assents to it: "Man is a stationary type" (*Dauertypus*); he continues at the same height, as concerns his hereditary attributes, *i. e.*, the average attainment and the degree of development of the race. [86]

However thankful we may be that the evolutionists usually accept this unity of humanity and human nature, and thereby show that life is stronger than doctrine, we must bear in mind that this unity does not rest on scientific grounds, but is derived from revelation. And yet it is an indispensable presupposition for history. For thereby only is a history in the true sense made possible, — a history of the world and a history of humanity, in which

all men, all peoples, nay, all creatures, are embraced, and
are held together by one leading thought, by one counsel
of God. And this unity is important for history in still
another sense. Eucken says with perfect truth: "A
type of human nature ever stands between the historian
and his sources." [37] Knowledge of history is possible, then,
only when the men who act on its stage, whenever and
wherever they may have lived, have been of like passions
with us. For when the historian wishes to give an account
to himself of their conceptions and emotions, of their
words and deeds, he can do so only by transporting himself
in his imagination into the characters and circumstances
of the persons he desires to depict. He must endeavor to
reproduce within himself their inner life, and thus to form
a plausible conception of the way in which they came to
act as they did.[38] He finds the key to explain the thinking and willing, the feeling and acting of his historical
personages, in his own spiritual life. The unity of human
nature and of the human race is the presupposition of
all history, and this has been made known to us only
by Christianity.

But this unity in its contents is entirely different from
that after which monism is striving. Monism always
understands by unity a universal principle, which is
abstracted from all that is particular, and which is then, as
a universal origin, made the ground of all that is particular. The psyche of man, for instance, is, according to
monism, a unity only when all psychic phenomena can be
deduced from one principle, whether from conception or
from feeling. The organisms are a unity when they have
successively originated from one original cell. The world
is a unity when all existence has developed itself from
one matter and from one force. Monism knows no other

unity than a genetic one, and can therefore never do full justice to the differentiation of the world, the difference between the inorganic and organic, between irrational and rational creatures, the dependence and liberty of man, — the difference between the true and the false, good and evil. The unity of monism is a dead, stark, uniform unity, without life and its fulness. This is plainly shown in the judgment which it passes upon the heroes of history, who are sacrificed to the idea, to the mechanical interaction of matter, to the one power which necessarily produces all. Against this view pragmatism continually raises protest, just as one-sidedly seeing in the great men the makers of history, and resolving the historic content in their personality, and ultimately arriving at the apotheosis and adoration of genius.

The unity which revelation makes known to us is of another kind and of a higher order. It is the unity of harmony, which includes riches, multiformity, differentiation. Just as soul and body in man are not genetically one and have not originated from each other, and yet form in the " ego " of man an inner organic unity ; just as the members of an organism are neither exclusively producent nor exclusively product of the organism, but stand in reciprocal relations with it and thus form a unity ; so the matter stands with every man and every people in history, and also with all humanity. Therefore history is so rich, its life so full, and therefore so many factors are at work in it. But therefore it is also that the monistic attempt to explain the entire process of history from specific biological, psychological, or economic factors is so mistaken. Life resists this view, the personality of man perishes in it. Over against it the Scriptures teach us that the unity of humanity does not exclude, but rather includes, the differentiation of man in race, in character, in attainment, in calling, and in many other things. Every man lives in his own time, comes into being and passes away, appears and disappears; he seems only a part of the whole, a moment of the process. But every man also bears the ages in his heart; in his spirit-life he stands above and outside of history. He lives in the past and the past lives in him, for, as Nietzsche says, man cannot forget. He also lives in the future and the future lives in him, for he bears hope imperishably in his bosom. Thus he can discover something of the connection between the past, the present, and the future; thus he is at the same time maker and knower of history. He belongs himself to history, yet he stands above it; he is a child of time and yet has part in eternity; he *becomes* and he *is* at the same time; he passes away and yet he abides.

All this Christianity has made us understand. But it does more than that. The special revelation which comes to us in Christ not only gives us the confirmation of certain suppositions, from which history proceeds and must proceed, but itself gives us history, the kernel and the true content of all history. Christianity is itself history; it makes history, is one of the principal factors of history, and is itself precisely what lifts history high above nature and natural processes. And that it says and proves by its own act; Christ came to this earth for a crisis; the content of history lies in a mighty struggle. Monism knows nothing about this; it schematizes everything with its before and after. It has only one model — earlier and later, lower and higher, less and more, not yet and already past. It knows no *pro* and *contra*, but thus it does despite to life, to the experience of every man, to the terribly tragic seriousness of history. Revelation is a confirmation and explanation of life when it says the essence of history lies in a mighty conflict between darkness and light, sin and grace, heaven and hell. The history of the world is not *the* judgment of the world; and yet it is *one of the* judgments of the world.

Furthermore revelation gives us a division of history.[39] There is no history without division of time, without periods, without progress and development. But now take Christ away. The thing is impossible, for he has lived and died, has risen from the dead, and lives to all eternity; and these facts cannot be eliminated, — they belong to history, they are the heart of history. But *think* Christ away for a moment, with all he has spoken and done and wrought. Immediately history falls to pieces. It has lost its heart, its kernel, its centre, its distribution. It loses itself in a history of races and nations, of nature- and culture-peoples. It becomes a chaos, without a centre, and therefore without a circumference; without distribution and therefore without beginning or end; without principle and goal; a stream rolling down from the mountains, nothing more.[40] But revelation teaches that God is the Lord of the ages and that Christ is the turning point of these ages. And thus it brings into history unity and plan, progress and aim.[41] This aim is not this or that special idea, not the idea of freedom, or of humanity, or of material well-being. But it is the fulness of the Kingdom of God, the all-sided, all-containing dominion of God, which embraces heaven and earth, angels and men, mind and matter, cultus and culture, the specific and the generic; in a word, all in all.

VI

REVELATION AND RELIGION

WE shall be strongly confirmed in the view that history as well as nature is rooted in revelation and needs it for its explanation, if we fix our attention upon one of its most prominent motive powers, namely, religion. The bare fact that religion exists already means much. Demons have no religion; they are no doubt convinced that God exists, but the thought of God moves them only to fear and hatred. We cannot speak of religion in animals; the idea of God is indispensable to religion, and animals entirely lack this idea, as they lack all abstract conceptions. The veneration of a dog for his master may show some resemblance and likeness to what religion is in man, but analogy is not identity.[1] On the other hand, religion is characteristic of all peoples and all men; however deeply a human being may be sunk in degradation, he is conscious of the existence of God and of his duty to worship him.

This fact is of extraordinary significance; however far man may wander from God, he remains bound to heaven; in the depths of his soul he is linked to a world of unseen and supernatural things; in his heart he is a supernatural being; his reason and conscience, his thinking and willing, his needs and affections have their ground in that which is eternal. And religion is the irrefutable proof of this. It is not thrust upon him by force or foisted upon him by deceit, but it rises spontaneously from his own nature, although it is nourished from without. The religion of man in the fallen state is no doubt always arbitrary, but at the same time also voluntary, service. Thereby every man acknowledges and confesses that he can be free only in absolute dependence; that he can be true to himself and be a human being only when serving God. The feeling of absolute dependence includes freedom; the subjection of man to God bears a character of its own, and is distinguished from that of demons and animals by being inseparably conjoined with his affinity to God. In religion these two things are always united, although sometimes the theocratic, and then again the theanthropic, element predominates.[2]

It is true there is an effort being made to remove religion from the central place which it occupies in the life of the individual as well as in the history of the race. This effort, however, is doomed from the outset to prove abortive, because it clashes with the unchangeable needs of human nature.

When the *Mercure de France* last year opened a discussion on the dissolution or evolution of religion, some, it is true, used the occasion to air their hatred of the church and religion or to predict their approaching disappearance. But even among those there were some who sought a substitute for religion in altruism and socialistically organized society, in morality, science, or spiritualism. And an overwhelming majority were convinced that religion, although its forms may change, nevertheless in its essential nature is ineradicable and will survive all the crises through which it may have to pass. They based their conviction especially upon these two considerations, that religion is deeply rooted in human nature,[3] and that science, which can make known only the inter-relations of things, but never their origin, essence, and end, will never be able to satisfy the needs of the human heart.[4] Beyond that from which science has drawn away the veil there always remains unexplored the do-main, sublime, immense, and silent, where the supreme power dwells on which we depend; and from the inner-most recesses of man's personality religion always rises anew.[5]

What is thus said of the present and expected in the future finds its foundation and support in the past; there are no peoples without religion, and history takes us back to no past in which religion is not already the universal possession of man.[6] And not only so, but from the beginning it has ever been the vitalizing element of all culture. Of course we must beware here of one-sided-ness and take care not to construe actuality in the terms of a theory. From his origin man has been not only a religious, but also a moral and corporeal being; various wants and powers have been implanted in him from the beginning of his existence, which have worked together harmoniously. Morris Jastrow's assertion that science, art, and morality have grown out of religion, is too strongly put; they rather have come forth together in intimate connection with one another, out of the several wants and inclinations of human nature as such.[7] No monistic abstract principle, but the totality of human nature has been the starting-point of all development; just as little as the need of food and drink, shelter and raiment, have there been developed immediately from religion, agriculture, and industry, science and art and the several constituent parts of culture; every one of them has its own root in human nature, and hence its own particular character and life. But religion certainly belongs, and always has belonged, to the most intimate movements of the human heart, and has made its influence felt upon the whole life, with all its experiences and activities. Most certainly other agencies besides religion have been at work in the development of science, philosophy, art, etc., as, for instance, curiosity, desire for adornment and sport, and the like. But the more deeply we sink ourselves in the past, the more we find religion, morality, knowledge, art, in fact all the elements of civilization together, undivided and undifferentiated. They do not yet exist independently side by side with one another, but lie still undeveloped, enclosed in the same germ. A complex, a totality of experiences preceded the differentiation. And among these those of a religio-moral kind took the first place. In this sense it may be said that religion has been the deepest cause of the process of civilization, the mother of arts and of all sciences.[8]

This consideration of human nature is of great importance for the investigation of the origin of religion. At present there is a tendency among men of science first to dissolve the organic connections in which religion appears in life, and then to investigate its origin. They treat religion as a chemist does the substances, which he separates from their actual connections and then analyzes into their component parts. Scientifically this is of high value, if only we do not forget that the process to which science subjects its object differs entirely from that which happens in actuality. There is no proof at all that the elements have all existed originally in an unmixed state; and similarly there is no ground for asserting that the factors which we at present discover in the religious life ever existed separately. Actuality presents a different appearance from theory. Life, full, rich life, is always first; the abstractions of our thinking come only later. When science in its search for the origin of things allows itself to be exclusively guided by the idea of evolution, and therefore ever endeavors to go back to the most insignificant beginnings, to the most meagre principles, it simply elevates the abstractions of thought into concrete powers, and in its interpretation of things takes refuge in mythology. No abstract principle, however, no simple power has been the origin of human life in all its richness, and no rectilinear law of evolution has directed the development. When we go back in the actual as far as possible to the origins, we find a human nature which already contains everything which it later on produces out of itself. Natural and spiritual life, religion and morality, knowledge and art, sense of beauty and consciousness of values, have been united in man from the beginning. The experiences of life are the background of all development and civilization.[9]

The researches of recent years into the origin of things, of religion and morality, science and art, family, society, and state, have put this in the clearest light. Of course we cannot speak here in the strict sense of the word of a scientific investigation, whether naturalistic or historical, for the elements of culture we have mentioned have always existed, as far as history carries us back. When Lubbock tried to prove that all peoples have passed through a phase of atheism,[10] he not only overstepped the limits of our empirical knowledge, but he also invented a condition which, if it ever had existed, would be totally unintelligible to us, in whose life religion forms an essential part.[11] We can form no conception of beings which are not animals, but men, and which yet wholly lack religion; they are unthinkable and impossible. The case is, in fact, the same with all the component parts of human civilization; men are not thinkable without some knowledge and art, without some kind of family and social life, without some conception of morality and justice. If, notwithstanding all this, science continues to attempt to penetrate behind all culture and to form a conception of the way in which all these phenomena arose in human life, it is in the nature of the case shut up to conjectures and guesses. This is frankly acknowledged by many. For instance, Oscar Hertwig, speaking generally of descent in the past, says: " When we try to trace the genealogical chains of the mammals, amphibians, and fishes in primitive times, we launch into a darkness which even the bright light of science cannot penetrate with a single ray, and scientific research is accordingly exposed to the danger of deviating from that path in which alone it can reach knowledge of the truth and consequently permanent results." [12] It is " a fatal and yet unavoidable necessity for the science which investigates the origins of the family, property, society, etc.," says Ludwig Stein, " that it is compelled to operate with hypotheses." [13] And with respect to the origin of religion it is agreed by Lehmann and Troeltsch, Tiele and Pfleiderer, and many others, that it is as impossible now as in former days to speak of a knowledge of these things, and we have to be content with conjectures and hypotheses.[14]

That these hypotheses may not hang wholly in the air an attempt is made to support them with data derived from embryology and anthropology, from palæontology and ethnography. Study of the animal and the child on the one hand, and on the other study of the so-called naturepeoples, is pressed into service in order to form in some sense an idea of primitive man still wholly without culture. But the method which is thus employed, and the results which some think they have obtained, inspire little confidence, and on better acquaintance evacuate the hope that along this road we shall ever reach any certainty about man's original condition.

Commonly the truth of the doctrine of the descent of man is tacitly presupposed. In Darwin himself this assumption had at least the foundation that he could explain it by means of "natural selection" and "the struggle for existence;" but although many have now discarded Darwinism in its original form, either altogether or in part, as an explanation of the development of living beings, they still hold the theory of descent unimpaired. As a working hypothesis the idea of evolution undoubtedly is of undeniable significance; it leads to the discovery of analogies which otherwise probably would not have been noticed, and offers a clue which opens a way through the labyrinth of phenomena. Nevertheless, science must never lose sight of the fact that it is dealing in it with an hypothesis and not, as Haeckel supposes,[15] with a "firmly established fact." Sober naturalists, who give ear to facts alone, express themselves differently, not only formerly through the lips of Virchow, but now also through the lips of Branco, Reinke, Wasmann, and others. Reinke, for example, acknowledged in 1900 : " We must confess unreservedly that there is not at our disposal a single unexceptionable proof of its correctness." Two years later, in still stronger language, he affirmed that science knows nothing about the origin of man. And at the International Congress of Zoölogists at Berlin, in 1901, Branco bore witness that palæontology knows no ancestors of man, but that man suddenly and immediately appears before us in the diluvial age as a perfect *homo sapiens*.[16] The mental and physical gap between animal and man remains at present as wide as it ever was. In the structure of the skull and brain, for example, the interval between the other mammals and the apes may possibly be bridged over, but not between the apes and man. Among all the mammals now existing there is not one which in this respect can be compared with man. Stanley Hall also has to acknowledge that what intervenes between the highest anthropoid brain of 500 cubic centimeters and that of the lowest man, 1150 cubic centimeters, is almost as lost as a sunken Atlantis. When he adds that all the ancestors of man have been accidentally extirpated, this is nothing but a makeshift, entirely without scientific value.[17] The common ancestor of ape and man is a mere invention of the mind.[18] All inferences from the animal to the original man lack thus firm scientific foundation. It is not without significance that many adherents of the doctrine of descent have recently turned their backs upon historical zoölogy and look for their salvation to experimental morphology.[19]

It may be doubted, however, whether this new science will be able to shed more light on the subject. The opposition to Haeckel's biogenetic law is growing in strength day by day. Geganbaur and Oscar Hertwig both intimate that ontogeny is a sphere where a lively imagination may no doubt carry on a perilous game in seeking phylogenetic relations, but where assured results are by no means easy to get at; and they warn against the false paths which lead to the construction of fictitious conditions, or even of entirely fictitious organisms.[20] The embryological forms of the mammals show, it is true, correspondences with amphibians and fishes, but this "ancestral similarity" does not, according to Professor Emery, authorize an inference to "ancestral inheritance." The simple germ cell is already a life-form, which comprehends a fulness beyond belief of great and small varieties, and which already is the product of a phylogenetic process of development. Further, the fertilized germ cells of the several species of animals differ as much from each other in their nature as the individuals which come forth from these germ cells. And finally, there is a very great essential difference between the stages of ontogenesis which pass into one another and the forms of an ancestral series which do not pass into one another at all. This is the reason why Hertwig finds the hypothesis improbable that our earth in a former period produced only one kind of cells; and in view of the hundreds of thousands of species of animals and plants prefers the polyphyletic supposition, according to which the organisms now living are not derived from one primitive cell, but from a large number of cells, which are already differently organized, and which in a former period have been produced in some way or other by the creative power of nature. Closer study thus leads in this domain not to uniformity, but to multiformity. Nature is far from being as simple as the advocates of the mechanical theory conceive it to be. There was not in the beginning the poverty of the monistic principle, but the fulness and wealth of created life.

The biogenetic law grows still more improbable when it is applied in detail, and the conditions of the life of the embryo, of childhood and of youth are considered a recapitulation of those of the ancestors of men and of the first men themselves. The small stature of human beings in youth certainly ought to prove that the original men were very small; but, according to Stanley Hall and others, they were rather of gigantic stature.[21] The late appearance of the teeth in children ought to be considered a proof that original men were toothless, but this also is not at all acknowledged.[22]   In the man of our time the brain is of early growth, and has reached its full size at the age of about fourteen years, but the doctrine of the descent of man postulates, on the contrary, a very late development for it in the phylogenesis.[23]   The heart develops before the blood-vessels, but in the history of the human race the reverse must have taken place.[24]   If the rudimentary tail of man is to be looked upon as an argument for his animal descent, then certainly the breasts of the male should be a reminder and a remainder of the period when man was androgynal ; but few are inclined to draw this conclusion.[25]   It is no wonder that Stanley Hall, having in mind all these considerations, reaches the conclusion that there are "many inversions" in the ontogenetic law: "ontogeny often reverses the order of phylogeny." [26]

A similar change is noticeable also with regard to the notion that the nature-peoples afford us the means of learning to know primitive man.   The name itself is misleading; nature-peoples are nowhere to be found, any more than wild or cultureless peoples.   The cultured peoples are no less dependent on nature than the so-called nature-peoples ; the difference between the two is not to be sought in the degree, but in the character of their relation to nature.[27]   And wild or cultureless peoples do not exist either.   The ridiculous fancies about men who formerly or even now clamber up into the trees like apes, covered over the whole of their bodies with hair, knowing nothing of fire, without language or religion, reappear, it is true, now and then; but they are antiquated.   All men and peoples, though they may be poor in culture, yet possess at least its fundamental elements, the erect walk, the average weight of brain, the hand and the thumb, fire and light, language and religion, family and society.[28] Furthermore, the nature-peoples do not form a separate group, and do not all stand on the same level; they cannot be dealt with all alike, nor brought together under a common name.[29] They are related to higher peoples by means of all kinds of links, and upon better acquaintance do not seem to be nearly so barbarous and uncivilized as at first they were thought to be. The savage of Australia does not stand intellectually below the level of other peoples of little culture. The decision about the Batakudes and other South American peoples is on the whole favorable. Among the Bushmen and the Esquimaux the imagination exhibited in their drawings, toys, fairy tales, and legends, is a clear proof of their capabilities.[30] There can then be no question of nature-peoples and civilized nations differing in fundamental endowment, as if the one were predestinated to barbarism and destruction, the other to progress and high culture. Repeated instances have occurred of transitions from the one group to the other. The Bedouins of Arabia, Syria, and Mesopotamia live now just as they did hundreds of years ago, but they have produced civilized races. Finns and Magyars have recently become cultured peoples, while their kindred are still living in the barbaric state. The Japanese have all of a sudden accepted Western culture, while the Mongols and the Kalmucks remain stationary at the old stage of civilization. Thus it has repeatedly happened that nature-peoples have become culture-peoples.[31] Missions, especially, furnish abundant proofs of this fact.[32]

While the nature-peoples are thus again being gradually looked upon as men, our eyes are being opened on the other side to the sins and imperfections of the culture-peoples. Experience has taught us that even here it is far from everything that glitters that is gold. Not only were the ancestors of the culture-peoples of to-day, for instance the Germans and the Gauls, who were idealized by Cæsar and Tacitus, poor in culture, but also with regard to many peoples, for instance the Chinese, the Mongols, the Thibetans, the Russians, it is a question to which of the two groups they ought to be reckoned. Rude and barbarous customs still prevail among the Russians, Letts, Bulgars, Magyars, etc.; and in general the so-called culture-peoples, when carefully considered, are far from standing on the high level which many ascribe to them. The percentage of those who occupy the highest round of the ladder is very low. Many individuals and circles among the culture-peoples fall below the nature-peoples in civilization. Vagabonds and pariahs, the enfeebled and deficient, such as we meet with in our large cities, are all but never found among the nature-peoples. The mass among those peoples is more intelligent than with us. Animism, spiritism, superstition, sorcery, belief in witches and ghosts, prostitution and alcoholism, crimes and unnatural sins, occur among the culture-peoples no less, and sometimes in more aggravated forms, than among the nature-peoples. When the nature-peoples become civilized, they gain much, but lose no less. Many beautiful qualities, such as faithfulness, truthfulness, simplicity, artlessness, sincerity, ingenuousness, are lost in civilization.[33] There are many to-day who are not far from thinking of the nature-peoples after the idyllic fashion of the age of Rousseau. Tolstoi and Nietzsche return along different paths to nature; in literature and art there is a reaction against the conventional, and a recurrence to the unconscious, instinctive, passionate life. Stanley Hall describes savages as amiable children: " Most savages in most respects are children, or because of their sexual maturity, more properly adolescents of adult size. Their faults and their virtues are those of childhood and youth. He, who knows them, loves them." [34]

Yet both theories are one-sided : equally that according to which the nature-peoples are semi-animals and that according to which they are innocent children. The notion that all peoples are on the road to progress is as incorrect as that they are continuously declining and degenerating. Neither development nor degeneracy covers the course of history ; this is wider than our thinking, and is not disturbed by the logic of our reasoning. There are peoples who have developed and have attained a high level of civilization ; it may even be not impossible that this development in some cases, as, for instance, in Peru and Mexico, has been autochthonous. But it is no less evident that a number of peoples have declined from a more or less high degree of civilization. This has been the case with many peoples of antiquity in Asia and North Africa, which have either totally disappeared or sunk into complete insignificance. [35] Virchow called the Laplanders and the Bushmen even "pathologically degraded, degenerated races," and Darwin, Spencer, Tylor, Wallace, Max Müller, and many others, have acknowledged the decline and ruin of many peoples. [36] Environment has had a great deal to do with degeneracy. " It is of great importance for the development of a people, whether it dwells in the midst of the inhabited world, where it is exposed to numerous influences, or near its margin ; peoples living on the margin of the inhabited world are mostly poor in culture

and few in numbers." [37]   The peoples cannot, therefore,
be arranged in succession, one after the other; it is arbitrary to place the nature-peoples at the beginning of the
genealogical table of the human race and to represent
their condition as the original condition of mankind. [38]
The theory of development which in every case maintains
apriori, "that the human race only knows aspiration,
progress, development, and no retrogression, decline and
decay," [39] is just as one-sided as the theory of degeneracy.
History declines to follow in its course a single straight
line.   Every people and every group of peoples, spread
over the globe, has its own life, and continues it in the
midst of the others. [40]   We must return from the "after-
one-another" to the "by-the-side-of-one-another," from
uniformity to multiformity, from the abstract theory of
monism to the fulness of life.

   The nature-peoples supply us, therefore, just as little as
embryos and children with the desired material for the
construction of original man.   The primitive man, wherewith the historian of our day operates, is nothing but
a fiction [41] of the same kind as the *contrat social*, of
which Rousseau made use in order to explain the origin
of society, and as the ape-man, who is placed by zoölogy
at the beginning as our common ancestor, and, according
as circumstances require, is thought of sometimes as an
ape and sometimes as a man.   In the same manner Wundt
says: "It is impossible to exaggerate the enormousness
of the gap which separates the man of to-day from primitive man.   But we must not think of this gap in such a
way, as if no connection existed any longer between them,
or as if the narrow path of a single thought were the only
one to lead from one side to the other. . . . Every view which
conceives of primitive man in a one-sided manner puts it-

self not only in contradiction with the facts, but deprives itself also of the possibility of comprehending a psychological development.   For every change of motive, however vast it may be in some cases, presupposes at least this, that some germs of the motives which come into activity later on, were already present originally." [42]   Primitive man, in other words, must be constructed physically and psychologically in such a manner that an ape and a man can be derived from him.   Thus you can make whatever use of him you like ; you wield a two-edged sword.   If you desire to explain the animal or the animal character in man, you ascribe to primitive man the qualities of the ape; if, on the contrary, you wish to explain man, you acknowledge in him as easily the necessary human qualities. [43]   Primitive man accordingly is a worthy counterpart of the animated atoms, the personified powers of nature, the apotheosized natural laws, the deified evolution idea.   In reality he has never existed ; he is nothing but a poetical creation of monistic imagination.

This is gradually becoming understood by many.   We have already remarked that Oscar Hertwig looks upon the polyphyletic hypothesis as much more probable than the monophyletic, and thus assumes that the creative power of nature in the beginning produced at once a great number of variously organized primitive cells.   Just as Haeckel, not being able to give a satisfactory explanation of them, declares matter and force, motion and life, consciousness and will to be eternal, so Hertwig places the idea of species already in the very first cells which were produced by the creative power of nature.   Whether, however, we assign priority to the cells or to the organisms proceeding from them, or, in other words, to the egg or to the chicken, amounts to much the same thing.   The starting-point in both cases is not a monistic principle, but the multiformity of life, and the miracle, and faith in miracles as well, remains in either case equally great. Sociology also is beginning to see, now and again, that the sociological problem cannot be solved by the single formula of imitation (Tarde), local association or clan (Mucke), division of labor (Durkheim), struggle of the classes (Gumplowicz), blood-relationships (Morgan), or consociation (Schurtz).[44] Many accordingly assume the existence from the beginning of what lies to be explained. Gustav Ratzenhofer, for example, maintains that society has not in the strict sense of the word been originated : man did not create society, but society man ; the human race was from the beginning subject to its social nature; the social is what is original, the individual is derived.[45] According to Zenker even property did not gradually come into existence, but existed from the beginning. " Without social life and self-consciousness, that is, with common life and without personal work, the pithecoanthropos would never have been able to lift himself out of his animal state." [46] The theory of original promiscuity, which was advocated by Lewis Morgan and found favor with many, has later on been strongly contradicted by Westermarck, Starcke, Grosse, and others.[47] Among economists, according to Schmoller, a conviction is growing more and more towards unanimity, that a psychologico-ethical view of social life is necessary which shall recognize not only the emotions and passions, but also the ethical powers in man, and shall investigate political economy in connection with the state, religion and morals; "all great social communities are a result of human nature in general, founded on language and writing, on custom, law, morals, religion, and intercourse." [48] In general men have become more cautious in the application of the theory of evolution along single- and straight-lined processes of development.[49]

This is also apparent in the investigation of the origin of religion. History does not lead us back in this domain, either, to the beginnings; all beginnings, said Schelling, are from darkness to light. If we are nevertheless determined to seek out a beginning, we are driven to conjectures which endeavor to support themselves upon the psychology of the child and the savage. Nature-peoples furnish us, however, very little material for the investigation of the origin of religion, because religion has already long existed among them all and is intimately interwoven with their whole life. Instead of offering a solution of the problems which the man of culture proposes to himself, the savage is himself a problem. This is also the case with the children; no more than the animal can the child serve to explain the adult; the adult, on the contrary, is needed to explain the child. It is extremely difficult, accordingly, to penetrate into the life of the child soul and to understand it truly.[50] Moreover it will not do to compare present-day children with, and to take them as an example of, original adult men. For our children on the one hand have advantages far above any enjoyed by primitive men, by their birth and education in the midst of a rich, cultured life; and yet on the other hand they, as children, are far behind the adults of the past ages in the development of bodily and spiritual powers. If the comparison contained any truth and entitled us to a conclusion, it could only be that primitive men received and learned their language and religion by communication from others; that is, ultimately by revelation of God.[51]

The many and manifold theories which have been

presented as an explanation of religion have all again
been abandoned one after the other. They all have the
defect that they derive religion from non-religious factors, and either cannot find the transition, or, if they
indicate such a transition, always presuppose religion;
they thus oscillate between a *metabasis eis allo genos*
and a *petitio principii*. The result of all the research is
accordingly the humble confession, *ignoramus*, we do not
know. How religion arose, and out of what causes, "is
entirely unknown to us," says Troeltsch, "and just as in
the case of morals and logic, will always remain unknown
to us. An absolute equivocal generation is denied to
us." [52] Openly or secretly all turn back to an inborn
disposition, to a *religio insita*. Just as matter and force,
life and consciousness, society and state, so also the religion which is to be explained is already assumed in the
explanation. Troeltsch does this, but also Schroeder, who
is certainly an adherent of the doctrine of descent, and
speaks, therefore, of *Untermenschen* ("undermen"), but
nevertheless presupposes already in them a divine spark,
which develops them into men. Tiele goes back to an
inborn feeling and need of the infinite, and even Hugo
de Vries speaks of the need of religion as an inborn
quality of man.[53] In the beginning, therefore, there did
not reign the dead unity of monism but the totality of
human nature.

If, however, religion as *religio insita* is an essential element of human nature, it points directly back to revelation. We stand here before essentially the same dilemma
as in the case of self-consciousness. If this is not a delusion or imagination, the reality of the self is necessarily
included in it; hence religion is either a pathology of the
human spirit, or it postulates the existence, the revelation,

and the knowableness of God. It is, as we have seen, necessary because of the peculiarity of human nature; and it is universal, as is apparent from the history of the human race and all the peoples. And wheresoever it manifests itself it is a relation of man, not to his neighbor or to the world in general, or to one of its parts, but to a personal being, who stands above nature and the world, and is therefore able to raise man above them and to unite him to himself. Religion is always a service of God, and hence it is either folly or necessarily implies the existence of God. Furthermore, faith in the knowability of God is inseparable from the existence of God, which is presupposed in and with the truth of religion; for a God who is wholly unknowable is practically for us a God who does not exist. Consistent agnosticism amounts practically to atheism. And finally, if God, even in however small a measure, is knowable, there can be no explanation of this except that he has revealed himself; for what we cannot perceive at all cannot be known, and what we cannot know at all we cannot love and serve, *ignoti nulla cupido*. All who recognize and defend religion as truth believe accordingly, whether they are willing to confess it or not, in the existence, knowableness, and revelation of God. Naturalism in the strict sense and religion are irreconcilable. All religion is supernatural, and rests upon the presupposition that God is distinct from the world and yet works in the world. Men may impose limits on revelation and not recognize it in nature and history, but only in their own consciousness; the thing itself remains in principle the same: religion has its foundation in revelation and derives from it its origin.[54]

The investigation into the essence of religion has led to the same result as that into its origin. When the study of religions came into vogue, it was thought that by means of comparative research the essence of religion might be determined, and thus the value of all forms of religion be estimated. But so many and such serious difficulties have been met with in the prosecution of this task that it may be reasonably maintained that it has now come to the dead point. It is undoubtedly impracticable for any one to obtain a thorough knowledge of all religions, or even of the principal religions, and to compare them with one another. Religion is of such a complex nature that it is scarcely possible to characterize accurately the essence of a single religion, or even of the religion of a single person. Very various opinions obtain among us of the essence of Christianity, of Romanism and of Protestantism; how, then, would it be possible to penetrate into the essence of all the different religions and to compare them with one another? To this must be added, that the study of the history of religions professes no doubt to be undertaken without any prejudice whatever, but facts disprove the assertion. Even the idea, from which it as a rule proceeds, that religion is neither an illusion nor a disease, but a necessary element of man's nature, a *habitus* and a virtue which has a right and reason to exist, — even this idea, I say, is an assumption of such importance that it is impossible to speak here of unprejudiced investigation; it is an assumption which from the outset binds and dominates the entire science. But every student of the history of religions approaches his task, whether he intends it or not, with his own conception of religion, which guides him in his investigation and serves him as a rule. If he proceeds, let us say, merely from the view that that religion is true which lies at the basis of all and manifests itself more or less purely in each, he thereby puts forth a dogma which is derived from philosophy and has far-reaching results for his investigation.   Already in the case of the physical sciences, and yet more so in the case of the sciences of the mind, it is impossible to begin investigation without assumptions, for they all are founded on ideas and canons which have their basis in the rational and moral nature of man.[55] This explains the fact that the search for the essence of religion has ended by resolving it into a vague, indefinite formula which is intended to embrace all religions, but cannot do justice to a single one of them, and which, as far as it contains anything positive, has given expression only to the notion which each investigator had formed beforehand of the essence of religion.[56]

Many have for this reason turned their backs upon this comparative historical investigation of the essence of religion, and have even run into the opposite extreme.   They say there is no universal, objective religion valid for all, and there is no essence which is everywhere the same and only clothes itself in different forms.   But religion is always something thoroughly personal, — a thing which concerns the individual man, and hence it is endlessly variant and incapable of being comprehended in a general definition.   He who desires to know it must watch it in particular men, and especially in the splendid specimens, the geniuses and heroes of religion, the mystics, the enthusiasts, the fanatics; they are the classics of religion.   It is not history but psychology which will tell us what religion really is.[57]   Even a man like Troeltsch, who persists in maintaining the historical point of view, and upbraids the psychology of religion with the lack of an epistemology, is compelled to confess that the expression "essence of religion" leads into error on account of its obscurity, and creates the false impression that it is possible "to answer with one stroke the different questions which are bound up with it in one and the same investigation." [58] As it was in the case of the origin, so again in the consideration of the essence, of religion, many turn back from abstract monism to the totality of religious life. There is not one principle which governs all religions and religious phenomena, and there is not one formula under which they all can be summed up.

The investigation of the essence of religion has, however, by no means been unfruitful. On the contrary, it has made as clear as the day that religion and revelation are bound together very intimately, and that they cannot be separated. All religion is supernatural in the sense that it is based on faith in a personal God, who is transcendently exalted above the world, and nevertheless is active in the world and thereby makes himself known and communicates himself to man. Let it remain for the present undetermined whereby and how God reveals himself, whether in nature or in history, through mind or heart, along ordinary or extraordinary ways. Certain it is that all religions, in harmony with their own idea, rest upon conscious and spontaneous revelation of God. This is confirmed by the consideration of what man seeks in religion. Siebeck divides religions into nature-, morality-, and redemption-religions. Tiele, however, rightly observes that, in a wide sense, the idea of redemption is common to all religions, and therefore all religions are redemption-religions. As to the evil from which redemption is sought, and the supreme good which men desire to obtain, their conceptions diverge widely. But all religions are concerned with redemption from an evil and the attainment of a supreme good. The first question

always is, What must I do to be saved?[59]   This being
so, religion everywhere, by virtue of its very nature, carries along with it the idea of revelation.   Religion and
science differ in many things, and in this too, that the
one owes the contents of its knowledge to divine revelation, the other to human investigation.[60]

To a considerable extent religion and science (philosophy) stand in relation to the same objects.   To separate
between religion and metaphysics, however often it may
have been attempted, is impossible ; religion is not merely
a certain frame of mind, an emotion of the heart, but it
always includes certain conceptions, and the emotions
are modified in accordance with the nature of these conceptions.   These conceptions of religion extend to man,
the world, and God, and hence enter the same domain
which science also tries to cultivate.   But religion gives
to its conceptions the character of dogmas which it accepts on divine authority ; science endeavors to obtain its
conceptions by means of independent investigation, and
has no other authority except reasoning and proof.   Now,
according to Tiele, all religious conceptions move around
three centres, — God, man, and the way of salvation.[61]
All these three elements are most intimately connected
with the idea of revelation.   Regarding the first element,
the doctrine concerning God (theology proper), this is
clear ; there is no knowledge concerning God, except
so far as he has revealed himself ; the distinction of
nature- and revelation-religions, in the sense that religions
may exist without appealing to revelation, is untenable.
But also in the case of the other two elements, the connection with the idea of revelation is clearly traceable.
For when religion carries along with it a distinct conception of man, it soars far above experience.   The religious

anthropology speaks of man's origin and destination, of his needs and ideals, of his disobedience and communion with God, of his sin and atonement,[62] — all of which are elements that cannot be obtained by means of empirical investigation and scientific reflection, but can be known, so far as they are true, only by means of revelation. Nearly all the religions have their reminiscences of paradise and their expectations of the future, and trace them back to revelation. And regarding the third element, soteriology, this also is either untrue or derived from revelation. For this part of religious dogmatics indicates the means by which communion with God can be restored, the power of evil broken, a new life begun, and the hope of abiding happiness realized.[63] Among these means a chief place is assigned in all religions to mediators, sacrifices, and prayer. Those persons are considered mediators through whom the Godhead makes known its revelations to man. Sacrifices, whatever theory of their origin and purpose may be favored, always include the idea that man is dependent upon God, owes everything to him, and is acceptable in his sight through a special service (*cultus*) distinguished from the ordinary ethical life. And prayer, which forms the heart of religion, has its ground in the belief that God is not only a personal being, but also is able to govern the world by his power, wisdom, and goodness, and make it subservient to man's salvation. Prayer never, not even in its highest form, loses this character; the petition for the remission of sins, for a pure heart, for communion with God, is as supernaturalistic as that for the healing of the sick or for deliverance from some danger to life.[64] Revelation is the foundation of all religion, the presupposition of all its conceptions, emotions, and actions.

Finally, all the attempts to classify the religions have led to the acknowledgment of the necessity of revelation. All the proposed divisions — into such as have grown and such as have been founded, into nature- and revelation-religions, into polytheistic and monotheistic, into particular and universal religions, etc., — suffer, according to the increasing conviction of many, from excessive one-sidedness; they ignore other elements, do no justice to the richness and variety of religious life, and all proceed tacitly from the Hegelian notion that the chapters which successively treat of the several religions represent so many steps in the development of religion. No one, however, believes that a satisfactory distribution has been found.[65] As little as natural phenomena, societies, and the peoples, can the religions be ranged one after the other in a formal system without violence to reality.

In view of this it is worthy of remark that the old distribution of religions into true and false has been revived in a new form. The more accurately the nature of the conceptions of the peoples was investigated, the clearer it became that they contain various elements which cannot be derived from one single principle. Thus it appeared that their religious conceptions are essentially distinct, not only from legends and fables, but also from myths. In the beginning of the last century, under the influence of the romantic school, the idea prevailed, and through the Grimm brothers found acceptance almost everywhere, that mythology was the real science of religion. This mythology accordingly arose out of nature-myths, was to be looked upon as the embodiment of religious, often sublime, ideas, but afterwards had faded into hero-sagas and fables. But deeper study has led to a different view. Myths, sagas, and fables no doubt often bear relation to one another; originally, however, they are distinct in origin and aim. "Myths are primitive philosophy, the most simple intuitive form of thought, a series of attempts to understand the world, to explain life and death, fate and nature, gods and cults. Sagas are primitive history, artlessly shaped in hatred and love, unconsciously formed and simplified. Fables, on the contrary, have grown out of and serve only the need of entertainment." [66] Religion is always distinguished from all these in that it is always connected with a cult.[67]

It is of still greater importance to observe that religion is more and more being recognized as distinct from magic. J. G. Fraser has no doubt attempted to explain religion just by means of magic,[68] and with him K. Ph. Preuss is of the opinion "that primitive human stupidity is the original source of religion and art; for both proceed directly from sorcery, which on its part is the immediate result of that prudence which proceeds from instinct." [69] This theory, however, is very strenuously opposed by Andrew Lang and others; we gather, says Tiele, no figs from thistles; superstition cannot be the mother of religion.[70] Superstition and magic are indeed often connected with religion, but they are neither the source nor the essence of it. They are rather to be regarded as morbid phenomena, which occur by no means only among the lowest, but also among the most advanced peoples and religions; and even in the present time in Christendom, not only among the common people, but relatively more markedly among the cultured and educated, where they number their adherents by the thousands; they are not "a lower stage or a first step of a religious development, but undercurrents of real religion." [71] If this distinction is correctly drawn, it follows immediately that it is impossible to reduce the religions and the religious phenomena among the different peoples to one head and to derive them from one principle. Monism as truly as the doctrine of evolution is contradicted by the facts. The religions have no common root; various factors, fetichism, animism, ancestor-worship, etc., have worked together in bringing them into existence.[72] Particularly have religion and magic different sources and must receive distinct explanations.

The great question in the history of religions is thus no longer, How in general did religion originate? but Whence do superstition and magic derive their origin? This is the problem that confronts us, namely, the old question, πόθεν τὸ κάκον? Existence, the good, the true, the beautiful are eternal and have no beginning; but becoming, error, falsehood, sin, shame, cannot be eternal and must have been originated in time. In superstition and magic ignorance in general and lack of knowledge of nature in particular certainly play a rôle. And yet "original stupidity" cannot be their only source. For not only do these morbid phenomena find credence in the highest circles of civilization even to-day, but even the most artless man distinguishes emphatically between the natural and the supernatural, although he draws his line of demarkation differently from us; and recognizes a domain which is subject to himself and governed by his knowledge and action.[73] To this must be added, that superstition and magic bear not only an intellectual, but also a moral character; they are errors of the head, but more especially errors of the heart. They furnish us proof that nature, but equally that God, is not known. The knowledge of nature and history also is intimately conjoined with that of God. Prophets and apostles had no knowledge of natural science, as it has been developed in these later centuries, but they had a very sound conception of nature, because they knew God and saw in the world his handiwork, and they left no room for superstition and magic. So soon, however, as the pure knowledge of God disappears, nature too in its true character is disowned, and either exalted into the sphere of the godhead or degraded to the sphere of a demoniacal power. And this mixture of God and the world, which results from vain speculations of the mind and a darkening of the heart, always was and still remains the origin of all superstition and magic.

But as sickness reminds us of former health, and aberration calls to remembrance the right path, so these phenomena of superstition point back to the original image of religion. Superstition and magic could not have arisen if the idea of another world than this world of nature had not been deeply imprinted on man's self-consciousness. They themselves are of a later origin, but they presuppose religion, which is inherent in human nature, having its foundation and principle in the creation of man in the image of God. Hence religion is, not only with reference to its origin and essence, but also with reference to its truth and validity, founded in revelation. Without revelation religion sinks back into a pernicious superstition.

VII

REVELATION AND CHRISTIANITY

THE arguments for the reality of revelation, derived from the nature of thought, the essence of nature, the character of history, and the conception of religion, are finally strengthened by the course of development through which mankind has passed, and which has led it from paradise to the cross and will guide it from the cross to glory.

We cannot reach the origin of the human race or form an idea of its primitive condition by the aid of animal, child, and savage; neither do biology, geology and palæontology give us any certainty with regard to its first abode or concerning the unity of the race. If there are no other sources and resources from which to draw our knowledge, we continually move in guesses and conjectures, and form for ourselves the image of an incomprehensible and impossible primitive man at the beginning of history.

Tradition, the testimony which mankind itself bears to its origin in tradition and history, points out a safer way to acquire knowledge regarding the oldest condition of the human race. In former times this was the method by which people sought to penetrate into the past. The Church Fathers derived all the wisdom they found among the heathen from the theology of the eternal Logos.[1] Augustine speaks of a Christianity which has existed since the beginning of the human race, and was of the opinion that the doctrine of God as the creator of all things and the light of all knowledge and action had been known to all the wise men and philosophers of all peoples.[2] Lactantius rejoiced in this unity of all peoples, and beheld in it a prelude of the great alleluiah which in the days to come will be sung by all mankind, although he complains that the traditions have been corrupted by poetical license and the truth often perverted into a delusion.[3] Both in earlier and later times in the Christian Church the truth and wisdom found among the heathen have been generally derived from a primitive revelation, from the continuous illumination by the Logos, from acquaintance with the literature of the Old Testament, or from the operation of God's common grace.[4]

No doubt the rationalism of the eighteenth century threw all these theories overboard, because it believed that it possessed in reason the only and sufficient source of all truth.   But it was cast down from this exalted pedestal by the philosophy of Kant, by the theology of Schleiermacher, and with more prevailing power by the rise of the romantic school.   When towards the end of that century Persian, Indian, and Egyptian antiquity gradually disclosed its treasures, the idea of an original revelation, a common tradition, a primitive monotheism, revived in wide circles.   A host of men — Schelling, Creuzer, Chr. G. Heyne, F. G. Welcker, O. Müller, Fr. Schlegel, Ad. Müller, and others — proceeded from this hypothesis and, often rather one-sidedly, elevated India or Egypt or Persia to the cradle of the human race and the source of all wisdom.[5] Traditionalists, such as de Maistre and de Bonald, carried this tendency to an extreme, maintaining that language, and with it all knowledge of the truth, had been communicated to man by God in the primitive revelation, and that this knowledge was now propagated by tradition

and had to be received on authority.[6]   Antagonism to the
autonomy asserted by the Revolution led these men to ignore
entirely the activity of reason and to deny all personal independence.   By these extravagancies the romantic school
digged its own grave; empirical science raised its voice
against it, called men back to reality, and at first imagined
that all the advance of culture as well as the origin of man
himself could be explained by means of minute variations,
occurring through an endless series of years.   But deeper
study and continued investigation, not only of the culture
but also of the history of the most ancient peoples, has
in this case too led to the acknowledgment of the just
claims that lay at the foundation of the old view.

In the first place, we have to consider the primitive
history of culture, which is best known to us through
many important and exact researches concerning the
oldest inhabitants of Europe.   The prehistoric men who
lived there no longer speak to us, and have left nothing
behind them in writing; hence our knowledge of their
condition always remains in the highest degree imperfect;
we cannot even directly prove that they possessed language and religion, morality and laws; there is here a
large domain for the play of the imagination.   Nevertheless they are known to us in part by means of the fossils
of their bones and skulls, by means of the relics of their
arms and tools, of their dwellings and graves, their food
and clothing, their furniture and ornaments.   And these
teach us that the original inhabitants of Europe stood on a
much lower level in culture, science, art, technic, etc., than
the culture-peoples of the present time; but in intellect,
talents, capabilities, in bodily and mental qualities, they
were men of like passions with us.   In elements of culture
they did not stand on a lower plane than many nature-

peoples of our day as, for instance, the Patagonians and Bushmen, whom we nevertheless reckon among men, and who have in common with other men the same mind and the same bodily structure.   In fact the study of the arms and tools which have been preserved proceeds on the assumption that those who made them were men; for we consider objects arms and tools only when they manifest intellect and reflection, thought and purpose, and hence are an evidence of the activity of the human mind. Schurtz is right in saying that "all material culture is a creation of the mind, and always serves to strengthen the body or to free it of burdens; the staff lengthens the arm, the stone strengthens the fist, the dress protects the body, the dwelling shelters the family." [7]   The original inhabitants of Europe, having left behind objects such as never have been conceived or made by any animal, — these bear incontestable witness to their mental gifts and their human nature.   When we consider, indeed, that they stood at the beginning of culture and had to invent many things which we, aided by their labor, simply need to modify and develop, we stand amazed at their inventiveness, and especially their artistic skill, which accomplished so much with such defective means and under such unfavorable conditions.

But there is still something further in ancient culture which draws our attention.   Notwithstanding all the differences caused by character and talents, wants and environment, soil and climate, there exists a striking likeness between the oldest culture which is met with in Europe and that which is found in other parts of the world and among other peoples.   For example dolmens, that is family graves, composed of five large blocks of granite, are found in all parts of the earth, with the exception of

Australia, and are ascribed on this account by some writers
on the history of civilization to a single race which had
spread through various lands.[8]   Axes, which mark the
boundary between the palæolithic and the neolithic conditions show great similarity to one another in the whole of
Europe and in Egypt; and the pottery which is found in
the latter country vividly reminds us of the forms which
are scattered through Europe.[9]   It is remarkable in this
respect, that numerous axes have been found in Southern-
and Central-Europe, made of kinds of stone which are not
indigenous to Europe, but are common in Central-Asia.[10]
The ornamentation by which the pottery especially is dec-
orated is the same which from time immemorial was used
in Egypt.[11]   The same species of cereals, wheat, barley,
and millet found in Egypt and Asia were later raised in
Europe.[12]   All the principal elements of culture in Europe
— tools, decorations, agriculture, cattle-breeding, dwellings, and graves — point back to the East, to Egypt and
Asia.   On this account Sophus Müller says that not only
has the more recent culture been influenced by the East,
but the oldest culture also did not grow up independently
in Europe, but was introduced from the East.[13]   In point
of fact, scientific research increases the probability of the
hypothesis that man did not originate in Europe, but
came across from Asia and Africa into Italy and Spain.
Even such an enthusiastic adherent of the doctrine of
evolution as Ludwig Reinhart testifies that, as Europe is
only an appendix of the vast continent of Asia, so also
the principal gifts of culture were for the most part not
acquired in Europe, but brought over from the ancient
civilized countries of Western-Asia.[14]

The remarkable excavations which have been undertaken in recent years in several parts of Greece and

especially in Crete, have confirmed this result of the history of civilization. They make it clear that Greece, long before the Hellenic culture proper, that is to say, more than a thousand years before Christ, passed through an extremely interesting period of culture, which is designated the pre-Mycenic and the Mycenic ages, the latter of which is intimately connected with the Egyptian civilization.[15] Some, it is true, such as Karl Penka, have been of the opinion that civilization really began in Northern-Europe and spread thence towards the South; others, like Solomon Reinach, have expressed the judgment that the civilization of Europe had an origin of its own, independent of Asia. But the arguments in favor of the contrary are so numerous and strong that the great majority of the experts are persuaded of the Egyptian origin of the Mycenic civilization. Just as in later days the art of writing, the brick-kiln, the coining of money, Christianity, etc., have been brought over from the south to northern Europe, so it happened with the other constituents of civilization. The south was the real source of civilization for Europe, although it is true that the north has greatly modified and developed the elements received, as, for example, the stone axe.[16] And Southern-Europe in its turn stood under the influence of Africa and Asia. The knowledge of metals penetrated from the East into southern Europe. Bronze objects found in the lowest strata of Troy, pottery and objects of worship in Crete, graves in large numbers, especially on the islands of the Archipelago, but also in Greece and Asia Minor, daggers and axes of bronze in the graves, ornaments wrought on the pottery in the form of spirals, lines, and female figures, — all these point to the civilization of ancient Egypt.[17]

The study of Greek philosophy points in the same direction. Zeller, Ueberweg and others succeeded in introducing into wide circles the idea that the philosophy of Thales and his fellow spirits was the result of opposition to religion, or at least of the emancipation of the mind from religion, and that philosophy had taken an antithetical position to belief in any form. But further research has brought to light the incorrectness of this explanation. As a rule, the philosophers were opposed to the superstition of the people and the superficiality of the masses, but we have no right whatever to represent them on this account as infidel and irreligious. On the contrary, re-religion and philosophy were still in their case one; they were not one-sided, materialistic, nature-philosophers, but on the contrary propounded a positive view about man and God. They investigated not only the essence of nature, but also the essence of man, his soul and its immortality. Moreover, the philosophy of Thales did not fall abruptly from the skies; a long time of preparation preceded it. According to the testimony of Pythagoras, Plato, Aristotle, the theologians and lawgivers were the precursors of the philosophers. The age before Homer was by no means one of rude barbarism, without history and without letters; but the Pelasgians brought over from Asia a treasure of religious conceptions, manners and customs. When the several tribes in Greece intermingled, there was born from their intercourse a new cult, the cult of the Muses, who formed the court retinue of the Doric god Apollo. Orpheus was in this period the great figure; singers and poets in their νόμοι regulated the worship of Apollo; the siege of Troy and the founding of the colonies in Asia Minor furnished new material for thought and hymn; Homer and Hesiod did not invent, but system-

atized the religious ideas and customs. Next to these
poets and singers appeared the politicians and the lawgivers, the wise men and the moralists, the theologians and
the mystics. Along with them appeared very soon on the
scene the real, afterwards so-called, philosophers. They
were men of like passions with the others, and stood not
outside the rich, full life of their time, but, as Heinrich
Gomperz has described them, as men of flesh and blood,
in the midst of it. The rich tradition which existed in
poetry and aphorisms, in theology and legislation, forms
the background of their philosophy, and is itself intimately
connected with Oriental wisdom. The greatest thinkers
of Greece — Pythagoras, Plato, Aristotle, and later Plu-
tarch and Plotinus — derived their wisdom, especially the
knowledge of the ideas, from ancient tradition, and further
on from divine revelation.[18] Of course this tradition was,
to a large extent, corrupted, especially through the imagination of the poets, and was more purely preserved in the
Orphic school than in the works of Homer and Hesiod.
But it was nevertheless the source from which philosophy
drew its most elevated ideas. Just as poetry and art,
so philosophy enriched itself from the precious treasure
which was preserved in tradition. The first problems on
which thinking tried its strength were brought to the
thinkers by life itself. Philosophy arose out of religion,
and the question which presents itself to us is, not how
philosophy later on assumed a religious character in
Pythagoras and Plato, but, on the contrary, how philosophy was born of religion and theology.[19]

The marvellous discoveries which have been made in recent years in the land of Babylon and Assyria enable us
now to trace further back this broad stream of tradition
which culture and history both indicate to us. A new

world has here risen out of the ground. New peoples
have appeared on the scene whose names were scarcely
known to us. As natural science has expanded our horizon above, beneath, and around us, so historical science
has extended it into an almost infinite past. They who
recognized the historical value of the book of Genesis of
course knew better; but for many there lay behind the
time of Moses nothing but a world of rude barbarism.
All this has now been changed. Penetrating into the
past [20] under the guidance, not of imagination, but of history, we encounter in ancient Asia not half-bestial men
and savage hordes, but highly civilized peoples and a
richly developed culture.

Not only do we find a land, the fertility of which
in that dry climate was increased by numerous canals
and channels of irrigation, under the superintendence
of a large multitude of officials, whose activity was carefully regulated. Legislation and jurisprudence also had
reached a high degree of development. The code of
Hammurabi contains decrees about marriage, about the
relations between parents and children and between free-
men and slaves, about the protection of honor and life,
about rents and leases, about feudal tenure, mortgage, inheritance, and penal justice. Trade and art rejoiced in a
rich measure of prosperity; architecture and sculpture,
metallurgy, the arts of the goldsmith, potter, and stone-
cutter produced works which excite even now our admiration, and had at their disposal even then a great
wealth of forms. Commerce flourished and moved along
excellent roads of communication which led from Babylonia to Western-Asia. Science also found its students,
especially astronomy, in harmony with the astral character of the religion, but also arithmetic, geometry,

chronology and geography, hieroglyphics and history. Not a few even maintain that the civilization of Babylonia, like that of Egypt, does not, so far as it is known to us, exhibit a picture of advance and bloom, but rather of retrogression and decadence. The oldest works of art in both lands are, in their opinion, far in advance of later productions in talent and in freedom and truth of conception. Otto Weber expresses this view thus: " The dogma of a gradual development from a lower to a higher level is not sustained by the history of the Oriental peoples. What history gives us leaves upon us, on the contrary, the impression of decadence rather than of an advancing civilization, which tries to find fixed forms; everywhere in art, science, and religion, this is confirmed." [21]

It has happened with the excavations in Babylon and Assyria very much as it happens with all discoveries. At first they were greatly overestimated and their importance exaggerated. Just as in former ages all the wisdom of the peoples was derived from the books of the Old Testament, and in the days of romanticism from India, Egypt, or Persia, so also there has arisen in sequence to the important discoveries in the land of Sumer and Accad a Panbabylonian school, which imagines it has discovered in Babel's astral religion a key to the religion and world-view of all the peoples. Certain similar features in the narratives of creation and the deluge, for example, so astonished men that borrowing or community in origin was at once assumed, the differences ignored, and even the precipitate conclusion formed that probably affinity and agreement existed in everything else too. Just as the points of resemblance between man and beast have been the occasion of a rash inference of common descent, so also the Panbabylonists, through the mouth of

Winckler, Zimmern, Jeremias, Mücke, Stucken, Hans Schmidt, and especially Jensen in his *Gilgamesh-Epos*, have made a fearful abuse of the argument from analogy. The Babel formula seemed to furnish the explanation of the entire history of the world. But this exaggeration need not cause much solicitude; all exaggerations hasten by and are succeeded in a short time by a calmer and more sober view.[22] And the result will be the recognition of the significant fact that the land of Babel was the cradle of the descendants of Noah and the starting-point of all civilization.

This fact receives strong confirmation from another side also. Not only the Babylonists and the Assyriologists, but also the ethnologists in a wider sense, supply us with strong grounds for the suggestion that the cradle of the human race stood in Central-Asia. We meet with striking points of agreement, in conceptions, manners, customs, institutions, between the most widely separated peoples. The state of society of the Greeks as described by Homer, for instance, shows remarkable resemblances to the condition of the ancient Irish, Welsh, Scottish Highlanders, and further to that of the ancient Norsemen, Araucanians, Massai, Turcomans, and the Kirgish. All the institutions, all the characteristics of the ancient ancestors of the Romanic, Germanic, Slavonic, and Semitic peoples, find their parallels in the primitive races which still exist or have recently become extinct. The similarity between the Semites and the American Indians is so great that some old ethnologists imagined that they had discovered in the aborigines of America the lost ten tribes of Israel.[23] Richthofen found astronomical conceptions in China which distinctly pointed back to Babylon. This led him to remark : " We stand here before one of the most remarkable problems which prehistoric times offer us in reference to the inter-communication of peoples." [24]   In a word, the study of history and civilization makes it more and more clear that Babylon was in ancient times the ancestral country of the human race and the source of civilization.   The peoples in Western-Asia stood in active communication with one another; there was no "spiritual isolation" (*geistige Sonderexistenz*) of the peoples, no Chinese wall which separated them from one another; a common tradition in the widest sense bound together all lands and peoples, — Babylonia, Arabia, Canaan, Phœnicia, and Egypt.   Whether the tribes and generations after the building of the tower of Babel took many elements of culture away with them from their original home, or whether these were in various ways conveyed to them or were developed through later communication, it is a fact that the hypothesis gains progressively in strength, that the same tradition and the same culture lie at the foundation of the conceptions and customs of all peoples.[25] Probably more light will be shed on all this as excavations are continued, the texts translated, and the researches of palæontologists and ethnologists further prosecuted.

But we are at least warranted in saying, even at present, that the so-called *Völkeridee* of Adolph Bastian has received a heavy blow.   The ethnologists have always been struck by the many and strong analogies which exist between even widely sundered peoples in all sorts of conceptions and institutions, manners and customs.   The celebrated and widely travelled Bastian thought this explicable on the hypothesis that human nature is everywhere the same, and that the several peoples have given birth wholly independently of one another to the same conceptions and customs; and this theory for a long time met with much favor. Dogs bark everywhere alike, the cuckoo utters everywhere the same note, and in the same way man everywhere forms the same ideas and performs the same actions.[26] Of course it cannot be denied that next to heredity variability, next to dependence independence, plays an important rôle, and it is well-nigh impossible to draw the boundary line where the one ends and the other begins. A frivolous game has often been played with formal agreement, affinity, descent, not only in the science of religion, but also in the science of philology.[27] But on the other side it must not be forgotten that the unity of human nature, on which Bastian based his argument, includes more than is actually derived from it.

It is, of course, easy to imagine that the animal-man stands behind the culture-man whom we meet with even in the primitive races, and that the interval between man and beast was bridged over in earlier times by many transition-forms which are now extinct and lost. This, however, is pure fancy, which has no rooting in reality. The facts are, that everywhere and always, so far as investigation can carry us, an essential difference exists between man and beast. Human nature is *sui generis;* it has its own character and attributes. If this be true, then the common origin of all men is necessarily given with it, without needing further proof; and in point of fact this hypothesis is accepted theoretically by many adherents of the doctrine of descent, and practically by almost all. This monogeny, however, again implies that the first human pair was either created by God or arose all of a sudden, by means of an enormous leap of mutation, to the height of human nature, and still further, that the oldest men dwelt together for a long time as one family. But there is involved in this not only the possibility but also the necessity of a common tradition. Human nature is not an empty notion, no purely abstract conception, but a reality, a particular manner of being, which includes distinctive habits, inclinations, and attributes. And this tradition was undoubtedly supported and strengthened for a long time by the intercommunication which the families and tribes kept up even after they had separated. Some tribes no doubt wandered so far away that they became isolated and impoverished in culture; others, however, remained in close proximity and came often in contact with one another. Commerce, intercommunication, intercourse, are, according to the latest researches, much older and more widely extended than is usually represented. There is nothing, therefore, that can be urged in itself as an argument against the existence of a common tradition.

Even Wundt acknowledges " that the historical testimonies do not of themselves exclude the hypothesis that all myths and religions have proceeded in prehistoric time from one single centre of origin, if only the possibility of such an hypothesis could be psychologically conceded." [28] Why this should be impossible is not easy to understand. For since human nature is one, the possibility is certainly implied in this, that conceptions may be taken over and further developed; and it is assuredly more readily explicable that peoples should have interchanged conceptions and customs than that they should have produced them all independently, and yet in close agreement. Moreover, however much a general tradition, the common property of all, may be denied, the same thing is acknowledged by all in a narrower circle. Wundt, for example, thinks it possible that in America, Oceania, South-Africa, and India " a flood of legends may have deluged vast territories." [29]

Every household, every family, every town, every people, in its turn is a centre around which spread out, in narrower or wider circles, conceptions and views, manners and customs. And the human race is similarly one large family, which in all its movements and in all its tendencies is dependent on its common origin and its original equipment. It is, as G. F. Wright correctly observes, a wise and holy arrangement of Divine Providence that succeeding generations are in a high degree dependent on preceding ones, and that the better-favored parts of the human race, to whom much is given, are made responsible for the communication of these gifts to the less favored.[30]

Through what channels this communication has been made it is often impossible to trace. This gap in our knowledge, however, cannot be adduced, as Wundt[31] supposes, as an objection to the fact itself. For in a number of cases we can say that such channels must have existed, although we possess no detailed knowledge of them.[32] Since the human race has been made of one blood, then certainly men at first dwelt together, and when they went forth to fill the whole earth they must also have carried with them conceptions and customs from the parental home to all parts of the world. The unity of the human race, which forms the basis of the unity of human nature, necessarily includes in it an original common tradition.

Of course a large measure of wisdom and circumspection is needed for distinguishing among the traditions and manners of the peoples between what has been brought from the original abode and what has been the result of later modification and mutilation, extension and augmentation, by the different peoples. Apologetics has sometimes taken its task here too easily, for general

phrases do not suffice here; every element of the civilization of mankind needs to be investigated carefully and
comprehensively before we are ready to draw conclusions.
And even after the deepest and most extended research
it will be found that we have very often to be satisfied
with a conjecture or a probability.

Nevertheless there are phenomena which point back
with great probability to a common origin. Among these
we find, for example, the knowledge of a single supreme
Being, which is found among various peoples. We have
no historical testimony to the development of polytheism
into pure monotheism; when polytheism comes no longer
to satisfy the intellectual circles, it is remodelled into
pantheism, which has in common with polytheism the
"nature-character" of the godhead, and dissolves the multitude of nature-gods into one nature-godhead. On the
other hand, we have many historical examples of monotheism not developing, indeed, but gradually degenerating
into polytheism and polydemonism. There are Christian
churches in the past, and in the present also, which furnish proof of this statement; and even among the most
cultured people there are some who, in our own day, turn
not only to Mohammedanism and Buddhism, but also
to the crudest forms of superstition and sorcery; sometimes even theologians and philosophers prefer polytheism to monotheism. Goethe himself once said that he
was not satisfied with one system, but was by turns
monotheist, polytheist, and pantheist.[33] We may also
see with our own eyes the theoretical profession of faith
in one God accompanied in practice by the adoration of
many angels and saints. The same phenomenon appears
among many peoples.

When some speak of "monotheistic currents" in the

Babylonian religion, very serious objections may certainly be advanced. But it cannot be denied, and is indeed recognized on all hands, that many nature-peoples in Africa, America, Australia, Mongolia, Tartary, and the Indian Archipelago, alongside of a practical religion full of superstition and sorcery, believe in a supreme good God, who is often called the great Spirit, the supreme Being, the Father, our Father. It may be that this belief in such a supreme Being has often been too much idealized, as, for example, by Andrew Lang; it is, no doubt, seldom worshipped, and even sometimes not conceived in a pure monotheistic form; it remains, nevertheless, in the religions of the nature-peoples a most remarkable phenomenon, which cannot be explained from Christian or Mohammedan influences, and as little from animism or ancestor-worship. And if now we do not forget that the religious worship of natural phenomena and spirits always already presupposes the idea of God, and that religion, according to many students of the philosophy of religion, is rooted in human nature as such, the hypothesis lies close at hand that we are confronted in this belief in the great Spirit with an original monotheism which preceded all polytheistic religions and is still at work in them.[34]

But not to insist upon this or other agreement in details, so much at least remains undoubtedly assured that human nature, both in body and soul, points back to the common origin of all men. In the fundamental ideas and fundamental elements of religion, morality, law, science, art, technic, — in short, in all the foundations of culture, — a unity exists which, from the viewpoint of the doctrine of descent, must be considered a miracle. According to the nominalistic point of view, represented, for example, by Professor William James, all men must be considered as not originally one, but as gradually becoming one. This view forgets that whatever can *become* one already *is* one in its deepest foundation, and it ignores, moreover, the actual unity which has through all the ages existed among men notwithstanding all differences. According to James, it is pure accident that our ancestors have followed precisely the line of thought along which we still travel, just as, according to Darwin, we owe it to pure chance that our women have not been trained like bees, and on this account refrain from killing their daughters. This, however, does not remove the fact that the methods of thinking and acting, which have been gradually invented by men and transmitted by heredity from generation to generation, have become inextirpably tenacious. Yea, according to James' own expressions, "these fundamental ways of thinking" have continually grown firmer and remain practically useful and indispensable.[35] We may therefore quietly set aside the hypothesis that these modes of thinking and acting, like men themselves, have come gradually into being; in reality, they form the immutable foundation on which all our civilization is built.

Thus it is in every respect. The human race is everywhere and always bound to its nature, to its origin, to its past. There are a multitude of ideas, a whole complex of views regarding the chief concerns of life which men have in common. They concern the idea of God as the almighty and all-wise source of all things, the world as established by wisdom, order and the reign of law, the unity and harmony of creation, the symbolical meaning of all things, the distinction between a world of things seen and unseen, the opposition of truth and falsehood, the struggle between good and evil, the memory of a golden age and a subsequent decay, the wrath of the gods and the hope of reconciliation, the divine origin and destination of man, the immortality of the soul and the expectation of a judgment, reward and punishment in the hereafter.[36] All these fundamental ideas form the beginning and the foundation of history, the principle and starting-point of all religion, morality, and law, the bond of all social relations, the germ and the root of all science and art, the harmony of thinking and being, of being and becoming, of becoming and acting, the unity of logic, physics, and ethics, of the true, the good, and the beautiful. All these fundamentals are given from the beginning in human nature; they are transmitted from generation to generation, and are at the same time grounded in the very nature of man, so that dependence and independence work together here. And they all point back to a divine origin: "all knowledge is," at least so far as principles and foundations are concerned, "of divine origin." [37] Knowledge in this sense flows from revelation.

To this original revelation is joined on that revelation which according to the Old Testament was bestowed upon Israel. The latter is built upon the former and rests upon it, and is at the same time the continuation, the development and completion of it. The distinction between what has come to be called general and special revelation does not begin until the call of Abraham; before that the two intermingle, and so far have become the property of all peoples and nations. Special revelation certainly is set antithetically over against all the corruption which gradually entered into the life of the peoples, but it takes up, confirms, and completes all that had been from the beginning put into human nature by revelation and had been preserved and increased subsequently in the human race. The earlier view, which exclusively emphasized the antithesis, no less than that now prevalent which has an eye only for the agreement and affinity, suffers from one-sidedness. The latter, however, is giving way gradually to another and better view. For a time the notion was prevalent that the history and the religion of Israel could be thoroughly explained if the books of the Old Testament were subjected to free criticism and redating like other literature. But when this historical criticism had analyzed and rearranged the books of the Bible, consciously or unconsciously under the influence of the doctrine of evolution, — after all this source-criticism, the problem of the religion of Israel remained still unsolved. Historico-critical investigation had not succeeded in destroying the peculiar and special character of this religion. And yet this was the motive which had given the impulse to this research. What profit was there in the analysis of the sources if Israel itself with its religion remained in the midst of the peoples unexplained? It is therefore that Panbabylonism has drawn away the attention of scholars and supplanted the historico-critical period by a religio-historical one. It has been right in suggesting that there may be a great difference and a long interval between the origin of ideas and institutions and their literary description; it has restored to honor the living tradition, and has shown that there are many other ways besides the literary one of exercising and receiving influence. For the field of religion especially these observations have been of great importance. For a religion is not invented by this or that thinker, and is not imposed upon a people from without, but is always a doctrine, a worship, a sum total of conceptions, rules, ordinances, and institutions which are linked to the past, live in the hearts of the people, and are transmitted from generation to generation. And religious and moral conceptions do not develop themselves after a logical method, as a result of apriori thought, but are often of older origin, exist side by side with each other, and develop themselves together in mutual connection. The simple and rectilinear theory of evolution comes in conflict with the complicated reality.

Thus the religio-historical method was right in reverting from literary criticism to the study of religion, and therewith from theory to life, from a system of abstract conceptions to the folk-soul, to the totality of reality. Its purpose, however, is to derive this totality, this complex of conceptions and prescriptions, not from Moses and the patriarchs, but from Babylonia. There, in its opinion, is to be found the source of the religion and worship of Israel, and even of the whole of Christianity. " Babel and Bible," says Otto Weber, " are products of one and the same world-view." [38] Continued research will result, however, here, as in geology and anthropology, in a reaction from one-sidedness, and soon in the agreement the unlikeness and the difference will also be noticed. In the meantime, however, this gain has been registered, that it is no longer possible to consider Israel as an island, separated by a wide ocean from the rest of the world. Israel stands as a people and in its entire religious life in relation with its environment, and also with the past. No sudden breach was made by the prophets of the eighth century before Christ between the past and the future. The narrative of creation and the deluge, monotheism and the worship of Jehovah, the laws and ceremonies of the cultus, the reminiscences of paradise and the expectations of the future, the idea of the Messiah and the Servant of Jehovah, and all the eschatological conceptions, are much older than the literary documents wherein they are mentioned. Babel does not lie behind the Bible, but behind the Scriptures lies the revelation which begins with the origin of the human race, continues in the tribes of the Sethites and Semites, and then flows on in the channel of the Israelitish covenant towards the fulness of time.

For although Abraham left Babylonia and was sent to dwell apart in a strange land, the God who manifested himself to him, and later to Moses and to Israel, is no new, strange God, but the God of old, the creator of heaven and earth, the Lord of all things, who had been originally known to all men, and had still preserved the knowledge and worship of himself in many, in more or less pure form.[39] The segregation and the election of Israel served the sole purpose of maintaining, unmixed and unadulterated, continuing and perfecting, the original revelation, which more and more threatened to be lost,[40] so that it might again in the fulness of time be made the property of the whole of mankind. The promise became temporarily particular, in order that thus it might later become universal. Israel belongs to the human race, remains in relation to all peoples, and is chosen not at the cost, but for the benefit of the whole human race.

Hence the peculiarity of the religion of Israel does not consist exclusively or primarily in its ethical monotheism. There are a number of elements in the history and religion of Israel which occur nowhere else, so far as is now known to us, and not even a parallel to which is found among other peoples. Among these are the name of

Jehovah, the cosmogony free from all theogony, the idea of the unity of the human race, the narrative of the fall, the week of seven days and the Sabbath, circumcision of all male children on the eighth day, prophetism which accompanies Israel through its entire history, the plan of salvation embracing all nations, ethical monotheism, the invisibility of God and the impossibility of representing him, etc.[41] And there are many more elements in the Old and New Testaments still whose explanation is sought by the Panbabylonists in the astral religion of Babel, but in such a manner that the far-fetched character and the artificiality of the derivation are manifest to all.[42] Nevertheless all these elements do not yet form the essence of the religion of Israel. They stand, indeed, in very close connection with it, and form with it an integral whole; but the substance of the revelation which came to Israel, and the core of the religion which corresponded with it in Israel, consist in something else.

In order to find this, we must go back to the prophets and psalmists, to Jesus and the apostles, and they all teach us unanimously and clearly that the content of the divine revelation does not consist primarily in the unity of God, in the moral law, in circumcision, in the Sabbath, in short, in the law, but appears primarily and principally in the promise, in the covenant of grace, and in the gospel. Not law, but gospel, is in the Old and the New Testament alike the core of the divine revelation, the essence of religion, the sum total of the Holy Scriptures. Every other view fails to do justice to special revelation, effaces its difference from general revelation, degrades the Old Testament, rends apart the two economies of the same covenant of grace, and even gradually changes the gospel of the New Covenant into a law, and makes of

Christ a second Moses. Paul, however, declares that the promise is older than the law, that Abraham already received the righteousness of faith, not by the law, which was in his days not yet in existence, but by the promise which was granted him by grace. The law was thus originally not joined to the promise, but was added to it later, that transgressions might abound, and accordingly the necessity and indispensableness of the promise might be ever more clearly revealed, and its contents ever more fully developed and at last completed. The law thus is temporal, transitory, a means in the service of the promise, but the promise is eternal; it had its beginning in paradise, was preserved and developed by revelation in the days of the Old Covenant, received its fulfilment in Christ, and is now extended to the whole human race and all the peoples.[43]

In this promise, given to the patriarchs and to Israel, there are three things included. In the first place, there is the free, electing love of God, who seeks, calls, and adopts as his own Abraham and his seed, by pure grace, without any desert or merit of their own. The new element, which enters in with Abraham and later with Israel, consists in this, that God, the knowledge and service of whom were gradually passing away, at a given point of time places himself in a most special relation to a particular person and people. This relation is not grounded in nature; it is not a matter of course; it does not exist by virtue of creation; it is not instituted on the part of man, by his conscience or reason, by his feeling of dependence or need. But it is an historical product; the initiative came from God; he so reveals himself as, by the act of revelation, to receive a particular person and people into communion with himself. The calling of Abraham,

the deliverance from Egypt, the institution of the covenant on Sinai, are accordingly the main pillars upon
which the religion of Israel rests.[44]　It is the sovereign
and gracious *will* of God which calls this federal relation
into life.　By this will, which injects itself into history and
establishes a new relation between God and his people,
God is once for all in Israel made free from nature and
raised above it.　God is no nature-power, as is the case
among the nations.　He is an independent person, has his
own nature and will, and a law and worship of his own
which, in the most stringent way, prohibit all idolatry
and image-worship.　The human race owes a great deal
to Babylon, many good things of civilization and culture.
But let us not forget that there have also come forth
from Babylon all superstition and magic.　It was Babylon
which made all peoples drunk with the wine of her for-
nication and sorcery.[45]　And it was Israel alone which,
by the revelation of God, was delivered from these bonds,
and in this respect Israel stood alone in the midst of all
peoples.

Because to-day we evaporate religion into frames of
mind, detach it from every object, and retain scarcely any
sympathy with the knowledge and worship of God, we
no longer feel the importance of this entirely unique
position of Israel.　The prophets and apostles, however,
thought of it very differently.　The true religion consisted
for them first of all in the knowledge and worship of the
true God, according to his will and in consonance with
his command.　They still knew the difference between
faith and superstition, between religion and magic, between theology and mythology.　Well, now, Israel is the
people chosen by God, which never had a mythology,
and has rescued the human races from the bonds of super-

stition and sorcery. The Bible did not come forth from Babylon, but in its fundamental thought is in diametrical opposition to Babylon, and has made an end to Babylon's spiritual dominion over the peoples. Granted that the chaos-myth, as Gunkel supposes, has had an influence upon Israel, that Rahab and Leviathan, Tiamat and Na-chash, were originally mythological conceptions; they have on Israel's soil, in the sphere of special revelation, totally cast aside this character. The poetical personification of natural phenomena is in Israel as strong as among other peoples; the thunder is God's voice, the light his garment, the lightning his fiery arrow, the storm his breath, the clouds are his chariot, and the like. But nowhere is this poetry presented as a description of objective reality, and never are these poetical conceptions combined and elaborated into a mythological narrative. Israel has no mythical feeling; by special revelation, by the intervention of God in history, by miracles, it has been profoundly convinced of the distinction between God and the world; the knowledge of God has expelled all myths. God no doubt works in nature and in history, but he transcends them as the free and almighty One; he has a character and will of his own. However personal and poetic the description of the phenomena of nature may be — though it may be said that the mountains clap their hands, that Tabor and Hermon rejoice, that the cedars gambol like calves, and that the whole creation listens and keeps silence, declares the honor of God and proclaims his glory — they are never represented as real, independent powers with which God has to struggle. The narratives also of the creation and the fall, of the deluge and the building of the tower of Babel, of the patriarchs and judges, are for the Israelite no myths, but history.

Israel's God is far exalted above nature, but by special revelation he brings about in the world a peculiar history.[46]

In the second place, God's pardoning grace is contained in the promise which was given to Israel. Although Tiamat and Nachash, Rahab and Leviathan, are no longer real, inimical nature-powers, yet certainly the Old Testament knows a power which opposes God. But this power must not be looked for in the abyss or the stars, nor in the sea or the mountains; on the contrary, it appears in history, in the world of men. It is sin, sin alone, which opposes God and with which he fights. It admits of no doubt that sin and sickness (misfortune, disaster, demoniacal possession), guilt and misery, forgiveness and deliverance, were in Israel's consciousness more intimately connected and much more closely interrelated than in ours. All the pious of Israel wrestled with the problem of the relation between them. But this very wrestling presupposes that there is, after all, a distinction between them; it can arise only when the just, convinced of his innocence, maintains himself in his religio-moral consciousness in the face of the suffering of the world. Therefore we owe to special revelation in Israel the purely ethical conception of the nature of sin, with respect both to its origin and to its essence and punishment. Sin is no disease, although disease is often the result and proof of it; it is not involved in existence itself, for every creature, as it comes forth from the hand of God, is very good; it consists in transgression of God's commandment. As God is distinct from nature, so also is his moral will distinct from the law of nature, the ethical from the physical, the "what ought to be " from " what is." The third chapter of Genesis, therefore, tells us just about the origin of sin; it cannot be explained except as a narration of how sin has entered into the world, and consists in transgression of God's command. The following chapters sketch for us the progress of sin, which is an imagination, a product of the heart of man from his youth. And when again after the deluge the stream of unrighteousness flows on its course, God chooses Abraham and his seed for a people of his own, that they may walk in holiness before his face.

But the electing love of God is at the same time a forgiving love. God not only elects and calls, but gives himself to his people; he joins himself to them, so intimately and tenderly, that he charges their guilt and transfers it, as it were, to himself. I am thy shield and exceeding great reward; I am the Lord thy God, who has led thee out of Egypt. The covenant with Abraham and his seed is built in a certain sense upon redemption and remission, and the walk before God's face to which the patriarchs and Israel were called is the duty of gratitude. The law which God gave his people, entered in after the promise, is built on the promise and is placed in the service of the promise. It was not a law of the covenant of works, but a law of the covenant of grace, a law of the covenant, a law of gratitude. It served the purpose not of acquiring righteousness and life, but of confirming these gifts to our consciousness, and of bringing them out in our walk before God's face. Nor was the ceremonial law a means to bring about reconciliation, but to maintain the reconciliation which already existed in the covenant relation. Prophecy revived from time to time the consciousness of this: it did not usher in a higher law, it did not establish a new religion, it was not the promulgator of ethical monotheism, but it had the covenant of God with his people for its pre-supposition and was built upon the regulation of their reciprocal relation in the law. Never did it call upon the people to make themselves God's people by keeping the law; it always started from the supposition that Israel had become God's people by election, and laid upon them the demand that therefore they must as God's people walk in his ways. Morality was in Israel grounded in religion. God forgives sins for his name's, for his covenant's, for his glory's sake.

That God forgives sin by grace, for his name's sake — the knowledge of this mystery we owe wholly to the special revelation which God granted unto Israel. We would value this more highly if we had a deeper consciousness of guilt. For the forgiving love of God is not a matter of course; it is not known to us from nature, or from history, or from our own intellect and conscience. On the contrary, appearances are against it, — we do not perceive it by sight or by touch ; it is a matter of faith. Nay, more than this : if God forgives sin for his own sake, then he must himself provide the atonement. For without atonement, without the shedding of blood, there is no remission of sins. In the ceremonial legislation God himself gave his people instruction in this matter; it pointed to the way in which God himself would bring about reconciliation. Man can as little make propitiation for his sin as he can forgive it himself. But God can do both, atone and forgive; he can do the one just because he can do the other. The tension, however, which existed between them in the days of the Old Testament, the time of the πάρεσις, is reflected in the consciousness of the Israelites, as a disharmony between righteousness and suffering, holiness and blessedness, virtue and happiness, but in this way contributes to prepare the way for its own solution.   For so in Israel's prophecy, psalmody and chokhma, the profound thought is gradually formed of a suffering which is endured on account of and for others; thus there gradually reveals itself the divine mystery of an innocent and atoning suffering, which is illustrated in Isaiah by the Servant of Jehovah, who is wounded for our transgressions, bruised for our iniquities, but upon whom was the chastisement of our peace, and with whose stripes we are healed.

In the third place the gospel in the Old Testament includes also the promise of God's unchangeable faithfulness. The more Israel's apostasy and unfaithfulness increased, making it ever more apparent how little reliance could be placed on man, the louder the prophets announced that God will not break his covenant and will not annul his promise. Mountains may depart and hills may be removed, but his loving-kindness shall not depart from his people, and the covenant of his peace shall not be removed forever. The prophets narrate the past of Israel, they explain the present; but they likewise foresee the future not as fortune-tellers and soothsayers, but as seers and watchmen upon the walls of Zion, as searchers according to the description of Peter, and as inquirers under the guidance of the Spirit into the salvation which in the future was to be obtained and given by the Messiah. Thus they see what others do not see; persevere in believing where others doubt; cling to the promise in hope against hope, and expect that God himself will in his own time realize and extend his dominion to all peoples through his Anointed One. As he is to complete his revelation through the Prophet like unto Moses and to procure the atonement through the Servant of Jehovah, so also is he to establish his kingdom on the earth through the

Anointed King. Theology leads through soteriology to
eschatology. The love of election passes over through
the grace of forgiveness into the full communion of God
with his people. In the future God will make a new
covenant, wherein the old promise, I will be your God
and you shall be my people, will be fully realized.

These are the contents of the gospel, which was preached
and intrusted to Israel. No criticism of the books of the
Bible can destroy this content. Election, gracious forgiveness and true, perfect communion, are the great
thoughts and the spiritual gifts which Israel has received
from God and in the fulness of time has communicated
to humanity. For in the Person of Christ, who is the
Son of God and also the Son of Man, who is at the same
time the highest prophet, the only priest and the eternal
king, all the promises have been fulfilled. He indeed is
the object of the conflict of the ages, at present fiercer and
more serious than ever before. Judged from the present
position of scientific investigation, it would seem as if
everything concerning his person and work is uncertain
and even unknowable. All kinds of hypotheses have
been erected and numerous attempts made to explain
the origin and essence of Christianity. Judaism and
Heathenism, apocryphal and Talmudic literature, political
and social conditions, the mythologies of Egypt and Persia, of Babylonia and India, are called upon to help us derive not only the world and man, religion and morality,
but also the Christian religion, from weak beggarly elements and the poorest possible beginnings. These investigations have an important value and contain a rich
promise. Through them the Christian religion will become
better known in its close connection with the world and
history, and the words and facts of the New Testament

will be better understood in their universal significance
and bearing.   But more than this, all these investigations,
provided they are not broken off half-way but carried on
to the end, will throw into ever clearer and clearer light
the uniqueness of the Christian religion.

For Christ, the mediator of creation, the life and the
light of men, the promise to the fathers, the desire of the
nations, the saviour of the world, and the judge of the quick
and the dead, is akin to all and to everything, and at the
same time distinguished from all and exalted above all.
Whatever may be adduced to elucidate and explain his
person and work, he appears now as ever on the pages of
the gospel before us and the whole world in his unique
superiority.   The central facts of the incarnation, satisfaction, and resurrection are the fulfilment of the three great
thoughts of the Old Covenant, the content of the New
Testament, the κήρυγμα of the Apostles, the foundation
of the Christian Church, the marrow of its history of
dogma and the centre of the history of the world.   Without these facts history breaks into fragments.   Through
them there is brought into it unity and variety, thought
and plan, progress and development.   From the prote-
vangel to the consummation of all things one thread runs
through the history of mankind, namely, the operation of
the sovereign, merciful, and almighty *will* of God, to save
and to glorify the world notwithstanding its subjection
to corruption.

This *will* of God forms the heart of pure religion and
at the same time the soul of all true theology.   For
according to the counsel of this will we are chosen, con-
formably to this will we are regenerated, through this will
we are sanctified.   In virtue of the good pleasure of this
will both that which is in heaven and on earth will be

gathered in one in the dispensation of the fulness of time under Christ as Head.   And in the whole course of revelation this will of God unfolds itself ever more clearly as the love of God, the grace of the Son, and the communion of the Holy Ghost.

VIII

IF Christianity were at one with itself, and there were no other religions, the recognition of its truth would be easier. But it is endlessly divided and torn to pieces. The one church, which was the centre of village and city in the Middle Ages, is completely demolished; on every side a number of sects arise around her, each laying claim to be the purest expression of Christian truth, and continually subdividing and multiplying. Beyond that, the religions of the various nations are latterly becoming much better known to us than in former centuries, and the relation which Christianity bears to other religions has become a serious problem. Among those religions there are some which number millions of adherents, and numerically considered may, therefore, put in a more telling claim to the name of world-religions than Christianity. They provide examples of strong conviction of faith, earnest piety, and self-denying devotion which bear comparison with those of Christian confessions. All the elements of religion — doctrine and ethics, consciousness of sin and forgiveness, comfort and hope, contempt of death and certainty of salvation, prayer and praise, assemblies and public-service — appear in all. The claim to divine revelation is common to all religions.[1]

This extension of the religious horizon would not have proved so undermining to faith in Christian truth had it not been accompanied by a keen criticism of the power

and value of human reason. In accordance with Scripture, Christian theology has always taught that sin involves also error, and thus has not only corrupted the
heart and will, but also blinded the understanding. This
doctrine of Scripture was especially reasserted in the
Reformation, in opposition to the Roman view that the
natural gifts have remained to men and only the supernatural lost. Luther, above all, was not on friendly terms
with reason; though the substance of this doctrine is
merely that intelligence has been blinded by sin, but not
extinguished, and by its nature remains able to understand unseen and divine things. The newer philosophy,
however, emancipated itself entirely from this Christian
conviction and placed its trust exclusively in the power
of reason, and was soon called upon to pass through an
unpleasant experience. Both Descartes and Bacon established a separation between faith and reason, leaving the
domain of faith to theology and satisfying themselves
with a position external to it. For a while they lived in
the illusion that they could very well dispense with revelation and faith, and could throw sufficient light upon all
that man needs for his religious and moral life by reason.
When this new philosophy, however, had reached the
highest point of its development, it was wrecked by its
own continued inquiry. In criticising revelation it had
forgotten one thing, — criticism of itself. Reason in this
newer philosophy took its starting-point in childish naïveté
from its own integrity and trustworthiness. But when
it had completed its work of demolishing revelation and
now came to itself and examined its own nature and content, it found itself quite dissatisfied with itself. Reason
found in reason its keenest inquisitor, and received its
sharpest criticism from itself. All that had appeared to

stand firm began to waver and to fall. The secondary attributes, the law of causality, the objective world of sense, the ideas of substance, personality, and self-consciousness, the world of supernatural and divine things — all appeared untenable and unknowable. Kant struck the balance of this critical process thus: the intelligence of man is confined to the world of phenomena, and does not know anything of what lies behind it. Reason is not merely blinded or weakened by sin; it is in its very nature blind and deaf and dumb in the presence of the spiritual world.

Whatever value we may attach to this critical philosophy, there can be no doubt that it has roughly shaken confidence in human reason, and has given a deep wound to the faith and conviction, to the spiritual security and moral will-power of the modern man. As on the one side it has declared man autonomous, and set him free from all objective forms and external authority, on the other side it has opened the door for a wild anarchy of thought. If the knowledge of God and of spiritual things is excluded from the domain of science, then not only is science bereft of moral character and made atheistic, but religion and morality also are left to individual caprice. Both become matters of private judgment and individual taste; each one can do what he will. That is an incalculable injury, not only for the schools, but still more for life; agnosticism produces ethical and practical indifference.

But naturally one cannot live on criticism and agnosticism. Although the agnostic view, that "scientific superstition," as Mr. F. W. H. Myers calls it, is embraced to-day by many learned men, it has never been the creed, nor is it now the creed, of the human race.[2] Questions continually arise in the mind for which every one necessarily seeks an answer. There are some beliefs for which man cannot afford to wait. What must I do to be saved? is a question of an urgency of a totally different kind from the cause of the tides or the meaning of the marks on the moon. Men must settle roughly somehow or other what they have reason to hope or to fear from the unseen world.[3] Auguste Comte's positive philosophy grew into a sociolatry and a positive religion which made humanity and its heroes objects of worship. The whole of the nineteenth century is full of endeavors to recover the loss that had been suffered, to heal the gaping wound. Kant himself began it. In order to find a place for faith he confined science to the knowledge of sensible phenomena; what he demolished by theoretical reason, he tried to build up by practical reason. After him first one and then another arose, to make a similar effort to find a way to the unknown land. Speculative reason and intellectual contemplation, mysticism of feeling and the moral power of the will, the faith of the church and the religions of the nations, were all summoned in turn to aid in penetrating into the supernatural world, and building up the knowledge of God on a new scientific, unassailable foundation. However these efforts may differ, they all have in common that they no longer subject themselves to any socalled external authority, but try to find out God through man. Theology has, since Kant's time, become theology of consciousness and experience, and thus loses itself practically in religious anthropology.

In this transformation of theology into the science of religion the new conception of science comes to light. Kant had already limited the power of the intelligence, because he was under the influence of the one-sided Newtonian explanation of nature and could recognize as scientific only a conception of the world which bore a strictly mechanical character.[4]   This mechanism is in wide circles no longer looked upon as a sufficient explanation of the world, so that philosophy has acquired a new value; but nevertheless, the idea still exists that there is only one science, or at most two sciences, namely, the sciences of nature and of history, and that accordingly there are only two scientific methods, the empirical and the historical.[5] Thus, if theology is to be a science, and the knowledge of unseen and divine things trustworthy, the same method must be applied in its domain as in those of nature and history.   Theology must become an empirical science.[6]

But in this way the word " experience " is made to play an ambiguous rôle.   When used in religion and theology, it has a wholly different significance from that which it bears in empirical science.   In the latter what is meant is, that, by consistent application of the empirical method, personal interest in the inquiry is to be excluded as much as possible, and that the phenomena are observed and explained in their purity and impartially; empiricism even calls to its help the experimental proof.   But when men speak of experience in religion, they mean it to be understood, on the other hand, that religion is, or at any rate must become, a personal matter through and through. Religion is, according to this interpretation, no doctrine, no precept, no history, no worship, in a word, not a belief on authority, nor a consent to truth, but arises from within, when the heart is touched and a personal fellowship established between God and our soul.   Now there is certainly such a religious experience; the devotional writings of all religions bear witness to it, and serve in their turn to feed and strengthen that religious life even more than Bible and catechism.[7]   But the mistake is when men fancy

they in this way make theology a science as exact as that of
nature, and thus arrive at a scientific knowledge of unseen and eternal things.[8]

For whatever meaning religious experience may have, it
is not and cannot be an heuristic principle. Experience
comes into being only when, first, there exists something
to experience, and afterwards this something is really experienced ; it cannot otherwise exist. Religion is without
doubt a matter of the heart; but it cannot be separated
from all objective knowledge of God through his revelation in nature and history, in Scripture and conscience.
A subjective religion is always preceded by an objective
religion, whatever this may be. Just as language presupposes the capacity for speech in the child, but yet is
learned from the mother, so also religious experience
arises out of preceding revelation. Every child grows up
in the religion of its parents, and thereby develops its
own religious life ; the pious teaching and example of the
mother awaken piety in the heart of the child. No less
than in sensation, science, and art, does this take place also
in religion. Man is never self-sufficient and independent of
the outside world ; he needs the earth to feed and clothe
him, light to see, sound to hear, the phenomena of nature
or the facts of history to observe and to know, and in the
same way revelation to awaken and strengthen his religious life. The heart cannot be separated from the head,
nor faith as trust from faith as knowledge. Even those
who look upon dogmatics as an exposition of pious feelings
recognize that these feelings nevertheless are due to external influences, as, for example, from the person of Christ.[9]
Experience does not come first, after which interpretation
follows, but revelation precedes, and is experienced in
faith.[10]

If we reject the empirical order and proceed in an opposite direction, we reach the so-called psychology of religion which has latterly aroused so much attention. There is no doubt that this young science, for which Pietism and Methodism prepared the way, and which is a direct fruit of the empirical psychology and theology, has a right to exist, and may be expected to yield important aid for the knowledge and guidance of religious life. It may be hoped also that the method which has been applied in this science by James, Starbuck, Coe, and others, will gradually meet the objections which to-day are properly urged against it. Finally, we may acknowledge that dogmatics, especially in the doctrine of the *ordo salutis*, must become more psychological, and must reckon more fully with religious experience.[11] But this does not alter the fact that the psychology of religion only inquires into the experiences of the soul and cannot form a judgment upon their right and value. It observes and describes the phenomena of religious consciousness, but it cannot pronounce upon their truth and purity. It regards religion, no doubt, as one of "the most important biological functions of mankind," [12] but it can never come to the question of its truth, it cannot elevate itself to a *logos* of religion, and therefore can never replace metaphysics or dogmatics.[13]

We may reasonably question even the anticipation of Coe, that this psychology of religion will be able to regain many who in our days have turned away from all religion.[14] For without underestimating the new conclusions which present themselves, and the important suggestions which have been derived from this new study of religious life, the results to which it has led do not support the expectations which Coe formed for them. This is very clearly manifested in the fact of conversion, to which

the greatest attention has been devoted. The psychology
of religion not merely conceives conversion as a "natural
and necessary process," [15] forming a part of man's biological development and connected intimately with puberty,[16]
but its investigation gradually loses sight of what must
be understood by conversion. In itself it has no standard
by which to form a judgment of what conversion consists
in ; it inquires into and describes conversion only as a
psychological phenomenon. But regarded from this point
of view the treason of Judas is as important as the penitence of Peter, and conversion is nothing other than one
of the many transformations of consciousness, or alterations of personality, which take place so frequently in
human life.[17] If all these religious phenomena are studied
only from a psychological standpoint, the result is that
they lose their character and their content is sacrificed
to their form. Conversion thus loses its special meaning ;
on the ground of certain analogies with other psychological phenomena it is confused and identified with them in
the same manner as in the religio-historical method. All
religions are first compared one with another, and then, on
the ground of some points of agreement, are identified
with one another. What conversion is and ought to be
no psychology of religion can teach us ; the Scriptures
alone can tell us that ; and if they do not tell it to us,
nobody knows.

    This remark applies not to conversion only, but also
to all special religious experiences, such as consciousness of sin, repentance, faith, hope, sense of forgiveness,
prayer, fellowship with God; and it applies as well to
religion in general. Religious psychology occupies a
neutral standpoint outside and above all religions, and
studies and compares the religious experiences of Ro-

manist and Protestant, Christian, heathen, Jew and Mohammedan, and feels itself naturally attracted by those persons and groups whose religious life bears a more or less eccentric character; mystics, fanatics, enthusiasts of all sects and confessions, form for it interesting cases which it eagerly inquires into.[18] But again the qualitative discrimination disappears from view; or rather the psychology of religion does not perceive it, and attends only to the psychological form of these phenomena; it does not penetrate to their core and essence. So it treats them all alike. Religion is everywhere the same as to contents, — only the form differs, — and every religion, wherever it appears, is therefore true and good. Thus James, for example, says that religion is quite " private " and "individualistic ";[19] all do not need to have the same religion; each one has his own God. So long as a man has use for his God, he cares little about who he is; " God is not known; he is used." In the house of the Father are many mansions; "all ideals are matters of relation."[20] The question even arises whether polytheism does not better correspond to the variety of religious experience than monotheism, for what is required is not an absolute power, but only one higher than that of nature.[21]

That this peculiar idea is not a private opinion of Professor James, but a necessary and general conclusion from the premises, is demonstrated by the fact that other men, though widely separated from one another, announce the same opinion. Some years ago, even, Schian declared that there is no such thing as an ideal type of faith and piety, but that each dogmatist presents his own type. If there is no infallible Scripture, " there can exist only a subjective and purely individual notion of what belongs to Christian faith." All ways are good, if they but lead to faith : not to what is contained in faith, for this differs endlessly, but to faith as trust in God as revealed in Christ.[22] Schian has received much support from others in this idea,[23] and Professor Herrmann too has given his adherence to it during the last few years. The strict Ritschlian distinction between religion and metaphysics, between judgments of value and judgments of being, has led him to supplant faith almost wholly by trust. Revelation, he says, is not an external thing, but " man receives the revelation, which is the ground of his religion, because the depths of his own being are opened to him." Religion is a new life, and rests upon an experience of the power of moral good, as Jesus has shown us. To trust in that power is to believe, to live, to be saved. And because religion is thus " the complete quickening of a man, there is no general religion, the same for every one, but there are only individuals in religion." [24] So we see that from the standpoint of religious psychology there is no longer a place for metaphysics, theology, or dogmatics, nor even for an " ethics of the religious personality." For every standard fails here ; there is no single law or rule ; the individual man is the measure of all things, also of religion ; God does not say how he will be served, but man decides how he will serve him.

Naturally such a consistent indifferentism does not please all, and in the long run cannot satisfy any one. Most of those who have followed Kant and Schleiermacher in taking their standpoint in the religious subject, try nevertheless to build up on that subject one or another view of the world. In truth, Kant himself set limits to knowledge in order to make a place for faith, and to find room, by reasoning on the nature and content of practical reason, for the reality of a moral government of the world. And

Schleiermacher, though striving after the liberation of theology from philosophy, could act in this way according to his conviction only because he believed he possessed in the religious feeling of absolute dependence an immediate revelation of the Infinite.[25]   The peculiarity of the whole mediating theology which spread over the world in the nineteenth century, and remains still to-day dominant in many circles, is its effort to attain a transcendent reality — which was only more or less a reflection of the old dogmatics — by means of speculative reasoning on the immanent requirements, needs, or experiences of the religious and ethical man.   Ritschl, it is true, set himself in opposition to this, and brought about a separation between religion and metaphysics which Herrmann espeially has carried forward.   But a powerful reaction theologically and philosophically has arisen against this separation, even among Ritschl's own followers.   We are witnesses in these days of a rebirth of philosophy, a fresh acknowledgment of the right of metaphysics; and in connection therewith of a fuller recognition of the spiritual life, of its norms and values of its religious and ethical nature.[26]

This new philosophy, however, appears in many respects different from that of former times.   The old problems always remain the same, but they return in quite another form.   Whilst formerly the procedure was often aprioristic, and the world was constructed out of the idea, now the opposite direction is taken and an effort is made to raise the real world of sensation and experience to its idea. The natural and mental sciences have brought much that is new into the field.   What has been said as to the source of mathematical axioms, the ideas of number, time, and space, matter and force, movement and law, the development of the whole organic life, in plants, animals, and humanity, the interpretation of history, of the origin and progress of state and society, presents so much that is important that nobody, and certainly no philosopher, can neglect it without great loss.[27] This applies also to psychology. Here above all continued study has shown that the so-called empirical psychology cannot suffice for the right understanding of the psychical life.

Researches into uncommon phenomena, such as telepathy and telæsthesy, hypnotism and spiritualism, faith- and prayer-healing, the intuition of genius and prophetic or poetic inspiration have demonstrated one fact beyond all doubt, — that the psychical life of man is much richer than his conscious intelligence and action. One may disagree over the names; but whether we speak of waking and dreaming, day and night, supraliminal and subliminal, intuitive and reflexive consciousness, in any case there is a great difference between what happens beneath and what above the threshold of consciousness. It certainly does not commend itself when Max Dessoir speaks of two personalities in one man;[28] for there always remains a weaker or stronger consciousness that both dwell in one and the same breast, and belong to one person.[29] But still a man may be so divided against himself, and so many alterations may take place in his consciousness, that he leads as it were a double life. Sometimes he seems to live in two worlds, which have nothing to do with each other. In many pathological cases, and especially in the so-called demoniacal possession, the apparatus of consciousness appears to become an instrument of a foreign, mysterious power. Apart altogether from these extremes, however, in every man there is present a difference between his subliminal and supraliminal conscious-

ness. Man tries to give direction to his life by his
consciousness, but that life itself has its origin in the
depth of his personality.   It must not be forgotten,
Coe says truly, that though reason is necessary to guide
the ship of life, feeling is the stream that propels it.[30]
Beneath consciousness there is a world of instincts and
habits, notions and inclinations, abilities and capacities,
which continually sets on fire the course of nature.
Beneath the head lies the heart, out of which are the
issues of life.

For this reason empirical psychology will never be able
fully to explain the psychical life. It may with the utmost closeness examine the phenomena of consciousness,
the sensations, the feelings, the passions, and it may try to
conceive their working mechanically ; it may even endeavor to explain the ego or the self-consciousness by
association of ideas ; but naturally it cannot penetrate
to what lies behind and beneath consciousness, and can
kindle no light in the secret places of the heart. Herein
the declaration may find its application that God alone
proves the hearts and reins of man.   Empirical psychology can inquire into the conditions of consciousness,
can even investigate the self-consciousness which slowly
arises in man and is subject to all kinds of changes. But
the question whether a hidden ego or an independent
soul lies behind it is beyond its reach. So soon as it occupies itself with this question it passes beyond itself
into metaphysics.[31] Let us put it more strongly still, —
in inquiring into the phenomena of consciousness, empirical psychology always takes its start from an abstraction ; it separates man from his social environment, the
psychical processes from their contact with life, and in
those psychical processes it again isolates definite phenom-

ena, such as sensations of time, space, color, wholly from the psychical life. No doubt there are gains to be registered by this method ; but we must abandon the illusion that human psychical life can ever find its explanation in this manner. For if science cherishes this illusion it degenerates into psychologism, historism, and relativism, and the fulness and richness of life are curtailed. In reality all these phenomena of consciousness, so far from being isolated, exist only in intimate mutual relations, and ever spring out of the depths of personality. The whole cannot be explained in an atomistic manner by a combination of its parts ; but on the contrary the parts must be conceived in an organic way by unfolding the totality. Behind the particular lies the general, and the whole precedes the parts. If, for example, we had to learn to see, we should be dead before the task was accomplished.[32] But just as the bird knows how to build its nest, so we bring with us from our birth all kinds of abilities and capacities. It is the instinctive, organic life which in sensations, in thoughts and actions, gives an impulse to us and shows us the way. Instinct and capacity, norm and law, precede the life of reflection. Man is not sent into the world unarmed, but is equipped in body and soul with rich gifts and powers ; he receives the talents which he has only to invest and augment them in the acts of his earthly life. Empirical psychology may thus possess an important pedagogical significance, but it takes its origin from, and also leads back to, metaphysical psychology. And thus it becomes manifest that empirical life is rooted in an aprioristic datum, which does not come slowly into existence by mechanical development, but is a gift of God's grace, and a fruit and result of his revelation.[33]

If psychology leads by serious reflection to a metaphysical reality, and this again to the idea of revelation, we are not far removed from the conviction that man, in the hidden places of his soul, yet belongs to another and a higher world than that of this earthly existence. Plato asserted that the human soul existed before its indwelling in the body, lived in the world of ideas, and preserved the memory of it in its earthly exile.[34] Others cherish the idea that man in the hidden side of his nature holds communion with the unseen world and can receive from it all kinds of manifestations and revelations. The Society for Psychical Research, established in 1882, aimed at inquiring into all the phenomena which belong to the domain of spiritualism,[35] and one of its members, namely, F. W. H. Myers, who died in 1901, arrived with others at the conclusion that man in his subliminal life possesses faculties and powers whereby, without the help of the body, he can hold communication with souls and spirits.[36]

Now there has always existed very great difference of opinion as to the nature and origin of hypnotic and spiritualistic phenomena, notwithstanding the exact research which has been devoted to them. On the one side an attempt is made to explain all these phenomena in a natural way, especially by suggestion, and this attempt is even extended to the miracles of Scripture ; and on the other side, men feel forced by the facts to assume in some or in many cases a supernatural interposition. It is unnecessary to examine here the correctness of these opinions ; for it is not impossible, *a priori*, that such an intercourse with souls and spirits, without the help of the body, may exist. If the human soul indeed exists from the beginning as a whole, and is not slowly produced by steps and stages in the way of mechanical evolution, then it is in itself super-empirical, and has part in another world besides this visible one.   It is then spiritual in its essence, and it is possible for it to hold communication with spirits or souls without the body.   The body evidently is the organ of the soul; it is not the body, but the soul, which sees and hears, thinks and acts, through the body.   Thus there is nothing absurd in the idea that the soul can exercise those activities in special cases without the organ of the body.   It is also remarkable that humanity, everywhere and in all ages, has acknowledged this possibility, that Scripture often presupposes it, and that it is included in the idea of revelation.   For revelation always supposes that man is able to receive impressions or thoughts or inclinations from another than this phenomenal world, and in a way other than that usually employed.

But when science undertakes to inquire into the phenomena which belong to such a spiritual intercourse, it exposes itself to serious dangers.   For naturally those who devote their time and strength to this study will not be contented with the phenomena as such, but in order to obtain completely trustworthy material for their work will adopt the experimental method, and will endeavor to produce such experiences in themselves or in others by artificial means. The seriousness of scientific study compels them to seek such intercourse with the world of spirits themselves. Such an intercourse is not within the circle of their common experience; if it is possible, it can only be reached in artificial ways, that is, by the help of means, all of which, however diverse, have the tendency to throw into the background the conscious supraliminal life and to set the subliminal consciousness to work.   If we do not lay stress on the injury which these artificially induced trance conditions may work to the bodily health, yet we must at least observe that it is silently supposed that subliminal life is the chief domain of the spirit. Just as the philosophy of the unconscious so spiritism and hypnotism inculcate the idea that consciousness is only a temporary and defective form of knowledge, and that true being lies in the unconscious; and the best way to come into contact with this being, and to obtain knowledge about it, is in the dream, the ecstasy, the trance. Nevertheless, whosoever intentionally robs himself of self-consciousness, reason, and will, extinguishes the light which God has given to man, annihilates his human freedom and independence, and degrades himself to an instrument for an alien and unknown power.[37]

For — and this is a second danger which threatens — nobody knows to what influences he abandons himself in such states of trance. It is easy to say, on the one side, that all is suggestion or hallucination, or, on the other side, that a real intercourse with spirits takes place; but nothing is really certain. By intentionally suppressing reason and will, and by going back from this world of revelation to a land of darkness, we lose all guidance and make all control impossible. The reality of the phenomena and revelations which take place in the ecstatic state remains uncertain; uncertain it remains also whether the spirits who appear are really what they represent themselves to be; and, again, whether the revelations which they give contain truth or lies, must be followed or rejected.[38] Let it be supposed that real intercourse is held with the spirits, still the alternative is ever before us whether we shall give ourselves unconditionally up to the phenomena and revelations thus received, in which case, just as in common human intercourse, we should become dupes of misleading and seduction; or whether we shall later on control the revelations received by the standards which conscience has given to us, in which case we should interpret them according to the view of the world and life, which is ours in conscious existence.

The history of occultism, whether in earlier or later times, demonstrates this. The complaint is common that the revelations which spiritualism and hypnotism impart to us are characterized by banality and are not worth the attention which is bestowed upon them; also that they contain nothing more than fragments of the world-view which the receiver already adheres to. Myers, for example, is of opinion that " psychical research " indicates the reality of the spiritual world, the immortality of the soul, and endless " spiritual evolution," and that it has established these beyond all doubt. In consequence of this he expects that religion in the future will no longer rest on authority and belief, but on observation and experiment, and in that way will in the long run bring about a " synthesis of religious belief." [39] But these ideas are so well known that there is really no need of revelation to make them known to us; they have been proclaimed at all times by pantheistic philosophy, and have only in later days received another, and, for our generation, more attractive form, through a peculiar combination of Darwinism and Buddhism, evolution and theosophy, Western intelligence and Eastern wisdom. It is so incredible that this pantheistic-theosophical world-view should be produced by the revelation of spirits that it could, on the contrary, be with more justice contended that the newer philosophy has in a high degree furthered occultism, and has strengthened the belief therein. And as to the expectation that religion will rest in the future on the results of psychical research, the remark may suffice that the religion which seeks its foundation in intercourse with and in the revelation of spirits denies the name and the essence of pure religion, and instead of this introduces pagan superstition. Belief in spirits leads among all peoples and at all times to spirit-worship. For if the spirits of demons or the deceased can be called up, hold communication with us, and reveal to us secret things, then naturally arises the notion that they are more or less partakers of the divine attributes of omniscience and omnipresence, and can help or injure us, at least in a certain degree. This belief leads unintentionally and of itself to the practice of adoration and homage. Occultism issues on the one side in unbelief and indifference with regard to existing religions, and on the other in the most abounding superstition, spirit-worship, and magic.[40]

There is only one religion which in principle condemns and prohibits all this superstition and magic, and that is Christianity. The Old Testament already contained the revelation that the Lord alone is Israel's God, and therefore he only must be worshipped and served; soothsaying and magic, inquiry of spirits and demons, are throughout forbidden. In the New Testament this worship of the one only true God is emancipated from all national limits, and is thus raised to its true condition as a worship in spirit and in truth. True there are prophets and apostles who act as organs of revelation, but they are still men, and enjoy no other honor than that which belongs to their office and vocation; even Mary, the blessed among women, is an ordinary member of the church. There is also, according to the Scripture, a realm of spirits; but the angels, notwithstanding the great power which is given to them, and the important task which is intrusted to them, are never objects of religious worship; while the attitude which is required to be taken toward the devils is so far from one of abject slavery that the only duty which we are commanded to fulfil toward them is to hate and resist them.

Christianity is the absolutely spiritual religion, because it is the only religion which sets religion in relation to God alone; therefore it is nothing else but religion; the idea of religion is completely fulfilled in it. For if religion is a reality, then necessarily it must consist in this, — that man, avoiding all idolatry, shall rightly acknowledge the one true God, trust only in him, subject himself to him alone in all humility and patience, expect all good things from him, love, fear, and honor him with the whole heart, so that he would rather renounce every created thing than do anything in the least against the will of God. Now, this is completely fulfilled in Christianity. It is purely a service of God alone, with exclusion of all creatures. God is the content and the subject, the beginning and the ending, the alpha and the omega, of religion, and nothing of the creature enters into it. On the other side the whole man is taken into fellowship with that one true God; not only his feelings, but also his mind and will, his heart and all his affections, his soul and his body. Christianity is religion alone, and therefore the pure religion, the full and complete, indissoluble and eternal, fellowship of God and man.

Christian theology, which investigates this religion, is on this account alone an independent and genuine science. As soon as the Christian religion is no longer acknowledged to be the pure, complete religion, but is thrown into a heap with all religions, theology ceases to be an independent science. There may still remain the study of the religious man (religious anthropology), and also psychological and historical inquiry into the religions of different peoples, perhaps also an endeavor to frame a philosophy of religion and a metaphysics, but there is no longer a theology, no longer an inquiry into the knowledge of God, and thus no standard for the judgment of religious phenomena.   There only remains positivism, psychologism, relativism.   Revelation, religion, and theology stand or fall together.

But if theology possesses a reason for and a right to existence, it brings with it, as an independent science, its own method also.   At the present time most people hold another opinion.   Because they have abandoned the self-sufficiency of the Christian religion, they cannot hold to a theology with a method of its own.   They suppose that there are only one or two scientific methods, namely, the physical and the historical.   And thus, if theology is to maintain itself as a science in the university, it must accept one of these two methods, and apply it logically to the whole domain of inquiry; in other words, it must become natural or historical science.   In this way it would lose its right to form an independent faculty in the circle of science, and would require, therefore, to be brought into the domain of the philosophical faculty.[41]

Whether one accepts this consequence or not, the principle on which the standpoint is founded violates science, and denies its richness and diversity.   True, if monism were the right world-view, and if all phenomena were purely modifications of one substance, then there would be only one science and also only one method.   It would be to deny its principle, to give an independent place to historical science by the side of natural science, and to defend the right of the historical method.   But the world is richer than materialistic or pantheistic evolution wishes it to appear.   A single factor never suffices for the explanation of phenomena in any domain.   Everywhere there is a richness of life and a fulness of being. There are different kinds of creatures and phenomena, each of which requires a special method according to its nature, that we may know and understand it. Religion and virtue, art and science, beauty and justice, cannot be handled and measured like bodies; yet they exist, and occupy a dominating place in existence. Reality does not arrange itself to fit our system, but our system must form itself in accordance with reality.

Life itself receives much greater injury from monistic doctrinairism than science. If the empirical and historical methods are the only paths to knowledge, then that wisdom which by nature is proper to every man, and is augmented and extended in the practice of life, loses all its value, and there arises between the schools and society a continually greater divergence and ever increasing opposition. For however science, with her inquiries and results, may serve, lead, and promote life, this life always and everywhere precedes science; it did not originate in science, and cannot wait for it. Family and society, work and vocation, agriculture and cattle-rearing, trade and industry, morality, justice, and art, have all an independent source and sustain their own character. The whole complete life, which reveals itself in all these domains and activities, can gratefully make use of the light which science kindles, but it flows from its own proper source and streams onward in its own channel. For both life and science it is, therefore, of the highest importance that the empirical knowledge, which is obtained in life, and the scientific knowledge, which is striven after in the schools, should support and strengthen one another; the wisdom of life is the starting-point and the foundation of all science, and the researches of the learned should not aim at extinguishing this knowledge of practical experience, but at purifying and augmenting it.[42]

This applies especially to religion. If theology acknowledges no other method than that which is usually taken in the sciences of nature and history, the religious man is not only totally dependent on the clericalism of science, but religion itself is robbed of its independence and freedom. This is recognized by all, so far as under the influence of Schleiermacher they strive to set religion free from all knowledge and assent, and conceive it as only trust in the heart. But this endeavor is a fruitless one. For religion does not spring up in every individual spontaneously, without outside influence, but always comes to development by connecting itself with the religious representations which are recognized in a definite circle as truth. The word "faith," which in Christendom expresses subjective religiousness, includes, along with the original religious habit which dwells in the heart of man, also the adjustment to representations which exist in this religion about God, world, man, etc.; it is at the same time knowledge and trust, and expresses the peculiarity of the Christian religion so well because this religion desires a knowledge of God which is at the same time trust, love, piety. Just because religion always includes knowledge, it comes into collision with science, and *vice versa*. This collision has existed through all ages and in all religions; the cause does not lie in arbitrary or occasional abuses of power, as would be the case if faith were nothing more than a matter of feeling; but the cause is that both, according to their several natures, move in the same domain and pronounce themselves on the same objects and phenomena.[43] And knowledge belongs so intimately to the essence of religion that religion,

if freed from all religious representations and limited
purely to feeling, would immediately lose its own character. For feeling has in itself no content and no quality;
religious, ethical, and æsthetic feelings do not exist independently of each other, but are distinguished by the
various representations by which feeling is awakened.
Monism, therefore, always promotes the confusion of religious and æsthetic feeling, and thereby weakens religion;
to limit religion to feelings does not maintain its independence, but undermines its existence.

After the criticism of " the pure reason," which Kant
has worked out from the standpoint of a mathematical-
mechanic science, and after the criticism of "the historical
reason," which has recently been developed by men like
Dilthey, Windelband, Rickert, over against the one-sidedness of the science of nature, a "criticism of the religious
reason" is still necessary. Theology is occupying itself
with this task in all lands; the formal part of dogmatics
is drawing thought to itself much more than the material
part. Yet it cannot proceed here by mere speculation.
Each science must borrow its form from the object which
it investigates, for method is determined by the object.
Now, if the object of theology is no other than the true
and pure religion, which appears to us in Christianity as
the fruit of revelation, then the inquiry after method results in this one and very important question: How
does the Christian religion itself represent that a man
comes to her, acknowledges her truth, and by her becomes
a true religious man, — that is, a Christian, a child of
God? Theology may afterwards reflect upon the answer
which the Christian religion gives, as she does also upon
other elements of truth; she has even the right, the duty,
and the vocation to do this. But she can never produce any

other method than that which is given by her own object. The plan of salvation in the Christian religion determines the method of Christian theology.

If we institute an inquiry into that plan of salvation, we are met by the fact that the Christian religion does not bring us merely into relation with persons and events of the past, but by means of revelations in history seeks to bring us into fellowship with that God who manifests his truth in that he is always the same, in the past and in the present. The Christian religion is an historical, but also a present, religion.[44] Whoever seeks fellowship with God, excluding all history, and revelation in nature and history, — that is to say, without Christ, — experiences a religious feeling which misses the objective reality, which feeds only on itself, and therefore also digests itself. He who frees himself from all connection with what is before and around him ruins himself by his autonomy. On the other hand, whosoever considers the Christian religion simply and alone as historical religion, and does not make it a religion of the present, wipes out in principle the distinction between Christianity and the other religions, and reduces it to a phenomenon which belongs only to the past, and loses its significance for to-day and the future.

The peculiarity of the Christian religion, then, as has been so often shown, and acknowledged even by opponents,[45] lies in the person of Christ. All other religions are independent, to a certain degree, of their founders, because those founders were nothing more than their first confessors. But Jesus was not the first Christian; he was and is the Christ. He is not the subject, but the object, of religion. Christianity is not the religion of Jesus, still less Jesus-worship,[46] but Christ-religion. Christianity is now as dependent on him, from moment to moment, as when he trod this earth. For he is not a person who lived and worked only in the past, but he lives and works still, is still Prophet, Priest, and King, and himself upholds the church, which he established, from age to age, and assures to her the victory. Christianity, according to its own confession, does not exist through the strength and fidelity of its confessors, but through the life and will of its Mediator. The stages of the application of salvation are as much, and in the same sense, his interest as the impetration of salvation. His will and his work is to make men truly religious, to bring them into fellowship with God, and that is also the will and the work of God himself. For the will of God to save the world was not only an annunciation of God's inclination in the past, but is an action, a deed, a work of God, which goes on from day to day. God is love; but that love is no quiescent attribute, but an eternal, omnipresent energy which realizes itself in the hearts of men. God is Father; but that Fatherhood is no mere title of honor, but an almighty, energetic power which regenerates men as his children and heirs.[47] Christianity is no mere revelation of God in the past, but it is, in connection with the past, a work in the midst of this and every time. The Father of Jesus works always hitherto, and he himself works also. All other religions try to obtain salvation by the works of men, but Christianity makes a strong protest against this; it is not autosoteric but heterosoteric; it does not preach self-redemption, but glories in redemption by Christ alone. Man does not save himself, and does not save God, but God alone saves man, the whole man, man for eternity. It is a religion, not of works, but of faith; not of merits, but of grace. Christianity proves itself in the plan of salvation to be the absolutely spiritual and pure religion. Man can add nothing to it, — salvation is God's work alone ; of him, and through him, and to him, are all things.

But this almighty and always active will of God is not realized without man, as antinomians of all kinds imagine, but in man, and through man. It is realized, according to the witness of the whole Scripture, in regeneration and faith, in conversion and forgiveness of sin, in sanctification and perseverance.   In other words, if we ask of the prophets, of Christ and his apostles, how man comes to a knowledge of the truth, and to a new life in God's fellowship, then they give the answer unanimously, — not by knowledge or action, nor yet by science or art, nor yet again by good works or civilization, but by faith and conversion.   Scripture has a richness of names for this plan of salvation ; it never gives a dry, dogmatic description, nor an abstract scheme of conceptions, but shows it to us in life, and gives us thereby a psychology of religion such as no scientific investigation, and no *questionaire* method can bring to light.   For all the steps in the way of salvation are God's work, the effect and fulfilment of his will ; but because they take place in man, and are realized in his consciousness and will, they may all be considered and described also from an anthropological point of view. The distinct individuality and experience of the prophets and apostles themselves appear in the different names by which the process of salvation is indicated.   But from whatever point of view this plan of salvation is considered, this is always the result, — that man, in order to become a child of God, does not need to be a cultured being or a citizen of standing, a man of science or of art, a civilized or a developed man. These are all good, but not one indicates the way to divine fellowship.   In order to become a sharer in this a person must be regenerated, changed, renewed, or, to use the most common term, a person must be converted. Conversion is the sole and the absolutely peculiar way to heaven.

In speaking in this way the Christian religion gains at once the consciences of all men. For there can be no doubt that, if there is really a redemption, this must consist before all things in redemption from sin. All men have a notion of good and evil, a conscience which accuses or excuses them, a consciousness of guilt and impurity, a fear of punishment, and a desire for redemption. But they often err as deeply about the character of sin as about the way of redemption. On the one side, sin is minified to an accidental and arbitrary act, from which man can eventually deliver himself by knowledge or act; on the other side, sin is considered as such an ineradicable evil that it is identified with being and nature itself. Confucius holds here the opposite view from Buddha, Mohammed from Mani, Socrates from Plato. And within the Christian church the same ideas and contrasts appear now and then. In our days some preach the doctrine that one must not take sin too seriously, because it is no habit, no condition, no bad inclination of the heart, but exclusively an arbitrary act of the will, which very easily arises from the conflict between the individual and society, between nature and culture, but for that reason also can easily be given up and conquered.[48] On the other hand, sin is represented as a mass of egoistic instincts and passions, which have been carried over by man from his former animal condition, which still hold supremacy over the altruistic inclinations in the savage and in the child, and anachronistically and atavistically exercise their influence in the criminal type.[49]

The two views approach one another in this way, that the innate egoistic inclinations, namely, the animality and sensuality, are of themselves no sin, that they also in later life, if they are yielded to in conflict with the interests of society, cause no guilt and no stain, but only betray a weakness and disease, which need cure. What the wound is to the body, that is the criminal in society.[50] In so-called "Christian Science" sin consequently is put into the same category as illness, and both are represented as an illusion, as an error in thought, which can only be cured by thought.[51] The fundamental error of heathenism thus returns, because the holiness of God is lost, and the gods are identified with the powers of nature ; and therefore the distinction between sin and misery, and accordingly between redemption from sin and relief from misery, is lost. Modern superstition and the increasing quackery rest upon each other. If the power on which man depends loses the character of personal holiness, man feels himself no longer a guilty sinner, but a powerless, helpless, miserable creature, and desires not an ethical redemption, but physical cure and bodily welfare. And if one cannot find these among the physicians, they are sought for amongst the charlatans and quacksalvers through superstitious and magic means.

The Christian religion alone maintains, in opposition to all these tendencies, the purely ethical character of sin. It does this by distinguishing between creation and fall. In all systems which identify sin with the substance of things, creation is changed into a fall, and the fall which Scripture relates is represented as the symbol of a remarkable progress in the life of humanity, as the rise from animal innocence into the state of human consciousness.[52] In reality, the whole order of things is thereby reversed; God becomes the author of sin, and the serpent the author of human progress. The Ophites acted, therefore, logically when they represented God as an unhappy demiurge, and the serpent as a blessed deity. In truth, in the voluntaristic-pantheistic philosophy of recent times it is not God who saves man, but man who saves God. Scripture restores the original order by distinguishing and separating creation and fall, but maintains thereby also the possibility of redemption. For if sin is identified with animality and sensuality, and has its origin in the descent and nature of man, then there is no redemption possible except by annihilation. Heaven is then no uppermost expansion of true life, but the extinction of all consciousness, will, and personality, the abyss of nothing, the sinking into everlasting death. On the contrary, if sin bears an ethical character, then redemption is possible, and conversion is in principle the conquest of sin, the death of the old and the resurrection of the new man.[53]

But in that case conversion is a necessary and moral duty for every man. If the Christian religion maintains the absolute necessity of conversion, it joins to itself again the witness of all consciences, the doctrine and life of the whole of humanity. Every man has the deep and ineradicable conviction that he is not what he ought to be; there is a schism between his duty and his inclination which he cannot deny and cannot do away with. Man is broken; his unity, his harmony has gone. And the strangest thing in this strange phenomenon is that he is not two men who struggle with one another, but he is in both cases the same man. It is our conceptions, ideas, inclinations and desires which are striving together and seeking to obtain the mastery; it is the same subject which excuses and accuses itself, which gives way willingly to

sinful desire, and is afterwards torn by repentance and
grief, which alternately springs up in joy and languishes
in sorrow.[54]   From the whole history of man resounds
a heart-breaking complaint over the disruption of life; it
finds its finest expression in the songs of the poets, but each
man knows it by experience; all religion is animated by it,
every effort toward reform proceeds from it, all ethics
assume the imperative tone after the descriptive one, and
every philosophy strives to set the heart at ease as well
as to satisfy the intelligence.   Men may differ as to the
nature and the reach of conversion, but its necessity is
established beyond all doubt; the whole of humanity proclaims the truth of the fall.

There is no doubt much diversity in the manner in which
conversion takes place.   Scripture makes it clear that by
conversion is meant a religious and moral change in man,
by which he deserts his sinful ways and learns to know,
love, and serve with his whole heart the true God, who has
revealed himself in Christ; but it at the same time allows
a wide application of this idea, and discriminates the process itself from the manner in which it is brought about.
It speaks of the conversion of Israel and of the heathen, of
individuals and of towns and of peoples, and it exhibits in
the examples of Nathanael and Nicodemus, Zaccheus and
Mary Magdalene, Paul and Timothy, different modes in
which conversion may be realized.[55]   In early times, when
Christianity was conquering a place for itself in the world
through the preaching of the apostles, conversion coalesced
with the resolution to abandon idolatry and to serve the
only living God.   The New Testament describes to us the
transition of Christianity from Judaism to the Greco-
Roman world, and is, in the first place, the book of the
mission which was fulfilled by the work of the apos-

tles.[56] When later the church obtained a firm foothold
in the world, and grew not so much through missions
among the heathen as by means of catechizing her own
children, conversion assumed another form, while re-
maining the same in essence. In infant baptism it was
confessed that conversion and regeneration differ, and
conversion is ordinarily a coming to consciousness of that
new life which has long before been planted in the heart.
An illustration of this is supplied also by revivals, which
do not occur among heathen, but only within the limits
of the Christian church. The psychology of religion also
suggests that the sudden conversions which occur in
revival-meetings need not be so sudden as they appear,
but may be a revivification of impressions and emotions
received sometimes years previously, and have sunk into
the heart beneath the threshold of consciousness, and by
the force of peculiar circumstances spring again into new
life.[57] It is a good work to awaken the sleeping churches,
and to stir up the unconscious life into conscious action,
but it is a fault if the organic existence of the church is
insufficiently recognized, involving as this does a mis-
understanding of the covenant of grace and too close an
identification of conversion with one definite form of conversion, which is therefore prescribed as necessary to all
and produced artificially. As soon as this happens, human
agency is confused with the work of the Spirit, the essence
is sacrificed to the form, and sometimes even to very
strange forms, and the earnestness and richness of Scripture is lost.

It may be remarked throughout Scripture that the
essence and the seriousness of conversion are never ob-
scured, and yet the rich variety of its manifestation is
continually exhibited. Mary and Martha were very dif-

ferent in religious disposition, but Jesus loved them both. The apostles differed in endowments and character, but they were all disciples of the Lord. In the Christian church, Augustine and Francis of Assisi, Luther and Calvin, Wesley and Zinzendorf, walked in various pathways, but still they were all children of the same Father's house, with its many mansions. So far as it is intended merely to give expression to the rich diversity of spiritual life, the distinction between "healthy-minded" and "morbid-minded souls" need not be condemned.[58] All have not the same experience of guilt and grace; the deeper knowledge of sin, and the richer comfort of forgiveness, are not the root, but the fruit of Christian faith.[59] The Gospel is so rich, and the salvation purchased by Christ contains so many and diverse benefits, that the most varied needs of men are satisfied by it, and the richest powers of human nature are brought to development. There are times in which the Gospel especially attracts, because it promises forgiveness of all guilt of sin; and there are other times in which it charms most, because it stills the thirst for a new, holy life.[60] The Gospel of the Synoptics, of John, and Paul, and Peter, and James, have awakened various sympathies in the different churches and among different peoples in different times and places. In every nation is accepted with God he who fears him and works righteousness.

Nevertheless conversion must remain conversion. What it is no science or philosophy can tell us, but we learn from Holy Scripture alone. If this does not tell us, or is not to be trusted in what it tells us, we are in despair as to the redemption of the world and the salvation of mankind. Philosophy may teach us through the lips of Kant and Schopenhauer — though even this always under the

influence of Christianity — that if sin is to be really eliminated from human nature, a sort of regeneration is necessary. But it can never proclaim the glad tidings that
such a conversion exists, nor can it show the way to obtain
it. The psychology of religion may bring into view the
phenomena which are connected with conversion from the
anthropological side, and illustrate them by analogies from
other regions, but it does not penetrate, as it itself acknowledges,[61] to the core and the cause of these phenomena. It even incurs the danger — if it abandons the
guidance of Scripture and presents these phenomena exclusively from an anthropological standpoint — of sac-
rificing the essence to the form and the kernel to the husk.
Viewed psychologically, all alterations of personality are
alike: the fall is as much a transformation of consciousness
as redemption and regeneration; the change of a virtuous
man into a drunkard or a voluptuary, a thief or a mur-
derer, is as much a " conversion " as the coming to himself
of the prodigal son and his return to his father's house.[62]
If certain phenomena which are often connected with
conversion are wanting, some rashly conclude that conversion itself has not really taken place, or was not wholly
necessary. By the side of the " twice-born " is ranged, then,
the category of the "once-born men," or righteous men who
have no need of conversion.[63] The diversity of religious
phenomena leads men rashly to the conclusion that conversion has no reality, that all " conversions " are in themselves equally real, and that each man can be saved in his
own way.[64] Thus under the psychological treatment the
essence of conversion is lost, just as life perishes under
vivisection. Pragmatism, which only takes into account
empirical phenomena, is nominalistic in principle, and becomes relativistic in result.

Scripture and experience are both in opposition to this levelling of all essential distinctions; for both testify that conversion is not one of those many transformations of consciousness which often take place in human life, but that it bears a specific character. Conversion can be said to be genuine only when a man is changed in his entire being in such a way that he experiences a hearty repentance and an inner horror of sin, succeeded by a lively joy in God and a sincere desire for the fulfilment of his will. True conversion consists only in the dying of the old sinful man, and in the resurrection of the new, holy man.[65] "All holy persons are twice-born persons,"[66] for by nature man does not possess that holiness and that deep and hearty love to God and desire for the fulfilment of his commandments. When Kant and Schopenhauer, and many others speak so much of the radical evil in human nature, they thereby bear witness to the truth. Stanley Hall rightly asks, "Who that is honest and has true self-knowledge will not confess to recognizing in his own soul the germs and possibilities of about every crime, vice, insanity, superstition, and folly in conduct he ever heard of?"[67] And James acknowledges in the same way that "healthy-mindedness is inadequate as a philosophical doctrine because the evil facts which it refuses positively to account for are a genuine portion of reality."[68]

Now there may be differences of opinion as to the possibility and reality of a conversion such as Scripture and the Christian religion teach. But if it exists, there can be no doubt that it has another source and another cause than the purely psychological operation of human representations and powers. The psychology of religion rightly says that it neither will nor can pronounce a decision.[69] James goes even further, and says that reality itself is revealed in the unconscious, that hidden powers and ideas work there, and that God's mercy is working through the "subliminal door"; and so he calls himself a supernaturalist, though in a modified form.[70] It causes no wonder that this supernaturalism is acknowledged in religious experience, for, if revelation in history, especially in the person and work of Christ, is denied, the truth and the right of religion can only be maintained by accepting a revelation in the religious subject. If religion is really communion with God, it includes his indwelling and inworking in the human soul. Scripture and theology, therefore, have always taught and maintained such a fellowship of God and man in their doctrine of the mystical union. But if this revelation in the subject is isolated from all objective revelation in nature and Scripture, in history and the church, it opens the door for all kinds of error. Finally, such a subjective revelation results in nothing beyond a "more," which works in the "subliminal consciousness" of man, and is interpreted by each one according to his nature and environment.[71] Pragmatism leads here also to indifferentism regarding all religions.

Such a religious indifferentism is, however, in conflict with all experience, and is in the strongest way contradicted by the Christian religion. For the conversion which brings us into fellowship with God never happens unmediatedly, but is always connected with representations and impressions which we have received at some time, shorter or longer, previously.[72] It always takes place in connection with historical Christianity, which in one or another form exists before and without us, and now enters into harmony with our own soul. It does not arise spontaneously out of and by ourselves, but causes us to live with fuller conviction in the religious circle wherein we were born and brought up, or into which in later life we have been introduced.   The religious representations are thus no subjective interpretations of our personal emotions; we formulate them as little as the child, who, though it brings with it the faculty of speech, does not produce speech itself, but receives the whole treasure of words from the lips of its mother. Man does not produce truth by thought in any domain, and certainly not in religion, but by inquiry and study he learns to know the truth, which exists independently of and before him.   Therefore religious experience is neither the source nor the foundation of religious truth; [73] it only brings us into union with the existing truth, and makes us recognize as truth what formerly was for us only an empty sound, or even was denied and opposed by us.   Conversion is not the source of truth, but the source of certainty as to the truth.   It bears witness in our heart as to the religious representations which existed outside of and before us.

So we have on the one side to maintain the dependence of religious experience on historical Christianity, and on the other side equally to recognize its independence and liberty.   Many know no other dilemma than either external authority, blind belief, intellectual consent to alien and hard dogma, or else free piety and individual formulation of religious life.[74]   But reality teaches us quite differently. Just as we with open eyes do not create the reality of the world, but only recognize it, — just as we by thought do not produce the truth, but seek and find it, — so also the religious man receives the reality of spiritual things which are presented to him by God perfectly freely and spontaneously.   He now sees them, where he was formerly blind; he understands now what he earlier as a natural man could not conceive; by re-birth he enters into the

kingdom of heaven; by loving the will of God he knows
that Jesus speaks, not of himself, but of the Father; he
hears and understands Jesus' voice now because he can
endure his word.

So one can understand that conversion produces and
generates an unwavering certainty as to the things which
the Christian religion teaches us. If it were nothing
more than a matter of feeling or sentiment, and were
confined entirely to the mysticism of the heart, it would
not be able to awaken such a personal interest in the
objective words and events of Christianity. But experience teaches otherwise. Conversion takes place in
connection with the Christian religion; faith, which forms
its positive side, is the substance of things hoped for, the
evidence of things not seen, because it is at the same time
cognitio and *fiducia*, a trustful knowledge and a knowing
trust. It is accompanied from its first existence by a group
of representations, is born in our heart in connection
with them, and binds us to them irrevocably. Conversion,
which is equally repentance and faith, sorrow and joy,
death and resurrection, changes the whole man in principle as to his being and consciousness, incorporates him
into another world of representations than that in which
he formerly lived. Those representations also depend
mutually on each other. Both psychologically and logically the representations which we receive in our conversion associate themselves with those which Christianity
includes within the circle to which we belonged from
birth or were later adopted into. It is not the least merit
of Christianity that it includes such an harmonious whole
of representations, which reconcile subject and object, man
and world, nature and revelation.[75]

This whole process of conversion, which begins with

the awakening of the consciousness of guilt and misery and develops itself into a hearty joy in God through Christ, is from the beginning to the end psychologically mediated. We do not here see God face to face, even if we descend into the depths of our own soul. Unconsciousness, ecstasy, hallucination, dreaming, and contemplation do not bring us nearer to him than the conscious life, as the mysticism of all centuries has fancied, for we walk by faith and not by sight. And not only so, but there arise in our own heart, in the world around us, and in the revelation of Scripture itself, all kinds of difficulties which we cannot resolve. But if we are convinced in our deepest soul that God will save us personally, and in its beginnings has saved us, then it is an unavoidable postulate of faith that this will also reveals itself outside of us in history, and that the world and humanity will not be led to an eternal death and a dark night and an unfathomable abyss, but to a never-ending day of light and glory. Above the power of nature and above the power of sin raises and maintains itself the almighty will of the Heavenly Father, who subdues wind and sea and all things.

Conversion and faith in our own heart are the operation and fruit of that will. Though they occur thus in a psychological way, which takes into account each man's character and environment, yet they are a revelation of that will which works in us both to will and to do according to his good pleasure. In and by our own testimony we hear the testimony of the Holy Spirit, which in its turn is added to the witness of Holy Scripture and of the church of all centuries. In this witness the souls of all God's children are secure; through the breakers of doubt it brings them into the haven of God's love.

IX

THE well-known preacher, J. Chr. Blumhardt, once said that man must be twice converted, first from the natural to the spiritual life, and then from the spiritual to the natural.[1] He thus declared, in somewhat paradoxical language, a truth which is confirmed by the religious experience of every Christian and by the history of Christian piety in all ages. The spiritual life, which is from above, strives again after what is above; it expresses itself in the sigh of the psalmist, — Whom have I in heaven but thee, and there is none upon earth that I desire beside thee; and it knows no higher desire than to depart and be with Christ, which is far better. It was under the influence of this inclination of the spiritual life that in the early days of Christianity ascetic life arose, and it is for that reason also that it has maintained itself till the present day in various pious circles. Other causes and considerations have, however, certainly added to that influence, which in primitive times gave origin and strength to this tendency of spiritual life.

When Christianity entered into the world, it was immediately called on to face a difficult problem. Christianity, which is based on revelation, appeared in a world which had long existed and led its own life. A society had been formed which was full of intricate interests. A state was in existence the citizens of which lived in safety and peace. Arts and sciences were practised and had been brought to great perfection. Morals and habits had assumed a fixed form. Conquests had created a powerful kingdom, and had brought in enormous capital. In a word, the Gospel of Christ found a rich natural life, a highly developed culture. And thus the question was inevitably raised how the relations between the two should be adjusted.

The different forms in which this question may be put show its importance and extent. For the problem always remains the same, whether one speaks of the relation between the preaching of the apostles and the Greco-Roman world, or between re-creation and creation, the work of the Son and the work of the Father, the kingdom of heaven and the kingdoms of the earth, sabbath- and week-days, Christianity and humanism, church and state, faith and science, theology and philosophy, authority and reason, the religious and empirical world-view, heaven and earth, divine gifts and human labor, revelation and culture. The problem which is present in all these forms of expression belongs not to a single period, but has been in order all through the ages, and will remain so till the return of Christ. And it does not belong to scientific thought alone, but forces itself upon every man in his every day life. All tendencies which present themselves in life and thought can be described and estimated from the standpoint they take respecting this principial question. Even systems which have broken with all religion and Christianity are compelled, by the force of reality, to take it into account. For though thousands exert themselves to set our present-day culture free from all the past, and to establish it on a new scientific foundation, in reality all our institutions of family and society and state are still resting on Christian principles, and all our morals and habits are still pervaded by the Christian spirit.

Therefore it is not to be wondered at that the first Christians did not solve this world-historical problem satisfactorily, and did not attain unanimity in the position which they adopted. There were those who looked so kindly upon culture that they failed to do justice to the rights and requirements of the Christian confession. There were others who turned their backs on the entire culture of the time, and sought their strength in renouncing it. The early Christians were nevertheless not essentially ascetics. They firmly believed that the earth is the Lord's, and the fulness thereof; and they considered themselves the new humanity, in which Jew and Greek found their unity and destination.[2] But the then existing culture was so intimately connected with all kinds of heathen practices that Christians could take little part in it without denying their faith, and needed to content themselves with practising the more passive virtues of Christian morality. In a world such as Paul describes in the first chapter of his epistle to the Romans there was, for a small, weak body of believers, no other than a negative position possible.

But this negative position nevertheless brought serious dangers in the long run. When in the second century dualistic and ascetic Gnosticism spread in its varied forms over the Roman empire, it did not fail of influence over many Christians also. The ascetic inclination which thus appeared was in the third and fourth centuries increased by the worldliness of the church, and strengthened by the infiltration of Stoic and Neoplatonic elements of thought.[3] From that time onward many sought solitude in order to pass their life in penitence, or to devote it to works of mercy. This anchorite life in the West underwent later an important modification, and was made use of by the church for all kinds of moral ends, — land-development and agriculture, science and art, the spreading of the gospel and the expansion of the church. But the church also felt the influence of this recognition of the monastic life, and developed a double way to the attainment of the ideal of Christian perfection by introducing the distinction between precepts and counsels. Perfection, to be sure, is the goal for every Christian, as much for the laity as for the clergy and the monk. But the vow of poverty, chastity and obedience is nevertheless the shorter and safer way to that goal. Ascetic life is a specially meritorious striving after perfection; monastic life sets apart a special class of men, and is a praiseworthy form of Christian life; marriage, family, social vocation, service of the state, property, and riches are not in themselves sinful, but place many obstacles in the way of the religious life; he who abstains from them acts better, and becomes the religious man *par excellence*.[4]

Though this asceticism is intimately associated with the doctrine and the life of the Roman Church, it has nevertheless, from the Reformation to the present day, exercised also a strong attractive power over many churches and sects in Protestantism. Anabaptism certainly cannot be fully explained from the monastic orders and sects of the Middle Ages; for whence came then its schism with the Roman Church, and its strong opposition to its hierarchy and forms of worship? But it adopted the old ascetic ideal, and tried to realize it by a radical reformation in the circle of believers. This reformation ended in separation, — separation, namely, between church and world, Christian and civil life, re-creation and creation, Spirit and Word, New and Old Testament; in a word, between the heavenly substance, which Christ brought with

him and communicates to his believers in regeneration, and
the earthly substance, which we receive from Adam in the
natural birth. The same dualism has in a modified form
since continued to work in many devout circles, and has
even received more lately strong support from all those
persons and schools which ascribe to original Christianity
an ascetic ideal of life. These, however, are themselves
divided again into two parties.

The first group is formed by those who, by inclination
or education, by their own experience or through exterior
influences, have learned to know the value of the ascetic
life, and therefore look with more or less of grief and
offence on present-day culture. There are not a few who,
in comparing the life of our time with that of Jesus, discover no connection or congruity, but only contrast and
opposition. If, they say, Jesus, who condemns the powerful and rich, despises earthly treasures, feels compassion
for the sick and poor, and seeks out the publican and sinner, is right, then present-day society, with its mammonism and capitalism, with its self-conceit and deification of
power, is quite wrong. They demand of Christians, If
you confess Jesus as the Son of God, and accept his word
as divine truth, why do you not follow his example and
walk in his footsteps? Why do you live in magnificent
homes, clothed in purple and fine linen, and fare sump-
tuously every day, and gather treasures which are corrupted by moth and rust? And why do you not give
your possessions away, feed the hungry, relieve the
thirsty, shelter the homeless, clothe the naked, visit the
sick and in prison, proclaim the gospel to the poor?
They explain to us and figure out how Jesus if he lived
now would behave, and what would be his conduct
towards the press and politics, towards the market and

exchange, towards the factory and parliament.[5] And some have taken the matter so seriously to heart that they have sought to put this moral ideal into actual practice. Tolstoi, for example, constructed a wholly passive ethics, from the commandment in the sermon on the mount, to resist not evil. The source of all misery is found, they declare, in society, with its lies and pretences; in the church, with her absurd dogmas; in the state, with its law and war; in the whole civil life of our time, with its marriage, castes, conventional forms, corrupt atmosphere, tobacco and alcohol. And escape from these miseries, we are told, is possible only if we turn our backs on all these institutions, return to nature, abandon altogether all force and justice, all wrath and punishment, and live again like children, simply and uprightly. Then the broken harmony between need and satisfaction will be restored, and happiness and peace return.[6]

On the other side are those who agree, no doubt, that original Christianity bore an ascetic character, but draw therefrom just the opposite conclusion, namely, that Christianity has had its day, and can no longer live with our present-day culture. In the estimate of the person of Jesus an important change has slowly taken place. After Rationalism had rejected the church doctrine concerning the person of Christ, men such as Strauss and Renan, Schenkel and Keim and Holtzmann took indeed a humanitarian view of the life of Jesus. But in their view Jesus, though not the Son of God, was still the true, ideal man, who established the pure religion by his word and deed, free from all sacerdotalism and ceremonial worship, who purified morals from all legalism, who as a human man shared in all the pleasures of life, and presented a moral ideal which deserves our admiration and imitation to-day.[7]

But in these last days, especially since the investigations of Baldensperger and Johannes Weiss,[8] an entirely new conception has in the case of many taken the place of this humanitarian idea. Humanitarian traits are not indeed entirely lacking from the figure of Jesus; yet according to the description given of him by the Synoptic Gospels he was a totally different kind of man. He was not a quiet, pious man, and not a philosophic teacher of virtue, but a prophet, an enthusiast, a fanatic, who lived under the impression of the speedy advent of the kingdom of God, and therefore exhorted his contemporaries to faith and conversion. As a man he was not nearly so great as the liberal theology has represented him. Although he was characterized by a praiseworthy willingness to help all misery, he was nevertheless a limited and superstitious man, believed in evil spirits and eternal punishment, was subject to visions and hallucinations, showed traits even of an hereditary epilepsy, paranoia, and finally attempted, when his preaching received no acceptance, to gain the victory by an act of force. His doctrine contained nothing new, but joined itself to the ideas and expectations of his time; his notion of the kingdom of God was not that of a moral community, but bore an exclusively eschatological character; and his ethics acquired, under Essenic, or even under Buddhistic, influences, an ascetic color. Perhaps he was originally an Aryan, or perhaps even he never existed, and his figure is the creation of one or another of the sects produced by the commotions of the age.[9] In any case his view of the world and life is not suitable for our time and circumstances. When he pronounces his woe on the rich, esteems occupation with earthly affairs an obstacle to the heavenly vocation, recommends the unmarried condition, and takes no thought at all of political and social life, he can be no example for us, and his ethics can supply us with no standard.[10] Nor does this opposition to Christian ethics concern subordinate points, but their kernel and essence. Christian ethics have laid to their charge legalism and heteronomy, seeking for reward and transcendent eudæmonism, withdrawal from the world and contempt of all culture, and especially of the senses and marriage. Nietzsche has endeavored, therefore, to reverse all its values. Instead of the morals of slaves which Jews and Christians have introduced, he wished to restore to honor the original morals of free men; his system may be called a logical aristocratic anarchism.[11]

If we are to speak of the relation which Christianity bears to culture, we must first of all give a clear account of what we understand by culture, and of precisely the kind of culture Christianity is to form a contrast to. The word "culture," which has come into use especially since the eighteenth century, along with other terms, such as civilization, enlightenment, development, education, indicates generally cultivation, improvement, and always presupposes an object which must be improved. This object may be indicated generally by the name of nature, for it always consists of something not made by man, but offered to him by creation. Culture in the broadest sense thus includes all the labor which human power expends on nature. But this nature is twofold; it includes not only the whole visible world of phenomena which is outside man, but also, in a wider sense, man himself; not his body alone, but his soul also. The faculties and powers which man possesses have not been acquired by him, but are given to him by God; they are a gift of nature, and these gifts are a means for cultivating the external world, as well as an object which must be cultivated. Thus there are two great circles of culture. To the first belong all those activities of man for the production and distribution of material goods, such as agriculture, cattle-rearing, industry, and trade. And the second circle includes all that labor whereby man realizes objectively his ideals of the true, the good, and the beautiful, by means of literature and science, justice and statecraft, works of beauty and art, and at the same time works out his own development and civilization.[12]

Such a culture has existed at all times, from the moment when man appeared on the earth and sought satisfaction of his manifold needs by labor. And from its first origin this culture has been closely connected with religion; in all ages and among all peoples these two are found together, and go forward hand in hand. It was not till the eighteenth century that culture was raised to a power which emancipated itself from the Christian religion and the whole ancient world-view, and sought to become an absolutely new, modern culture. Nobody, therefore, can declare that culture as such stands in contrast with religion, for all the preceding centuries raise a sharp protest against such an assertion. It can, at the most, be contended that our specifically present-day culture is in conflict with religion and Christianity.

But before this can be proved an exact definition should first be given of what is meant by modern culture. Immense difficulties present themselves when this is attempted, and the hope of attaining a clear and generally accepted conception seems illusive. In the first place, modern culture in some respects, and according to some estimates, forms an antithesis to that of former centuries. But this antithesis is not absolute. We are all, whether we will or not, standing on the shoulders of former generations. All our society, family, labor, vocation, state-craft, legislation, morals, habits, arts, sciences, are permeated still with the Christian spirit. The opponents of Christianity know this very well, and their antagonism against Christianity is so strong just because the Christian spirit shows itself all along the line, leavens everything, and exerts its influence even upon them notwithstanding themselves. Thought has often to a great extent emancipated itself from Christianity; but life goes quietly on, and is continually fed from the sources of the past. Modern culture would like to be absolutely modern, but it is not, and cannot be so; it is a product of, and thus also a moment in, history.

But even if we do not take into account this alliance with the past, and wish to judge modern culture on its own merits, we do not obtain the unity and clearness which are necessary in order to form an exact conception of it. For modern culture is an abstract name for many phenomena, and forms no unity at all. Not only are there innumerable factors which have contributed to its development, but it is also in the highest degree divided in itself. Everywhere, and in all domains, in politics, social economy, art, science, morals, instruction, education, there are parties, tendencies, and schools which stand in opposition to one another; the realms of justice and culture, church and state, faith and science, capital and labor, nomism and antinomism, combat each other, and proceed on different principles. Monism no doubt seeks here also for an abstract unity; but it sacrifices the diversity and richness of life to a theory, and blinds itself to the sharp contrasts which reality exhibits. It is, therefore, an empty phrase to say that modern culture is at strife with Christianity and religion; as to some phenomena it may be said with some appearance of right, but to others it is not in the least applicable.

Finally, we should consider that modern culture in the sense of an extensive group of various phenomena is not a finished thing; it is not complete, and not objectively placed before us; it has existed but a short time in the past, and is still developing from day to day. We are thus in the middle of it, and live in a "transition period," — an expression which says little of itself, because all time is a time of transition and change, but yet here embodies an old and well-known truth, in opposition to all who try to separate the present from the past and the future and make it absolute. Therefore nobody can say whither modern culture will lead us; one can surmise, guess, speculate, but there is no certainty at all. As to the phenomena which now already present themselves, and are included under the name of modern culture, the estimates of their value vary very much. There are some of them which are approved by nobody. Who, for example, defends the materialistic tone, the mammonism, the alcoholism, the prostitution so prevalent in these days? Who is blind to the defects which attach to our modern culture or to the dangers to which it exposes us? Each one is thus obliged, whatever religious or philosophical standpoint he may occupy, to apply a standard in his judgment of modern culture; he cannot accept it in its entirety; whether he will or not, he goes to work eclectically, and will approve some phenomena as in agreement with his own world-view, and dissent strongly from others in the name of that same world-view. And as to the future, the estimation of modern culture will depend upon the direction in which it moves, which nobody can foresee or foretell. Men are alternately panegyrists and grumblers, and the same man plays in turn the one or the other rôle according to what pleases or vexes him.

The assertion that modern culture is in conflict with Christianity is thus a meaningless phrase. Who ventures to assert that marriage and family, state and society, art and science, trade and industry as such are condemned and opposed by Christianity? At the most such an assertion may be made as to the manner and the direction in which these institutions and activities at the present time are developing or are carried on. This is no doubt what is meant. There are phenomena upon which a very different estimate is placed by many of our contemporaries from that placed upon them by the gospel of Christ. But it is mere presumption for them to identify their judgment with modern culture itself and to reject the whole of Christianity in her name. It may be explainable, for it makes an impression to say that culture, and science and state have antiquated Christianity; but it is not excusable, for it places the antithesis in a false light, brings confusion into the ideas, and is injurious to both Christianity and culture.

If we search out what in modern culture is antithetically opposed to Christianity and then reduce this to a principle, we shall arrive at the same idea which was found above to be irreconcilable in it with Christian faith. The complaint which many make against Christianity, its doctrine of faith and life, is based on its so-called heteronomy and transcendence. There is in modern society a striving after independence and freedom, such as was unknown in earlier times, or at least not recognized in the same degree. We meet with this among all men, and in every position and circle of life; science, art, industry, trade, labor, capital, all desire to govern themselves, and to be obedient only to the laws which are laid down for them

by their own mode of life. This striving in itself is not
illegitimate or unjustifiable, for men are not machines, but
free-thinking and free-living rational and moral beings.
But it undeniably often assumes a character which inter-
dicts existence, and the right of existence, to all objective
authority, to all external law, to every destiny of man
which passes beyond this earthly life. The legitimate
struggle for independence and liberty is transformed into a
theoretically proclaimed and practically applied autonomy
and anarchy, and these naturally place themselves in opposition to Christianity. For Christianity comes into
collision with such an autonomy, as does every religion.
It asserts all possible freedom and independence for man,
for it teaches his creation after the image and likeness of
God ; but it maintains at the same time that man is a
creature, and thus can never become or be absolutely independent ; it joins him to God, and binds him to his word
and will. When the apologists of modern culture accuse
Christianity of legalism, heteronomy, transcendent eudæmonism, etc., these are words which intentionally represent the matter in an unjust way and rouse prejudice
against Christianity ; but the matter itself is beyond dis-
pute. It is supernaturalism, which in point of fact forms
the point of controversy between Christianity and many
panegyrists of modern culture.

The Christian religion cannot abandon this supernaturalism without annihilating itself. There is even no
religion thinkable or possible without belief in a supernatural power. For all religion implies that God and the
world are distinct, and that God can work in the world,
enter into fellowship with man, and by that fellowship
can raise him above, and maintain him against, the world.
Because Christianity is the pure and true religion, it is not

less, but more supernatural than all other religions. For these religions dissolve the godhead into all kinds of natural powers, see everywhere in the world only the influences of good or evil spirits, and cannot therefore bring man into a true fellowship with God. But according to the Christian confession the one, all-wise, all-good, and all-powerful will of God lies behind the phenomena of nature and the events of history, and this will breaks down all resistance in the world and humanity and leads them in the face of their opposition to salvation and glory. This is the idea which underlies the whole of Scripture; on it Moses and the prophets, Christ and the apostles take their stand; the Christian church is built on the great facts of creation, incarnation, and resurrection; the gospel as it is preached by Jesus himself in his earthly life embodies this same counsel and will of God.

It is not open to doubt that it was not as a poet or philosopher, as a scholar or artist, as a politician or social reformer, that Jesus appeared among the people of Israel. What is new and peculiar in the person of Christ consists in this — that he was more than Solomon and Jonah, or one of the prophets; that he is the Messiah, the Son of God, sent by God to seek the lost, and save sinners, to proclaim the gospel to the poor, and to preach the acceptable year of the Lord, to declare the Father, and to reveal his name. What he came to bring to earth is therefore a blessing of unspeakable value, namely, the kingdom of heaven, not as a community which could be founded by human endeavor, but as a heavenly, divine treasure, embracing righteousness, salvation from corruption, eternal life, and obtainable only through regeneration, faith, and conversion.

We may differ on the question whether Jesus was right in this preaching of the gospel, and whether the knowledge of God and eternal life mean the highest good for man. There are many at least who deny and controvert this, and seek to set Christian morals aside in favor of the ethics of individualistic or social eudæmonism. Now Christianity leaves full room for the ethical culture of our own personality in the midst of society, but there is a notable contrast between the two systems of ethics, which cannot be disguised or obliterated. Christian morals lays stress upon sin and grace, the ethics of evolution proclaims the natural goodness of man; the former regards man as a lost being, who needs salvation, the latter sees in him the one creature who can reform and save the world; the first speaks of reconciliation and regeneration, the second of development and education; for the one the new Jerusalem comes down from God out of heaven, for the other it comes slowly into being by human effort; there divine action moves history, here evolution is the all-directing process.[13]

But this is certain,—if the gospel is true, then it carries with it its own standard for the valuation of all culture. Jesus has shown this distinctly in the attitude which he adopted towards all earthly things and natural relations. He was no ascetic: he considered food and drink, covering and clothing, as good gifts of the Heavenly Father, and was present at wedding-feasts and dinners. And he was as little an epicurean, who thinks only of himself and cares only for himself; he was continually moved with compassion for all kinds of misery. Neither shallow optimism nor weak pessimism finds in him an ally. But although he did not despise natural institutions and blessings, still he does not undertake to estimate them as such or to determine their inherent value. That was not the work which the Father had given him to do. He accepted the social and political conditions as they were, made no endeavor to reform them, and confined himself exclusively to setting the value which they possessed for the kingdom of heaven. And in that connection he said, that nothing a man possesses in this world — food or drink, covering or clothing, marriage or family, vocation or position, riches or honor — can be compared with that pearl of great price which he alone can present. It must all be abandoned, if necessary, for the gospel's sake, and the treasures of earth are often a great obstacle to entrance into the kingdom of God. In a word, agriculture, industry, commerce, science, art, the family, society, the state, etc., — the whole of culture — may be of great value in itself, but whenever it is thrown into the balance against the kingdom of heaven, it loses all its significance. The gaining of the whole world avails a man nothing if he loses his own soul; there is nothing in creation which he can give in exchange for his soul.

The truth of this declaration can be denied only by the man who shuts his eyes to the awful seriousness of real life. Not only does Scripture teach that man has lost himself, and may lose himself more and more, but our own experience also testifies to this. Man is lost before God, for he does not give himself to God, and does not serve him in love, but flies from him, and hides himself from his presence. He is lost for his neighbor, for he abandons him in his need, and sacrifices him to his own interests in the struggle for existence. He is also lost for himself, for there is a cleft between his being and his consciousness, a dissension between his duty and his desire, between his conscience and his will. That is the reason why we seek diversions in the world; instead of re-collecting our thoughts we scatter them, and in proportion as with our

representations and imaginations, with our thoughts and
desires, with our inclinations and passions, we move in
various directions, we lose more and more the centre of
our own life. Man is ever losing himself more and more.
No treasures are able to compensate for the spiritual loss
of our soul, for when the soul is lost all is lost. Nothing
fills the emptiness, nothing replaces the loss, nothing
covers the poverty. For this reason Christ brought the
kingdom of heaven to earth; he implants it in the hearts
of men, and thereby gives them back to God, and their
neighbor, and also to themselves. Peace with God carries
with it for man peace with himself also; the cleft between
his conscience and his will is filled up; the discord between his being and consciousness is reconciled; his soul
with all its powers is brought back to unity in the fear of
God's name. His duty becomes his choice, and his choice
his privilege. Conversion is a turning back to God, but
at the same time a coming to one's self.[14]

If this is the content of the gospel, — namely, that God
maintains and renews the ethical ideal of man by his
merciful and powerful will in the way of forgiveness and
conversion, — then the reality of this content may indeed
be denied, but it is inconceivable that such a gospel should
be opposed to culture. Much rather is it, if we may so
say, the most important element of all culture, — principle and goal of what all culture in the genuine sense of
the word strives after, and must strive after. There are
indeed many who think that the development and progress of the human race principally or exclusively consist
in the improvement of material welfare. But this materialistic view of life is strongly contradicted by man's rational and moral nature. Heart and conscience witness to
us all that man cannot live by bread alone; "life is not

the highest good." It is not religion only, but philosophy, which has at all times proclaimed this. Its chief representatives have declared, without exception, that the destiny of man and humanity must bear an ethical character, and that that ethical character must take the first place; the good is the same as the divine, and is raised high above the sensual world; ethics goes further than physics. So powerfully does this idea of the value of the good work in the heart of man that material culture, which began to flourish in the last century and for some time cast a certain glamour over materialism, soon gave way to a strong reaction in life, and by the disappointment which it brought caused the heart of man to thirst again after idealism and mysticism. Even Haeckel has felt this influence; he has continued, indeed, to call his world-view materialistic, but he has raised his monism to the rank of religion, and regards as its kernel the worshipping of the true, the good, and the beautiful.[15]

Now as soon as culture wishes to be ethical culture, not in name, but in fact and in truth, it loses all ground for accusing the gospel of enmity against it, and it cannot do itself greater service than by honoring the gospel as the chief and highest power making for culture. It cannot bring a valid objection even against the supernatural elements which are included in the gospel, because as ethical culture it rests on metaphysics, and on deeper introspection proves to be based indeed on revelation. Thus, it is historically proved that culture has not had an independent origin and development, but from its first commencement is bound up with religion in the closest way. The higher elements of culture especially, such as science, art, and morality, are indebted to religion for their origin and growth. The oldest science of which we have knowledge,

in Greece, Egypt, Babylon, and India, was theology;
philosophy originated in religion, and only later brought
forth various particular sciences.[16]   Art among the people
of old bore a specially religious character;[17] and among all
men of ancient times we meet the tendency to regard
moral laws as divine commandments.[18]   Science, art, and
morality are cognate in origin, essence, and meaning with
religion, for they are all based on the belief in an ideal
world, the reality of which is assured and guaranteed only
by religion; that is, from God's side by revelation.[19]

No doubt an endeavor has recently been made to make
ethical culture independent of religion.[20]   But this attempt is still new and limited to a small circle, and it
probably will have little success.   It is a dishonor for religion, to be sure, to serve as a police agent, or as a watch-
dog of morality.   Religion and morality are not bound
together in this external and mechanical way, but they are
in alliance with each other organically, by reason of their
inner nature.   The love of God includes that of our
neighbor, and the latter is reflected in the former.   For
good presents itself to us all from our earliest youth in
the form of a commandment.   Neither autonomic nor evolutionary ethics can make any change here.   The child does
not gradually create moral laws by instinct or reflection,
but is brought up in a circle which has possessed those
laws long before, and which imposes them on the child
with authority.[21]   As we look around us among the nations
and examine the history of mankind, we are witnesses of
much vacillation and variety, but a fund of moral laws is always and everywhere found.[22]   Every man acknowledges
that in morality a law is laid upon him which obliges him
to obedience in his conscience.   If this be so, then in this
wonderful phenomenon we have to do either with an

illusion, a dream, an imagination of mankind, or with a reality which is raised high above the empirical world and fills us with deepest reverence. For if the moral law or the ideal good indeed exists around and above us, then it must be grounded in the world-power and be one with the Godhead. God alone is the source, and thus also the guarantee of the reality of the moral law, of the objectivity of duty, the ethical vocation and destiny of man. In so far all ethics is also heteronomous.

Philosophy, particularly since Kant, has strongly controverted this heteronomy, and it is right in its opposition if this heteronomy be thought of as a moral law, which comes to us from without, is forcibly imposed upon us from above, and finds no echo in our own spirit. Such a merely external law may be, perhaps, a natural law, but in no case can it be a moral law. Such a view of the heteronomy of law might be acceptable, accordingly, to those moralists who think that man was originally an animal, and has become man by external influences, either by the pressure of society or by the discipline of the state; but it has no attractions to, and is quite superfluous to, Christian ethics, which is based on Holy Scripture. For Scripture teaches that man was originally created after God's image, and bore the moral law in the inmost recesses of his heart; that even in the state of sin he is still bound to the ideal world by his reason and conscience; and that the dissension which now exists between duty and inclination, according to all experience, is, in principle, reconciled in regeneration and conversion. As Jesus said that it was his meat to do the will of his Heavenly Father, so Paul testified that he delighted in the law of God after the inward man; and all sincere Christians humbly speak the same words.

Autonomous morality and ethical culture cannot raise objection to this doctrine, for it is the ultimate fulfilment of what they themselves mean and wish. It is rightly said that good must be the inner inclination of man. Good does not in a social-eudæmonistic way borrow its standard and nature from the consequences of human actions, for these consequences are external, often accidental, and almost always incalculable. Man is not good by the operation and fruit of his actions, but the actions are good because, and in so far as, they are a revelation and expression of the good will of man. There is therefore, according to Kant, nothing in the world which can be considered as good without limitation except a good will. The philosopher therein simply repeated in other words what Jesus had said : A good tree alone can bring forth good fruit, and a man can only bring forth good things out of the good treasure of his heart.[23] This declaration of Scripture even avoids the one-sidedness of Kant, who makes it seem as if good can be achieved only if it is accomplished by the intellectual sense of duty alone without the co-operation of the heart. In place of this intellectual rigorism, which always produces by reaction emotional romanticism, Christian ethics maintains that the whole man must be good in intellect and will, heart and conscience. To do good is a duty and a desire, a task and a privilege, and thus the work of love. Love is therefore the fulfilling of the law.

But again, if this is the kernel of Christian morality, with what right can the charge of enmity against culture be brought against it ? For it is it alone which makes true culture possible, and places it on a firm foundation. Ethical culture rightly declares that man must be good internally, in the roots of his being, in the core of his will ;

but it feels itself obliged, after honest consideration, to confess that such men do not exist, and that it cannot create them. All culture, whatever significance it may have, just as all education, civilization, development, is absolutely powerless to renew the inner man. For it always works externally, and does not penetrate into the heart of man. It may fashion, prune, restrain, bridle, form; it may force life to run in harness; it may cultivate legalism and even morality. But that is nevertheless not *the* good, the genuine, inner, spiritual good; it is no true *Sittlichkeit*. As long as ethical culture thinks itself sufficient, it is exposed to serious danger. For adhering firmly to its ideal, and esteeming itself able to realize it, it will hedge man about on all sides, and lay upon him command on command, rule upon rule; or it will, after many endeavors, convinced of its powerlessness, abandon the height of the moral ideal, give the leadership to the will, and permit every one to live himself out in accordance with his own character. Phariseeism and Sadduceeism are no uncommon phenomena on philosophical and practical ground. Thus the true, and the good, and the beautiful, which ethical culture means and seeks, can only come to perfection when the absolute good is at the same time the almighty, divine will, which not only prescribes the good in the moral law, but also works it effectually in man himself. The heteronomy of law and the autonomy of man are reconciled only by this theonomy.

Ethical culture accordingly can neither in the source nor in the essence of morals be independent of the metaphysical foundation; and finally much less can it dispense with it in the definition of the goal of morality.[24] As long as it remains *diesseitig*, it cannot give to the question, What may be the goal of the moral action?

any other answer than that this is to be found either in the individual man or in humanity. In the first instance, whether it wishes to do so or not, it sacrifices the community to the individual, and in the second it sacrifices the individual to the community. But nature itself distinctly proves that neither of these may be lowered to a mere means to the other; the individual and the community are not subordinate to one another, but coordinate with each other. If both are thus to maintain their independence and be brought into agreement, this can be accomplished only when men rise above both, and posit a goal for moral action outside of both. Another consideration enforces the necessity of *Jenseitigkeit* still more strongly. Neither humanity nor the individual can have the origin or the goal in itself. There was a time when they did not exist; they are transitory, and near their end. In the universe they occupy a temporary, transitory place; they are a means, and not an end, and certainly no final end, because they are not their own origin.

But if neither the individual man nor humanity can be the final end, because they are creatures, then the question is unavoidable what this final end is. Ethical morality, which reflects, must go beyond this world of visible things; it cannot maintain its standpoint within humanity. But then there are only two paths open, — either humanity, with all its culture, is a means for the unconscious, unreasonable, and purposeless world-power, or it is a means for the glorifying of God. The first can, and will, and may never be believed by humanity, for it is tantamount to suicide. The second, that man and humanity exist for God's sake, from him, and through him, and to him, upholds their moral, spiritual value far above the whole inanimate universe, and brings indeed the true, the good, and the beautiful to eternal triumph. This alone gives peace to the understanding and rest to the heart. Ethical culture must be a philosophy of revelation or it cannot exist.

Now the peculiarity of all revelation is, that while it posits principles and lays foundations, it charges men with the application of these principles and the building upon these foundations. Creation was the first revelation, the principle and foundation of all revelation; but, on the other hand, every revelation is also a creation, a divine work, in order to accomplish something new, to make a new commencement, and to unlock the possibility of a new development. From nothing, nothing could begin; all evolution supposes a germ; all becoming proceeds from being. Thought and speech, life and history, science and art, have all had their commencement in principles which are laid down by God's creative power. The whole special revelation which has its centre in Christ has no other content and no other meaning than to lay this firm foundation whereon the new humanity can be built. Christ is the head, and the church is his body; Christ is the cornerstone, and believers are the living stones of the divine building. Nothing can be changed in this foundation; it is laid, and remains for all time. But when it is laid both in deed and word, in nature and history, in the world of being and consciousness, then the independent work of the church begins with the development of doctrine and life, of organization and worship. Revelation from God's side always opens a way for "discovery" by man.[25]

This is applicable also to culture. In the measure that it considers more deeply its own essence, it arrives at the discovery that it is rooted in metaphysics and founded on revelation. It rests on data which God himself established, and is certain of its rights and value only because God is creator, regenerator, and consummator of all things. The creation of the first man shows this; the subduing of the earth, that is, the whole of culture, is given to him, and can be given to him, only because he is created after God's image; man can be ruler of the earth only because and in so far as he is a servant, a son of God. But man has not continued to build on this foundation; the development of the human race has not been normal; there has always on a time of flourishing followed a time of decay and ruin for culture. Then God takes, as it were, the development into his own hands by raising up great men, by causing new races to appear, by creating events of a world-wide significance; he demolishes the sinful development and raises culture from its abasement, and opens out to it a new road. This is particularly manifest among the Israelites, in Abraham, Moses, the prophets, and finally in Christ. Culture, therefore, sinks into the background; man must first become again a son of God before he can be, in a genuine sense, a cultured being. Israel was not a people of art and science, but a people of religion; and Christ is exclusively a preacher of the gospel, the saviour of the world, and founder of the kingdom of heaven. With this kingdom nothing can be compared; he who will enter into it must renounce all things; the cross is the condemnation of the world and the destruction of all sinful culture.

But it is wrong to educe from this pronouncement that the gospel must be at enmity with culture. For although the gospel limits itself to the proclaiming of the requirements and laws of the kingdom, it cannot be set free from the organic alliance in which it always appears in history and Scripture. For, in the first place, Christ does not stand at the commencement, but in the middle of history. He presupposes the work of the Father in creation and in providence, especially also in the guidance of Israel; yea, the gospel asserts that Christ is the same who as the Word made all things and was the life and the light of all men. As he was then in his earthly life neither a politician nor a social reformer, neither a man of science nor a man of art, but simply lived and worked as the Son of God and Servant of the Lord, and thus has only been a preacher and founder of the kingdom of heaven, he cannot have come to annihilate the work of the Father, or his own work in creation and providence, but rather to save it from the destruction which has been brought about by sin. According to his own word, he came not to judge the world, but to save it.

Secondly, for the same reason, the preaching of Jesus cannot be separated from what has followed after the cross. The gospel goes back in the past to creation, and even to eternity, and stretches forward to the farthest future. Christ, who as the Word created all things, and bore the cross as the Servant of the Lord, is the same who rose again and ascended into heaven, and will return as Judge of the quick and the dead. In his exaltation he regains what he denied himself in his humiliation; but now it is freed from guilt, purified from stain, reborn and renewed by the Spirit. The resurrection is the fundamental restoration of all culture. Christ himself took again the body in which he bore on the cross the sin of the world; he has received all power in heaven and earth, and is exalted by God himself to his right hand as Lord and Christ. The demand which has been made from

many sides of late, as earlier by many sects and monastic
orders, that we should return from the Pauline and
Johannine Christ to the so-called historical Jesus, the
gospel of the Synoptics, the sermon on the mount, and
the parables, is not only impracticable, because in the
whole New Testament the same dead and risen Christ
meets us, but mutilates the gospel, leads to asceticism, and
creates an irreconcilable dissension between creation and
re-creation, Old and New Testament, nature and grace, the
Creator of the world and the Father of Christ.

Such a dissension may be proper to Gnosticism and
Manichaeism, and also to the Buddhism nowadays ad-
mired by so many, but it is in direct contradiction to
Christianity. The truth and value of Christianity certainly do not depend on the fruits which it has borne for
civilization and culture: it has its own independent value;
it is the realization of the kingdom of God on earth; and
it does not make its truth depend, after a utilitarian or
pragmatical fashion, on what men here have accomplished
with the talents entrusted to them.   The gospel of Christ
promises righteousness and peace and joy, and has fulfilled its promise if it gives these things.   Christ did not
portray for his disciples a beautiful future in this world,
but prepared them for oppression and persecution.   But,
nevertheless, the kingdom of heaven, while a pearl of great
price, is also a leaven which permeates the whole of the
meal; godliness is profitable unto all things, having the
promise of the life which now is, and that which is to
come.   The gospel gives us a standard by which we can
judge of phenomena and events; it is an absolute measure
which enables us to determine the value of the present
life; it is a guide to show us the way in the labyrinth of
the present world; it raises us above time, and teaches us

to view all things from the standpoint of eternity. Where could we find such a standard and guide if the everlasting gospel did not supply it? But it is opposed to nothing that is pure and good and lovely. It condemns sin always and everywhere; but it cherishes marriage and the family, society and the state, nature and history, science and art. In spite of the many faults of its confessors, it has been in the course of the ages a rich benediction for all these institutions and accomplishments. The Christian nations are still the guardians of culture. And the word of Paul is still true that all is ours if we are Christ's.[26]

REVELATION AND THE FUTURE

ALTHOUGH the Christian religion is not at enmity with culture in principle, still there is no gainsaying that it attributes only a subordinate value to all the possessions of this earthly life. The value of the whole world is not so great as that of the righteousness of the kingdom of heaven, the forgiveness of sins, and eternal life in fellowship with God. In this respect the Christian religion is in direct opposition to the view of the world taken by the modern man, and is neither prepared nor fitted for compromise with it. The question between them concerns no less than the highest good for man.

Therefore not only is Christianity accused to-day of rather opposing than furthering culture in the past, and of adopting towards it at the present day a repellent and hostile attitude, but men go further and declare that it has had its time, and cannot be a factor in the development of the future. If modern culture is to advance, it must wholly reject the influence of Christianity, and break completely with the old world-view. There must be inaugurated a *Kulturkampf*, compared to which that of Bismarck against the Jesuits was child's play. For Christianity in its essence, and consequently in all the forms which it has adopted in its several confessions, is always occupied with such supernatural subjects as eternity, heaven, God, etc.; it gives a bill of exchange for the life hereafter, which perhaps will never be honored, and makes men indifferent to this life; it does not stimulate to activity, but recommends as the highest virtues, patience, forbearance, obedience, and contentment.

The present century, on the contrary, is wholly *dies-seitig;* it believes no longer in unseen things, but reckons only with those which are seen and temporal. After the disappointment caused by the French Revolution, a deep, general dejection reigned in Europe under the Napoleonic *régime.* But oppression occasioned a rebound. When the hour of liberty struck, humanity awoke to a new life and went to work with unimagined courage. Its energy was crowned, and at the same time increased, by the brilliant successes which were achieved in science and technic, in society and state. Discoveries and inventions, with their application to life, showed what man could accomplish by his skill and labor. Within half a century humanity was, as it were, reborn, and the surface of the earth was renewed. What the forefathers in former ages, what even the preceding generation had not dared to think or dream of, now came to pass in reality. Humanity stood amazed at its own creations.

In the measure in which self-confidence grew, confidence in God, belief in miracles, consciousness of misery, the urgency of prayer, and longing for redemption decreased, at least in many circles. Kant had boldly spoken the word, — *du sollst, also du kannst,* — and the humanity which trod the stage of the nineteenth century adopted this motto. It perceived in itself a necessity, a will, a power, and an obligation to reform the world ; and with this pressure it felt its strength awaken, and an irresistible desire to set to work. The modern man no longer feels himself a miserable creature, who has fallen from his original destiny, and no longer regards the earth as a vale of tears, which has taken the place of the original paradise. He can conceive nothing more wonderful than this beautiful world, which has evolved itself from the smallest beginnings and has reached its highest point of development in grand and mighty man.[1] He is in his own estimation no mere creature, but a creator and redeemer of himself and society.[2] More and more he becomes his own providence.[3] And he is so, and becomes so through his work, for labor is creation. By labor men are divine, and become continually more godlike. Labor must therefore be the foundation of religion and morality, and also of the entirety of modern society.[4] In earlier times, no doubt, both outside and within the bounds of Christianity, labor was estimated as of great moral value, but there was nevertheless no system of morals built upon it, either by the Greeks, who despised labor, or by the Christians, who considered this life as a special preparation for eternity, or yet by the new moralists, who deduce the moral law from the subject, that is, from the categorical imperative. But among such men as Ihering, Wundt, Höffding, Paulsen, Spencer, and Sidgwick, we see ethics becoming more and more a section of sociology, which perceives in labor for himself and for others the calling and destiny of man. For labor reconciles the egoistic and social instincts and takes into captivity the whole human life.[5] Labor is " the meaning of our existence." [6]

This awakening of human energy is reflected in the world-view which now receives the strongest sympathy. Till now the whole world was riveted to absolute conceptions, such as substance and essence, spirit and matter, soul and faculties, ideas and norms. But now everything is changed; there is nothing firm, unchangeable, steadfast;

there is no *status quo*, but only an eternal movement.[7]
Physics and chemistry dematerialize themselves, and seek
their foundations in pure mathematical proportions; psychology has closed the account with substance and the
faculties of the soul, and only reckons with psychical
phenomena; logic, ethics, and æsthetics withdraw themselves from the government of fixed aprioristic norms,
and seek to build themselves up on psychology and
sociology; the atomistic world-view has given way in late
years to the energetic, and the absolute is no longer considered as a being, but only as a becoming; "will is the
real substance of the world."[8] If Descartes pronounced
his *cogito ergo sum* as the principle of philosophy, the new
world-view proclaims her *moveo ergo fio ; vivere* is now no
longer *cogitare*, but *velle ;* in a word, modern wisdom can
be summed up in this short epigram of Proudhon : *Affirmation du progrès, négation de l'absolu.*[9]

As this world-view is a precipitate of modern life, so in
its turn it influences that life and gives it direction and
guidance. The century in which we live is distinguished
from all preceding ones by its restless activity, by its
exploitation of physical and psychical forces, but at the
same time also by its endeavor to obtain the greatest
possible results from the smallest possible expenditure
of power.[10] The activities of men move in the most
divergent directions, and cross each other every moment, so that nobody can obtain a clear view or give
a complete account of them. And yet it seems as if
all this manifold and many-sided labor accomplished
to-day by men under the sun, is animated by one spirit,
is directed by one aim, and is made serviceable to one end,
namely, the improvement of the human race. Men live
to-day in a land of abundance, but there still remains

a longing for a richer and more durable happiness. This earthly life is confidently declared the sole home of man ; yet men seek even here below another and better dwelling. And therefore there are not wanting reformers who earnestly reflect on the miseries of this life, and recommend ways and means not only for the deliverance, but also for the perfecting of humanity.

In the first place, there is being made an attempt, which should be remarked, to improve the racial qualities of mankind in an artificial way. Individuals follow one another like small, unsubstantial waves from an unlimited ocean of being, but are all nevertheless equipped with free and active powers. They must therefore not be passive in the routine of nature, and must not lose heart from the thought that man remains eternally the same and is capable of no improvement or perfecting. The Christian religion may offer in its doctrine of the inheritance of sin such a comfortless view; but this dogma, that man is radically corrupt, must be saved by Christ, and can never become holy and happy by his own power, is the most demoralizing of all the articles of the Christian faith, and ought to be opposed and eradicated with determined strength. In its place must come the comforting conviction that man is still always becoming; he has already raised himself above the animal, and is moving in the direction of the *Uebermensch*. The evolutionary process, of which we have evidence all over the world, presses on not only forward, but also upward, to meet the light, the life, the spirit.[11] It is only necessary that man understand this process, and take an active part in it; he must feel his responsibility for the carrying of the process through by man, and for its advancing through him to a higher type of being. It seems as if the physical development of man has reached its end, at least so far as its basal structure is concerned; but all the more necessary now is the spiritual development, that is, the conscious, intentional, systematic work of man towards his own perfecting. And to this belongs in the first place the improvement and ennobling of the human race.

But now we are faced by the fact that, as Karl Pearson expresses it, "the mentally better stock in the nation is not reproducing itself at the same rate as it did of old; the less able and less energetic are more fertile than the better stock." [12] And that is not all; but in all lands the law allows, apart from certain limitations of age and consanguinity, complete freedom to marriage, so that it is possible for all kinds of weak, sick, incurable, and degenerate people to be united in marriage and to give birth to unfortunate children, and in this way to promote the steady deterioration of the human race. Nobody can deny that such a deterioration takes place. While hygiene does its best, on the one side, to prolong the life of the weak as much as possible, the number of these weak beings is continually increasing by the complete freedom of marriage. Weismann may assert that propensities which are acquired during life are not inherited, but the fact still remains that the physical and psychical condition of the parents influences that of the children. Insanity and crime, tuberculosis and alcoholism, and all kinds of venereal diseases are increasing among all nations; increasing numbers of inmates are sent to hospitals and prisons; and all this lays on the community a burden which in the long run it will not be able to bear. Therefore it is our duty to devote the greatest possible attention to marriage, and to the people between whom it is concluded.

In the first place, it is necessary that the act of propagation be restored to honor. Ascetic Christianity has
imprinted the stamp of impurity on it, and humanity therefore will never become better by returning to this mode
of thought. But it will enter the path of self-perfecting
when it turns its back on all asceticism and comes to
understand the holiness of propagation. The act of generation is not impure, but a holy sacrament, and all conception is immaculate. True progress will come when
humanity returns to the classic honoring of the strength
and beauty of the body and regains the old respect for
the divinity of propagation.[13]

But with this restoration to honor of the propagation of
the race earnest investigation must be combined. The
science of "eugenics," which was already inaugurated by
Francis Galton in 1883, and for which he not long ago
founded a research-fellowship at the University of London,
must become a science which subjects to exact inquiry
everything that bears upon propagation and heredity, and
endeavors to discover the laws by which these are
governed. Such an inquiry has not yet been prosecuted
far enough to warrant the deduction of conclusions on
which legislation might be founded. But public opinion can be instructed, and the way for new legislation
respecting matrimony may be prepared, and the state can
at any rate begin to make medical inquiry obligatory
before marriage, forbid marriage in definite serious cases,
and so prevent the birth of unfortunate children. Artificial selection shows how genera and species may be
modified among plants and animals ; if this selection is
applied also to the human race, it will promote its well-
being and improvement in the highest degree.[14]

In close alliance with this attempt to ennoble the

human race by artificial selection is the effort which is making for the perfecting of humanity by a radical reform in education. Many opinions exist as to the nature of such a new education. Some accept in principle the perfect equality of man and woman, defend free marriage and free love, and would withdraw education as early as possible from the family and delegate it to the community. Others, on the contrary, esteem the woman in every respect distinct from man, and wish to maintain and re-establish her in the rôle of mother and educator of her children. According to these, biology and anthropology prove that woman, who, in her whole physical and psychical development is much more closely allied to the child than man, and lives by instinct, intuition, and feeling more than he, is on this very account a much better representative and supporter of the human race; she is more " reminiscent of the past," more " prophetic of the future," and therefore superior to man. In the new philosophy of sex, of which biological psychology already dreams, the woman and the mother will stand " at the heart of a new world," become the object " of a new religion, and almost of a new worship." The mothers are the most valuable portion of the people, and must therefore be liberated in the future from all other cares than those of motherhood, and be treated by state and society with the highest honor.[16]

But whatever difference of opinion on this or similar points may exist among the reformers of pedagogy, all agree that education requires radical changes and must be built up anew on a scientific basis. Education is of far too great importance for the future of humanity to be abandoned to caprice or chance. Education is " man's chief problem, and the home, school, state, and church are valuable exactly in proportion as they serve it," yea, "the highest criterion of pure science is its educative value." [16]   And the science which must be the principle and foundation of education is genetic psychology.   This teaches us that man has slowly risen from the animal, and repeats in his development as embryo and suckling, as child and boy and youth, the different stages of phylogeny.   The soul of man is thus not complete, but as it has become, so is it still becoming; it does not stand alone, but is cognate with the souls of the animals and plants and all creatures; it strikes its roots deeply into the past, as the tree does into the ground, is the product of an immemorial heredity, and can and must be conceived and explained by the history of the human race.   We shall never really know ourselves until we know the soul of the animals, and especially that of those which are in the line of our descent.[17]

He who takes into account the lesson of evolution quickly comes to the conclusion that the present-day system of education is one great error.   Up to now men have given almost exclusive attention to the soul of man, and to its hereafter.   They have taken their start from ideas, fixed norms, unchangeable conceptions, and have placed before themselves as their chief aim to implant maxims and dogmas, and to fill the head with representations and ideas which are in opposition to nature, and can therefore never be assimilated.   This education has neglected the body, fatigued the brain, weakened the nerves, suppressed originality, slackened initiation, and the consequence is that the children on leaving school have possessed no independence, and have had no eye to see and no ear to hear. They have been completely estranged from life; and what is of more importance, the education which has alone been hitherto procurable has shown its incapacity, especially, in that during its continuance men have retained the same nature and the same defects; it has not eradicated a single sin or brought about any moral improvement whatever.[18]

Instead of this a new system of education must be instituted which in the first place is to be characterized by an honoring of the child. The child has been hitherto governed peremptorily and from without, but in the future the child must be placed in the centre, must be considered in whatever peculiarity it may have, and must be developed according to its own individuality. It is now the era of the child. The child is born good, for there is no hereditary sin; every defect in the child is only a hard shell, which contains the germ of a virtue, which as such has the right not to be eradicated, but to be trained. There must be no question of punishment or breaking of the will; if the child is not good in later life, then it has been a victim of its parents and teachers, and upon them lies the guilt. They have to bow to the superiority of the child; a child is only another name for majesty.[19]

Further, this great reformation must be wrought in education, — it must return from school to life, from books to nature, from theology and philosophy to biology. In the life of the child sense, nature, and the body are in the foreground. Before consciousness awakens, and intelligence and judgment are formed, the child is passion, desire, movement, will. Formerly men said that life was thought, but now we see that life is will. Will is the essence of the world, and the innermost nature of man; first life, then thought; first the natural, then the spiritual. The muscles make forty-three per cent of the weight of the human body, and are the organs of the will and the

creators of all culture. Man is one-third intelligence and
two-thirds will. The "age of art" must thus take the
place of the "age of science." The body with its members
and organs ought to be developed before all things ; manual
labor, gymnastics, sports, and all kinds of play ought to
take up a large, yes, the principal part in education. For
mere knowledge produces a serious danger ; better ignorance than knowledge which does not develop the strength
of man ; "muscle-culture" is at the same time "brain-
building " ; power must accompany knowledge.[20]

As to the knowledge which must be communicated in the
various schools of instruction, the natural sciences ought to
take the place which was formerly given to the so-called spiritual sciences, literature, history, theology, and philosophy.
The science of nature must form the groundwork of all
teaching, and the common possession of all civilized people. For even the spiritual sciences can no longer be
understood and practised with benefit, if they do not rest
on the basis of the science of nature. Without knowing
man in his prehistoric life, they cannot attain their full
development. If they have latterly advanced, and have
reached assured results, they are indebted for this to the
application of that method which is used in the sciences
of nature. This, then, is the indispensable foundation for
all other sciences and for all culture. Nobody ought to be
nominated to any important office, therefore, or to be accepted as a member of parliament, or as a minister of the
state, unless he has acquired a solid knowledge of nature.
In a word, the old world-view must be replaced in all
schools by the world-view of the doctrine of evolution.
Then only will a great future stretch out before education,
for knowledge of nature has not merely an intellectual,
but also great practical, technical, and ethical value.[21]

But a reformation which will usher in a new era for
the human race cannot confine itself to a change in the
system of education. If reformation must consist principally in replacing the old world-view by that of evolution,
then educational reform is but a single step in a long road,
and there remains a great deal to do. For the old world-
view — that is, that conception of world and life which has
been formed under the influence of Christianity — is so intimately interwoven with our whole being, with all our
thoughts and actions, that to eradicate it would seem almost a hopeless task, and if it could be accomplished,
would throw humanity into a violent crisis, the consequences of which no one can foresee. Church, and state,
and society, religion, morality, and justice, marriage, family, and school, habits and laws, and our whole culture
are, notwithstanding many foreign elements which have
intruded from elsewhere, built on a Christian basis and
animated by the Christian spirit. He who desires such
a reform may, no doubt, make a beginning, but who
knows what the end will be, and who can estimate the
cost? None the less, if such a reformation is to be
wrought, it cannot be satisfied with a mere change in
the system of education; it must proceed to a total
rebuilding of society.

However, even if we do not reckon with the conscious
will of man, there is already at work in present-day society a hidden force which affects it, as it were, in heart and
reins, and distinguishes it from all earlier forms in a very
remarkable way. We may approve or disapprove of this
movement, but the trend of modern society is in the direction of freedom, autonomy, and democracy. All boundary lines which formerly separated men, and all bonds
which encumbered their movements and activities, have

been broken down one after another. All forms of servi-
tude — slavery, bondage, feudalism, and subordination —
are thought to be opposed to the independence and dignity
of man; even service for wages appears to the modern man
humiliating, and is accounted merely another form of
slavery. All the relations which have grown up between
men in the course of the centuries are more and more losing their organic, moral, and natural character, and are
being replaced by voluntarily formed contracts. Liberty
of religion and conscience has been succeeded by freedom
of habitation and occupation, of trade and intercourse, of
union and association, of writing and thinking; and
thought has so much outstripped discipline that the most
absurd ideas arouse the greatest admiration.

Specialization and multiplication of occupations go hand
in hand with this autonomy. The number of trades
which were organized as guilds in Germany in the eighteenth century were counted by tens; they are now to be
numbered by thousands, and continually increase, almost
from day to day. Labor is endlessly differentiated and
specialized. All activities which are auxiliary to the pro-
vision of the necessities of life have become independent
occupations. The machine which has replaced the imple-
ment in the hand of the workman, and operates much
more quickly, uniformly, cheaply, and powerfully than any
human power, increases the division of labor, and makes
the simplest article into a product which is accomplished
by the co-operation of many hands. And this specializing
of labor may be observed not only in material, but also
in spiritual domains. There was a time when one could
say of a person that he knew everything that was written
in books, but such an encyclopædic knowledge is not possible now, even for the greatest genius; sciences are di-

vided and multiplied, and are so far removed from the common centre that the investigator in one science is a complete stranger in the disciplines of the others, and does not even understand the terms employed in them.

With this specialization of labor is combined, contrary to what would perhaps apriori be expected, an increase in social dependence. It is usually said that the French Revolution has made men free and equal, but to tell the whole truth one has to add that it has replaced personal by social dependence. We depend on each other now more than ever. Nobody, no man, no city, no village, no people, and no state is independent any longer. We have no food and no drink, no covering or clothing, no warmth or light, no furniture and no implements, which are not procured for us by the community from day to day. Each man has significance only as a part of the whole, as a " labor-unit of the social organism "; if he be left to himself, and excluded from the social body, he is powerless and loses his value. This life in community, which forms such a remarkable trait in the society of to-day, is indebted for its growth in a large degree to the decline of the value of personality.

And this social dependence is continually increasing; the organization of society is progressing from day to day under our eyes. Society has already become a most artificial system of manifold and complicated relations, a gigantic organism, wherein all members are closely connected; but all agree that the socialization of society proceeds without intermission; we are carried steadily forward in the direction of what Lamprecht calls the " bound enterprises." The anarchy which reigns in the production of goods, the abuse of power of which the trusts are guilty, the law of parsimony in labor, the caprices of de-

mand and supply, and the conflict of capital and proletariat, — all this leads to social organization and demands help from the all-embracing state. And the
state has already traversed a good part of this way.
Private enterprise has been replaced in many departments by the service of the community; one circle of
life after another loses its independence. Jurisprudence,
army, navy, taxation, the postal system, telegraphy, trams
and railways, instruction in all kinds of schools, the care
of libraries and museums, of health and cleanliness, of
poorhouses and asylums, the exploiting of water and
heat supply, of gas and electricity, fire- and police-depart-
ments, roads and canals, parks and theatres, savings banks
and insurance companies, and many other interests, are
wholly or in part withdrawn from private enterprise and
given into the hands of local or national authorities.

Well, then, social reformers say to us, if these things
are so, what can we do but help on and direct, promote
and complete, this powerful movement which is already
proceeding? We are working in the same direction if we
break down finally the last barrier which separates men,
and that is capital, private property. The Reformation
has procured for us religious freedom; that is, the equality
of all men before God. The Revolution of 1789 gave us
political liberty, — the equality of all men before the law.
A third reformation is now in order, — the establishment
of freedom in society, and the equality of all men in respect to the possessions of culture. What good are religious and political freedom for men if social equality is
withheld from them? What value has the declaration of
the rights of man if the right to labor and food and pleasure
remains unsecured? As Protestantism has prepared the
way for liberalism, and liberalism for democracy, so now

democracy ought to be fulfilled in socialism. The motto of liberty, equality, and fraternity will be completely realized only when the community, leaving the means of enjoyment and the ratio of consumption to the individual, possesses itself of all means of production, — land, factories, and implements, — and, systematically regulating the whole production, divides the product among all citizens, according to their merits or necessities. In a word, the reformation of society will reach completion only in the socializing of all the possessions of culture.[22]

Men cherish the boldest expectations on the faith of all these reformers. Marx, it is true, held the opinion that he had set socialism free from utopianism, and had established it on a firm, scientific basis. His effort was to conclude an alliance between the suffering and the thinking part of humanity and to make science serviceable for the proletariat. Therefore he made a study of present-day society, tried to learn the laws which govern its development, and endeavored to show that the old society could produce an entirely new one by way of evolution. He refused indeed to draw up a complete description of the future state, but he did not shrink from proclaiming his expectations concerning it, and thus he ceased to be a scientific inquirer, and came forward in the rôle of a prophet. And when he further not only published the results of his inquiry, but also made it the basis of a programme which was to be adopted and realized by a definite party, he threw off the toga and put on the mantle of a preacher of repentance and a reformer. Even Marx thus could not escape from utopianism; and the socialism which operates under his name is, as a doctrine concerning a future society, no scientific school, but a political party. The society of the future naturally is no subject of ex-

perience and investigation, but an object of hope and
expectation, of desire and endeavor. This is sufficiently
proved by the fact that socialism, in consequence of the
serious criticism which its anticipated future state has
aroused, has finally abandoned all details and left to the
future what the future shall bring forth.[23]

Nevertheless it can never completely abstain from fram-
ing a description of the future state, either with respect
to its own members or those who are outside; for after all
each man wishes to know, to a certain extent, in what direction and to what end he is led by such a radical change in
society. If the ideal which men strive after cannot be
described, or on being described betrays to all its imprac-
ticability, all confidence is lost and all obedience is at an
end. Hope alone keeps socialism alive; "the vision of the
future is for every present circumstance the strongest
bearer of power."[24] Socialism, therefore, ever seeks its satisfaction in the forecast of Bebel, that the future state will
bring a condition of happiness and peace for all men. The
state with its ministers and parliaments, its army and
police, will not be necessary in the new society, for all
those relations of possession and power in the behalf
of which they have been called into being will have
passed out of existence. All men will receive equal posi-
tions in life and a suitable subsistence. Each will have
to accomplish a definite work; but this work will require
only a few hours a day, and for the remainder of his time
each man may devote himself, according to his free choice,
to spiritual occupations, to companionship, to pleasure.
There will no longer exist distinctions between rich and
poor, idle and industrious, learned and ignorant, the population of city and country, because there will no longer
exist commerce, trade, money, or unequal division of

pleasure and labor.   Each one after the necessary labor
will do what he pleases, so that according to his free
option one will become a musician, another a painter, a
third a sculptor, a fourth an actor.   Even diseases will
disappear more and more, and natural death, the slow
dying of the powers of life, will become more and more
the rule.[25]

Socialism does not stand alone in these utopian expectations.   It has had its predecessors in Plato and Thomas
More, in Campanella and Morelly, St. Simon and Fourier,
Proudhon and Comte, and in many other theologians and
philosophers, in many religious sects and political parties.
Humanity as a whole has always lived, and still lives, in
hope, notwithstanding all empiricism and realism.   Men
paint the future state in very different colors ; and according to the different conceptions each one has of the highest
good, represent that future state as a kingdom of morality
(Kant), or humanity (Herder), as a kingdom of liberty, in
which spirit fully penetrates nature (Hegel), or as a
Johannine church, which will at the end replace the
church of Peter and Paul (Schelling); as a world in
which ideal or material possessions are the chief enjoyment.   But such a future is expected by every one ; all
religion, all philosophy, and all views of life and the
world issue in an eschatology.   And not only so, but all
systems have in common that they finish the world's
history with to-day, and hereafter expect only a world
era wherein the hope and the dream of humanity will be
realized ; [26] all eschatology which lives in the heart includes the belief in a speedy *parousia.*

This ineradicable hope of humanity is full of potent
charm.   And if to-day it springs up with new strength, shuns
no exertion, esteems all opposition conquerable, and strives

to introduce the new era for humanity by all kinds of reformation, it compels respect and stimulates to activity. When Ludwig Stein preaches a social optimism, which wages war on all Nirvana-philosophy and turns its back on all conservatives and pessimists; [27] when Metschnikoff proclaims in the name of science the coming day of the abolition of all sickness, the lengthening of human life to a good old age, and the reduction of death to a gentle, painless fading away; [28] when Stanley Hall tells us that the world is not old, but young, that the twilight in which we live is not that of the evening but of the morning, that the soul is still always becoming, and is capable of a much higher development; [29] when James declares that the world is, or becomes, that which we make it: [30] when all these men appeal to our responsibility, to our consciousness of duty, to our power and energy, then our hope is rekindled, our courage is raised, and we are stimulated to go forward immediately without further hesitation.

Nevertheless it should be observed that while this optimistic activity seems to depend only on man, and to feel not the least need of divine help, yet on the other hand it breaks through the circle of immanent thought and action, mounts to transcendency, and seeks strength and security in metaphysics. The doctrine that man is corrupted by sin and cannot sanctify and save himself by his own strength is commonly accounted the most fearful of all errors; autonomy and autosotery reject all heterosotery. But at the same moment when all transcendency and metaphysics are denied, the human being is exalted above his usual state and is identified with the divine. The superhuman task of transforming present society into a state of peace and joy requires more than ordinary human power; if God himself does not work the change, hope can be cherished only when human power is divinized. This is in fact the intimate idea of that philosophical theory which Strauss has most clearly formulated, that the infinite is not realized in a single man, but only in humanity; humanity being the true unity of divine and human natures, the man becoming God, the infinite spirit descending to finiteness, the child of the visible mother nature, and of the invisible father spirit, the doer of miracles, the saviour of the world. What humanity confesses concerning Christ, and pronounces in its idea of divinity, is merely a symbol of what it finds in itself, and what it is. Theology is mainly anthropology; the worship of God is humanity adoring itself. Comte, therefore, was quite consistent when he substituted the worship of humanity for the worship of God.[31]

This deification of man proves clearly that no eschatology is possible without metaphysics. But this is shown still more clearly by another fact. Culture, ethics, idealism, all striving after a goal, must always seek alliance with metaphysics. Kant reversed the relation between them, and tried to make morals entirely independent of science; but on those morals he again built up practical faith in a divine providence. In the same way, any ethical system which aspires to be true ethics and to bear a normative and teleological character, not falling into merely a description of habits and customs, is forced to seek the support of metaphysics. If man has to strive after an ideal, he can gain courage only by the faith that this ideal is the ideal of the world and is based on true reality. By banishing metaphysics, materialism has no longer an ethical system, knows no longer the distinction between good and evil, possesses no moral law, no duty, no virtue, and no highest good. And when the immanent-humanistic philosophy of Natorp, Cohen, and others endeavors to base ethics exclusively on the categorical imperative, it loses all security that the "ought" will one day triumph over the "is," and the good over the bad.[32] Whatever one believes to be the highest good, this highest good is either an imagination, or it is and must be also the highest, true being, the essence of reality, the meaning and destiny of the world, and thus also the bond which holds all men and nations together in every part of the world and saves them from anarchy.[33]

The Christian finds his assurance of the triumph of good in his confession of God's sovereign and almighty will, which, though distinct from the world and exalted above it, still accomplishes through it its holy purpose, and, in accordance with this purpose, leads humanity and the world to salvation. But he who rejects this confession does not therefore escape from metaphysics. It sounds well to call man the rebel in nature, who, when it says "Die!" answers, "I will live." [34] But with all his wisdom and strength man is powerless against that nature in the end, unless it be subject to a will which maintains man in his superiority above it. That is the reason why, even when theism is denied, the true reality, the world-will which is hidden behind phenomena and very imperfectly manifested, is nevertheless always thought of as analogous to that of man, and especally as an ethically good will. Notwithstanding all his self-confidence and self-glorification, man is, in every possible world-view, incorporated in a larger whole, and is explained and confirmed by that totality. Metaphysics, that is the belief in the absolute as a holy power, always forms the foundation of ethics.

In our days evolution takes the place of such metaphysics. The modern man derives his faith and animation, his activity and his optimism, from the idea of evolution, which according to his belief governs the whole world. If he endeavors restlessly to establish a holy and happy kingdom of humanity on earth, and stands firm in his belief in its realization notwithstanding all difficulties and disappointments, this can be explained only in one way, — that he feels himself borne on by the true reality, which is hidden behind the oftentimes very sad phenomena. Striving and laboring to attain his ideal, he believes himself in harmony with the innermost motive-power of the world, with the mysterious course of nature. To work, to endeavor, to strive, to become, is the deepest meaning of the world, the heart and the kernel of true reality. The doctrine of evolution thus takes the place of the old religion in the modern man.[35] It is no science; it does not rest on undeniable facts; it has often in the past and in the present been contradicted by the facts. But that does not matter; miracle is the dearest child of faith. All change in the world, as if it were nothing, is identified with development, development with progress, progress with material welfare or ethical culture, with liberty or morality. Although monism in its different forms denies that the absolute power which rules the world has personality, consciousness and will, yet it always speaks of this power as if it were a person. Consciousness, instinct, will, labor, endeavor, development, aim, and holiness are unintentionally ascribed to it; it is even identified with absolute divine love in a naïve way, which is in direct antagonism to the scientific pretensions of the speakers. And love is then called " the original of all social forces, the creator and reconciler of all; the only true God is love." [36] Just as the pagan treats his idol, so modern man acts with the idea of evolution.

The superstitious character, which is more and more taken on by this idea, is clearly seen in the contents of the optimistic expectations which are cherished concerning the future of the human race. For these expectations involve nothing less than that human nature in the future, either slowly by gradual development, or suddenly by leaps of mutation, will undergo radical change. In the future state there will be no longer any sickness or crime, no envy or malice, no enmity or war, no courts of justice and no police, but contentment and peace will be the portion of all. Now it is possible to say that sin and crime are owing to circumstances alone, and thus will disappear with the reformation of the environment. But this is nevertheless such a superficial judgment that no refutation of it is necessary. Every man knows by experience that sin is rooted in his own heart. If there ever is to be a humanity without sin and crime, holy and blessed, then it must be preceded by a radical change in human nature. But such a change is not too great for the expectation of the optimists, for they are assured of it by evolution. Man has advanced so much in the past that we may cherish the best hope for the future. He was an animal, and became a man, — why should he not become an angel in the future? As by immanent forces alone life has proceeded from the lifeless, consciousness from the unconscious, intelligence from the association of representations, will from feeling, spirit from matter, good from evil, what should hinder man from conquering in course of time all sin, putting an end to all misery, and establishing "the kingdom of man" on earth once for all, the more because he himself by exertion can lead and promote the evolutionary process? Thus the idea of an *Uebermensch* is intimately connected with the idea of evolution. Darwin himself believed in it, and comforted himself for the suffering of this present time with the hope that man in the far future would become a much more perfect creature than he is now; [37] and the optimistic evolutionists join in this expectation: man is still in the making, he is still at the beginning of his development, —a rich, beautiful future lies before him.[38]

But although this future may speedily appear, it is not in existence yet, and it is not likely that it will dawn in the days of the present generation. What profit all these expectations for the men who now live, and each day draw nearer to their end? Socialism scoffs at the Christian faith, which promises a bill of exchange on eternity; but eternity is after all more worthy of our trust than an insecure, doubtful, and distant future. So the doctrine of evolution has found itself suddenly confronted with the question, what significance the eschatological expectations have for the individual. In the materialistic period, which lies behind us, it had for this serious question only a contemptuous smile. But the belief in a future kingdom of humanity is always confronted by the problem of personal immortality. And the doctrine of evolution assumes now in its new idealistic form quite a different bearing towards this problem.[39] Why should it be impossible to introduce this immortality into its system? If man in the long process of his development has raised himself by his intelligence high above the animal, probably he can make himself immortal by continual development. Of course it is improbable that all men who have already lived and borne that name have reached such immortality, for the transition from animal to man has been very gradual; and it is also possible, as the adherents of conditional immortality assure us, that even now and in the future not all men will be able to advance so far, but only they who ethically work out their own self-perfecting. But in itself there is no reason why man by his own development should not become immortal.

Death certainly cannot be thought of as a catastrophe, as a punishment of sin, as a judgment which is executed upon man. It is simply a normal phenomenon, a gradual transition, such as often takes place in the organic world. The egg becomes a chick, the caterpillar becomes a butterfly; and so man advances, as at birth so at death, into another form of existence; he changes his clothing, — he lays aside the coarse, material body, and continues his life in a finer, ethereal body. So Darwinism successively brings us into company with Swedenborg and Jung Stilling, Davis and Kardec, Madame Blavatsky and Mrs. Annie Besant, Mrs. Eddy and Elijah Dowie, with all the theosophists and spiritualists of recent times. And it is not to be wondered at that many adherents of the evolutionary doctrine are at the same time advocates of spiritualism.[40] For all these tendencies are produced by the same root idea: they are all strongly opposed to the Christian doctrine of creation and fall, of hereditary sin and ethical impotence, of redemption by Christ and salvation by grace; and they declare instead that all is eternally becoming, that in an absolute sense there is no coming into existence and no dissolution, but only a change in the form of existence. This leads to the consequence that, as Haeckel has equipped substance, ether, and atoms with spirit, soul, conscience, and will, so men have truly existed eternally; and it is no wonder that preëxistenceism has again gained many adherents to-day.[41]

But although there may be difference of opinion on this point, human development is a part of the great

evolutionary process and is bound to fixed laws. Man
is what he does, and perhaps already has done, in preceding states of existence; all that happens to a man
upon earth, his external as well as his internal condition is a strict consequence of his behavior and actions.
There is place only for merits, for the law of reward of
man's works; there is no grace or forgiveness in the
course of nature. The ethical law is the same as the
natural law; everywhere karma reigns, — the law of
inevitable consequences. Therefore there exist also differences among men, not in origin and disposition, by divine
ordinance, but by the use or misuse which they make of
their gifts. Men do not run with equal ardor; they do
not exert themselves with the same vigor. There are sar-
cical, psychical, and pneumatic men; and according to
their work in their earthly existence they continue their
life after death. Death is no death, but life, — a form of
transition to a higher existence. The deceased do not
even know that they have died; they keep a body, they
see and hear, think and speak, consider and act, just as
they did here upon earth. Perhaps they continue their
intercourse for a shorter or longer time with men on
earth, as spiritualism teaches; or they return in another
body to the earth, as theosophy assumes; or they continue
their purification in some other way.[42]

But whatever evolution thinks about the future, it affords no rest for the mind and none for the heart, because it takes away from us the Lord of the world.
If there is no being, but only becoming, then there is
no final state, either on this side of death for humanity, or on the other side for the individual man. The
doctrine of evolution is even mortally wounded by this
eternal process, because the idea of a never-ending devel-

opment means a process without aim,[43] and thus no longer a development. For every state exists only to make way for another; as soon as the kingdom of man came into existence it would pass away, and this the more because, according to the testimony of science, the present world and the present humanity cannot last eternally.[44] If there is no omnipotent and holy God who exists above the world, and is for it the goal and resting-place of its strife, then there is no final end, no completion of the process of the world, and no rest for the human heart. It is then an empty sound even to speak with Höffding and Münsterberg of the eternal preservation of values,[45] for all value disappears with personality; or to take refuge in a mysterious Buddhistic Nirvana, as is proposed by Schopenhauer and von Hartmann, wherein all life, consciousness, and will sink into an eternal, hypnotised condition.[46] From the standpoint of evolution there is place only for an eternal return, as was already assumed in Greek philosophy by Heraclitus and the Stoics, and in these later days has been advocated even by Nietzsche. Nietzsche was first a pessimist, pupil of Schopenhauer and Wagner; later he became a positivist, and, rejecting all metaphysics, took his standpoint in reality as the one true world; still later he combined with this the doctrine of the *Wille zur Macht;* the real world became for him an ocean of powers, which *is* not, but eternally *becomes,* which has no origin and aim, but continually rises and falls, appears and disappears. Although he draws from this creative energy of the *Wille zur Macht* the belief in the appearance of the *Uebermensch,* and takes this as the aim of the process of the world, yet it is self-evident that this belief is in direct opposition to his positivism, as well as to his doctrine of the eternal return. The

Uebermensch is not only a pure product of his imagination, but can only be a transition form in the process of the world.[47] An optimism which is exclusively built on evolution is always transmuted into pessimism if one ponders a little more deeply.

This is apparent also in the so-called meliorism of James. If pragmatism is opposed to idealism, and takes its standpoint in the empirical world, it cannot attain to an eschatology. One may with Comte require from science that it give us the power to look forward and predict the future; [48] but Ostwald rightly says that our knowledge of the commencement and end of the world is null,[49] for the world is so enormously great, and human society so complicated, that nobody can calculate with any certainty how they will develop in the future. Every one who holds strictly to experience must protest against a metaphysics of evolution which speaks of an infallible and eternal progress. All this belongs to the province of faith, and is not able to withstand a logical and ethical criticism. On the ground of empirical reality we can only resign ourselves to ignorance; we know not what the future may bring, or how humanity will be developed. The only thing we have to do is to fulfil our duty. We cannot stop the process, but we may perhaps bend and guide it a little. Let us take the world as it is, and make the best of it. Perhaps the future will be better than we think.[50]

This meliorism certainly does not bear witness to strong faith and great courage. It has to all intents abandoned the whole world to pessimism, and maintains itself only by holding fast to duty. But this isolation of the categorical imperative from the totality of life, in which it is presented to us in man and humanity, has in no small measure contributed to the appearance and spreading of

a pessimistic feeling in the nineteenth century ;[51] the system of Schopenhauer depends closely on Kant's criticism.
If the essence of things is unknowable, the misery of man
cannot be fathomed. For metaphysical need is born in all
of us, and the thirst after the knowledge of the absolute
cannot be uprooted from the heart. Our condition would
be more tolerable if religion did not consist in fellowship
with God, or if that fellowship could be realized and enjoyed without consciousness. But what we do not know,
we have not, and we love not. The special needs of our
time are therefore caused by agnosticism. Trust is under-
mined not only in science, but also and principally in ourselves, in the witness of our self-consciousness, in the
value of our religious and ethical perceptions, in the
power of our intelligence and reason. Doubt is awakened
in all hearts, and the uncertainty causes our convictions
to sway hither and thither; we are moved by every wind
of doctrine, and weakened in our will by the yeas and
nays which resound on all sides.

Nobody can predict how the human race will overcome
this disease. Philosophy, which has revived in late years,
assuredly is not fitted for the task. For it is itself infected
in a great measure by the disease; it is uncertain in its
starting point, is in doubt concerning its own task and
aim, and is divided into all kinds of schools and systems.
There is no question of a steady progress in its history; it
has, especially in the period of Kant, broken more down
than it has built up, and its defenders not infrequently
give utterance to the opinion that the advantage which it
has produced consists solely in the enlightening of insight
into the essence of human knowledge, and that aside from
this it is mostly a history of instructive and important
human errors.[52]

The ethical autonomy also, which formed for Kant the basis of his metaphysics, offers in its isolation no sufficient security. For if the whole world is ascribed to the operation of a blind process, it cannot be understood how consciousness of duty could obtain a firm foothold in this stream of becoming. Evolution, which is everywhere else recognized, does not respect this apparent immutability, but penetrates into the essence of the moral man, analyzes his views, shows the sources from which his opinions are drawn, and shrugs its shoulders over the eternity of moral duty and moral laws.[53] But apart from this serious objection, moral autonomy may uplift and animate man for a short time; it may fill him with admiration, as does also the starry sky above his head; and in days of self-confidence it may stimulate him to restless effort, but it can give him no comfort in hours of repentance and bitter agony. It is good for the Pharisee, who knows no other law than reward for service, but it is pitilessly hard for the publican and sinner, who need God's grace. And such poor sinners are we all, each in his turn. The strongest among men have times in which they feel miserable, and as desolate as the prodigal son. The " healthy-minded men " are not separated from " the morbid-minded " as a special aristocratic class, but often themselves pass over into their opposites; optimism and pessimism alternate in every man's life.[54] Fichte, the philosopher, affords us a striking illustration of this. In the first period of his philosophic thought he felt no need of God, and was content with the moral world-order: in the beginning of things there was not being, but doing; not the word, but the deed; the non-ego was nothing but the material of duty, and the fulfilment of this duty the highest blessedness. But later, when serious experi-

ences had enriched his life and thought, he returned
from doing to being, from duty to love, from striving to
rest, from morality to religion. The more deeply we live,
the more we feel in sympathy with Augustine, and the
less with Pelagius.[55] Knowledge of law awakens the need
for grace.

Present-day culture offers still less security for a glad
hope. There are still many who are enthusiastic about
science, and anticipate from its technical applications the
salvation of humanity. The cries of science, progress, and
liberty are continually heard on the lips of free-thinkers.[56]
But the hollowness of the sound reveals itself to any
keenly listening ear.   Culture brings with it its blessings,
but also its dark shadows and serious dangers ; it develops
attributes and powers in men which are highly valuable,
but it does this almost always at the cost of other virtues which are not of less value; while it promotes
reflection, sagacity, activity, and strenuous striving, it
suppresses the unbiassed opinion, the childlike naïveté,
the simplicity and the guilelessness, which often belong to
the natural life.[57]   Intellectual development is in itself no
moral good, as rationalism has dreamed ever since Socrates' day, but may be used equally well for evil as for
good ; it can be serviceable to love, but it may also become a dangerous instrument in the hands of hate ; not
only the virtuous, but also the criminal, profit by it. What
da Costa said of the invention of printing, that it was a
gigantic step to heaven and to hell, may be applied to
all scientific and technical elements of culture.

We are indeed witnesses in our own developed society
that sin and crime increase frightfully, not only in the
lowest ranks of population, but quite as much in high
aristocratic circles. Unbelief and superstition in all forms ;

adultery, unchastity, and unnatural sins, voluptuousness and excess, avarice, theft, and murder, jealousy, envy, and hatred, play no less a part in the life of cultured humanity than among the lower races. Art and literature are not infrequently handmaids to all these sins, and the plays, which in such centres of civilization as Paris and Berlin are given before the *élite*, seriously raise inquiries whither we are bound with all our civilization.[58]

And at the same time with these iniquities the cleft becomes wider between religion and culture, between morality and civilization, between science and life, between the various classes and ranks of society. Legislation is almost powerless here; internal corruption, moral degeneration, and religious decay cannot be removed by a law of the state; on the contrary, every law has to reckon with the egoism and the passion of men, if it does not wish to be doomed to complete impotence; if law does not find support in conscience, it does not touch life. Besides this, legislation is put more and more into the hands of the people, so that it is not seldom made the servant of party interests. Complaints about the shady side of parliamentary government increase in all lands;[59] the state, which is above all, and has to further the interests of all, tends to become a ball in the strife of parties, and a powerful means by which the majority tries to suppress the minority. The benefit of liberty itself, in religious, social, and political domains, comes very seriously into question in many countries, such as France.

There is even reason for the question, whether the theory of evolution does not promote in a high degree this continual triumph of the power of the strongest. For though it believes in progress in this sense, that the material gives birth to the spiritual in the way of gradual

development, it also teaches that in the struggle for life
the unfit perish, and only the fittest survive. Therefore
opinions greatly differ on the relation between Darwinism
and socialism; according to Virchow, Loria, Ferri, and
others, Darwinism is serviceable to socialism, but Haeckel,
O. Schmidt, Ammon, H. E. Ziegler, and H. Spencer maintain, on the contrary, that the principle of selection bears
an aristocratic character.[60]   In any case, we are witnesses
to this remarkable fact, that a social aristocracy is raised
against a social democracy; the *Herrenmoral* of Nietzsche is also defended on economical grounds; capitalism
is deeply despised and fanatically opposed, but it gains
also strong support and passionate defence;[61] and art in
late years very seriously protests against social levelling,
and makes a strong plea for riches and luxury, for the
genius and aristocracy of the mind; it is highly normal,
it is said, that the many should live for the few and the
few live at the cost of the many.[62]

The same fact also presents itself internationally in the
mutual relations of the nations.   The cosmopolitanism of
the " Enlightenment " was not only exchanged in the nineteenth century for patriotism, but this patriotism was not
infrequently developed into an exaggerated, dangerous,
and belligerent chauvinism, which exalts its own people
at the cost of other nations.   In its turn this chauvinism
was fed and strengthened by the revival of the race-con-
sciousness which in Gobineau and H. St. Chamberlain
found its scientific defenders.   Not only in the different
parts of the earth, but also often among the same people,
and in the same land, races are sharply opposed to each
other, striving after the chief power in the state, and
supremacy in the kingdom of the mind.   This race-
glorification acquires such a serious character, and so far

exceeds all bounds, that the virtues of the race are identified with the highest ideal. *Deutschtum*, for example, is
placed on a level with Christendom, and Jesus is considered as an Aryan in race.[63]

Economical interests besides sharpen the competition
between the nations. Though this competition still bears
outwardly a peaceful character, it widens the gulf between the nations, feeds egoism, stimulates the passions,
and may on the smallest occasion break out into a war
which would surpass all previous wars in devastation.
From a kingdom of peace, which shall embrace all nations, we are farther away than ever. Many men have,
indeed, dreamed sweet dreams of such a peace, or at least
of a palace of peace and international arbitration; [64] but
they have been sadly undeceived, and forced into fresh
reflection by the sudden apparition of Japan. Just as
many in the state are returning to monarchy and des-
potism, and wish again to accord the first place in society
to aristocracy and capitalism, so others in international
relations defend the arming of nations, the conflict of
races, and sanguinary war. The effacement of all differences between the nations is not, according to their
opinion, the highest aim to be striven after. An amalga-
mated humanity would cause, without doubt, an impoverished civilization and a weakening of human life. Of
course race-hatred and contempt for foreigners are not
approved on this account; but it is said that strong
nations, just like strong individuals, will respect most
the rights of others and will be most merciful to their
defects. And though this diversity between nations and
races may now and then cause a war, history proves that
such a war has been a source of strength and welfare for
many peoples, and for humanity as a whole.[65] War is,

according to Moltke, an element of the world-order, as it is established by God, in which the noblest virtues of men are developed, such as courage and self-denial, faithfulness to duty, and self-sacrifice; without war the world would become a morass, and would sink into materialism.[66]

If we take into account all these facts, it is not to be wondered at that culture is often treated with deep disdain, not only by Christians, but by the children whom it has fed and nourished. There are those — and their number increases — who, with Buckle, notwithstanding the intellectual development which has taken place, do not believe in any moral progress and speak only of a circle of development.[67] Others go still farther, and are of opinion that the human race, just in consequence of culture, is retrograding physically, psychically, intellectually, morally, and socially, and that safety can be obtained only by a radical change, namely, by a return to nature, or even to the animal state in which men originally lived. The great number of reformers who appear to-day in every domain of thought and action, indeed, sufficiently shows that culture, with all its blessings, does not content the heart, and does not meet all the needs of the soul. Evolutionists and socialists, though glorying in the conquests which the man of culture has made, vie with each other in condemning present-day society, and build all their hopes on the future. But that future is distant and uncertain; for he who considers the moral corruption which has attacked our culture at the core, and takes into consideration the perils which press upon us from without, — the red, the black, and the yellow peril, — feels the anxious question rising within him, whether our whole modern culture is not destined sometime to devastation and annihilation like that of Babylon and Egypt, Greece and Rome.[68]

Thus it appears that neither science nor philosophy, neither ethics nor culture, can give that security with regard to the future which we have need of, not only for our thought, but also for our whole life and action. This need of security cannot be voided by saying that every one must do his duty and leave the future to itself. For though there is great truth in the Christian motto, " Blind for the future, and seeing in the commandment," such true resignation is not born of doubt, but of faith, and does not leave the future to itself, but to God's fatherly guidance. The need of security concerning the future and the ultimate end of the world, therefore, always remains with us, because everything we value in this life is inseparably connected with the future. If the world at the end of its development is dissolved in a chaos, or sinks back into everlasting sleep, the value of personality, of religious and ethical life, and also of culture, cannot be maintained. The weal and woe of man, and the safety of our souls, are closely interwoven with the final destiny of the world. Therefore, in order to live and to die happily we need a consolation which is firm and durable, and gives security to our thought and labor. All world-views, therefore, end in an eschatology, and all efforts at reformation are animated by faith in the future.

If neither science nor culture, nor the combination of both,[69] can give us such security, the question remains whether there is anything else in the whole world in which we can trust at all times, in adversity and death, with our whole heart? Now history teaches, with a distinctness which precludes all doubt, that there is only one power which can give such a security, and can awaken such an absolute confidence in the heart always and everywhere, and that is religion. While science can boast of only a few martyrs, religion counts its witnesses by thousands and tens of thousands. Who would be ready to sacrifice his life for a purely mathematical or scientific truth? If we wish to find the security which gives us rest in life and death and keeps us firm in the midst of the storms of doubt, we must seek it in religion, or we can find it nowhere. All certainty concerning the origin, the essence, and the end of things, is based on religion. As soon as a world-view attacks these problems, it is met by the alternative, either to content itself with guesses and doubts, or to take refuge in a religious interpretion of the world. Comte thought, indeed, that religion and metaphysics belonged to the past, but none the less made his positivism serviceable for the preaching of a new religion; and Herbert Spencer did not explain how he, in his philosophy, could accept an unknowable power behind phenomena, and could give expression to the suggestion that this power is the same as that " which in ourselves wells up in the form of consciousness." [70]

The reason why religion alone can create such a security lies at hand. First, it always includes faith in a divine power, which is distinct from the world, far above it, and can govern and guide it according to its own will; and, secondly, it puts man himself personally into connection with the divine power, so that he sees in the affairs of God his own affairs, and allied with God can defy the power of the whole world, even unto death. But this idea of religion has only come to its true and full embodiment in Christianity. For all religions which exist without the special revelation in Christ, and equally all confessions and world-views which differ from it, are characterized by this common peculiarity, that they identify God and the world, the natural and the ethical, being and evil, creation and fall, and therefore mix up religion with superstition and magic. There is only one religion which moves on pure lines and is conceived altogether as religion, and that is Christianity.

In this religion God is the creator of all things. The whole world is the work of his hands; matter itself is made by him, and before its making was the object of his thought. All being and becoming thus embody a revelation of God. This revelation is the starting point of the unity of nature, the unity of the human race, the unity of history, and is also the source of all laws, — the laws of nature, of history, and of all development. The ideas and norms which govern religious, ethical, and social life, and appear in the self-consciousness and the thought of humanity, are the product of this revelation of God. In a word, that the world is no chaos, but a cosmos, a universe, is the silent postulate of all science and art for which they are indebted to the revelation which Christianity makes known to us. Nature and grace, culture and cultus, are built upon the same foundations.

But this revelation is not sufficient. God is creator: he is further the reconciler of all things. There is much evil in the world, — natural and moral evil, sin and misery. Christianity is the one religion which connects these two kinds of evil and yet distinguishes them. Sin does not lie in matter, nor in nature, nor in the substance of things, but it belongs to the will of the creature; it is of ethical nature, and thus capable of being expiated, effaced, extinguished. It can be separated from the creature, so that it disappears and the creature remains intact, yea, much more, is restored and glorified. For God is above the world, and is also above sin and all evil. He allowed it because he could expiate it. So he maintained through all centuries and among all men the longing and the capacity for redemption, and wrought that redemption himself in the fulness of time, in the midst of history, in the crucified Christ. " God was, in Christ, reconciling the world with himself, not imputing their trespasses unto them." The cross of Golgotha is the divine settlement with, the divine condemnation of sin. There it is revealed that sin exists; it is no fiction which can be conquered by thought, no external defect which can be obliterated by culture; but it is an awful reality, and has a world-historical significance. But although it exists, it has no right of existence; it should not exist, and therefore it shall not exist.

For God is the creator and redeemer, but also finally the restorer and renewer of all things. The history of mankind after the resurrection of Christ is the execution of the judicial sentence which was passed on the cross, of the sentence which in Christ condemns sin and absolves the sinner, and therefore gives to him a right and claim to forgiveness and renewal. The cross of Christ divides history into two parts, — the preparation for and the accomplishment of reconciliation; but in both parts, from the creation to the cross and from the cross to the advent, it is one whole, one uninterrupted work of God. Christianity is as religion much more than a matter of feeling or temperament; it embraces the whole man, all humanity, and the totality of the world. It is a work of God, a revelation from the beginning to the end of the ages, in word and in deed, for mind and heart, for the individual and the community. And it has its heart and centre in the person and the work of Christ.

Christ occupies in Christianity quite a different position

from that which Zarathustra or Confucius, Buddha or
Mohammed, hold in the religion which was founded by
each of them.   Christ is not the founder of Christianity,
nor the first confessor of it, nor the first Christian.   But
he is Christianity itself, in its preparation, fulfilment, and
consummation.   He created all things, reconciled all
things, and renews all things.   Because all things have
in him their source, their being, and their unity, he
also gathers in one all things under himself as Head, both
those which are in heaven and those on earth.   He is
Prophet and Priest, but also King, who does not cease
his work until he has delivered the kingdom perfect
and complete to God the Father.

This one equally sovereign and almighty, holy, and
gracious will of God, which meets us and speaks to our
conscience in the person and the work of Christ, is the firm
basis of our certainty, of our certainty concerning the past,
the present, and the future.   For nobody can deny that if
there is and works such a will, then the origin, development, and destiny of the world are certain; then the life
and fate of every man who identifies himself with this will
of God and makes God's cause his own is assured now
and for eternity.   But the world of science and art, culture and technique, knows nothing of such a merciful will
of God.   It can advance no further, with all its thorough-
ness and sagacity, than the postulate that there must be
such a will of God.   But even this result of human
knowledge and effort is a significant fact; for it contains the confession that the whole world, with all its
development, is lost and must perish if it is not sustained and guided by an almighty will, which can cause
light to appear out of darkness, life out of death, and
glory out of suffering.   What eye has not seen, nor ear

heard, neither has entered into the heart of man to conceive otherwise than as a wish or a sigh, is revealed to us in the gospel. Jesus Christ came into the world to preserve it and to save it. This is the content of the gospel and the testimony of Scripture in spite of all criticism and opposition. By this testimony the prophets have lived, and the apostles and the whole Christian Church, and by it men will live till the end of time. For the truth of this testimony lies outside and beyond the bounds of all criticism in the system of the whole world, in the existence of the Christian church, and in the need of the human heart. The world cries: Such a will of God ought to be, if I am ever to be saved; and the gospel says: There is such a will of God; lift your eyes to the cross. Between the world as it exists around us, with all its laws and all its calamities; between culture, with all its glory and all its miseries; between the human heart, with all its aspirations and all its pains; between this whole universe and the will of God as it is made known to us in the gospel, there exists a spiritually and historically indissoluble unity. Take away that will, and the world is lost; acknowledge that will, and the world is saved. Revelation in nature and revelation in Scripture form, in alliance with each other, an harmonious unity which satisfies the requirements of the intellect and the needs of the heart alike.

This result of a philosophy of revelation is finally confirmed by this, that the will of God, which, according to the gospel, aims at the salvation of the world, yet acknowledges fully here and hereafter the diversity which exists in the world of creatures. Monism in all its forms sacrifices the richness of reality to the abstract unity of its system. It asserts that all that exists is but the development of one matter and one power; it sees in the diversity only modifications of the same being; it dissolves even the contrasts of true and false, of good and evil, of right and wrong, into historical moments of the same movement, and it concludes with the declaration that the world at the end of the process returns to chaos, to darkness and death, perhaps after a while to begin anew its monotonous round. The eschatological expectations which present themselves under the name of the restitution of all things, hypothetical or absolute universalism, and conditional immortality, also have received so much sympathy only because man closes his eyes consciously or unconsciously to reality and transforms the wishes of his heart into prophecies of the future. By the magic formulas of monism and evolution men make the world to be and to become in the past, present, and even in the future, everything they please. But reality scoffs at these phantasies; it places before us the sorrowful facts that the power of evil raises itself against good, that sin does not annihilate man, but hardens him spiritually, and that virtue and happiness, sin and punishment, are not in proportion to each other here upon earth as all hearts and consciences require. And yet since this is what really exists, it must in some way be in accordance with the holiness and goodness of God.[71]

The gospel is suited to this reality, and is quite in agreement with it; it takes and acknowledges the world exactly as it is shown to our unbiassed view; it does not fashion it after a prescribed pattern, but accepts it unprejudicedly, with all its diversities and contrasts, with all its problems and enigmas. Man is indeed what Scripture describes him, and the world appears as Scripture shows it to us. A superficial view may indeed deny it; deeper experience and more serious inquiry always lead back again to the acknowledgment of its truth; the greatest minds, the noblest souls, the most pious hearts have repeated and confirmed the witness of Scripture from age to age. Scripture therefore does not stand isolated in its contemplation of the world and life, but is surrounded, upheld, and supported on all sides by the *sensus communis* of the whole of humanity; there is neither speech nor language where its voice is not heard. The world certainly was not originated in a monistic way, and it does not exist in this way. From the beginning it has shown a great variety, which has had its origin in divine appointment. This variety has been destroyed by sin and changed into all kinds of opposition. The unity of humanity was dissolved into a multiplicity of peoples and nations. Truth, religion, and the moral law have not kept their unity and sovereignty, but are confronted by lies, false religion, and unrighteousness. So the world was, and so it still remains. In spite of all striving after unity by means of world conquest, political alliance, and international arbitration, trade unions and economical interests; in spite of the advocacy of an independent, positive, and common world-language, world-science, world-morality, and world-culture — unity has not and cannot be realized. For these forces can at the most accomplish an external and temporal unity, but they do not change the heart and do not make the people of one soul and one speech. The one true unity can only be brought about by religion, by means of missions. If there is ever to be a humanity one in heart and one in soul, then it must be born out of return to the one living and true God.

Although the gospel lays this missionary work on the

consciences of all its confessors with the greatest earnestness, yet it never flatters us with the hope that thereby the inner spiritual unity of mankind will be accomplished in the present dispensation. The idea of a millennium stands in direct opposition to the description of the future which runs through the whole of the New Testament. Jesus portrays to his disciples much rather a life of strife, oppression, and persecution. He promises them on earth not a crown, but a cross. The highest ideal for the Christian is not to make peace with the world, with science, with culture at any price, but in the world to keep himself from the evil one. We have no guarantee that the church and the world will not as fiercely strive with one another in the future as in the first centuries of Christianity. We have not the least assurance that, in spite of all preaching of tolerance, a persecution which will exceed all previous oppressions will not break out against the church of Christ before the end of time. On the contrary, there is great danger that modern culture, progressing in its anti-supernaturalistic course, will be stirred up to anger against the steadfastness of believers and attempt to accomplish by oppression what it cannot obtain by reasoning and argument. At any rate, this is what the teaching of Christ and the apostles predicts of the last days.

Because it recognizes this reality the gospel cannot end in a monistic formula; there remains difference, there remains an opposition, until and, indeed, even after the advent. Heaven and hell in what concerns their essence are no products of imagination, but elements of all religious faith, and even postulates of all thought which seriously takes into account the majesty of the moral world-order, the ineradicable consciousness of justice in the heart of man, and the indisputable witness of his conscience.[72]   But in contradistinction to all other religions Christianity teaches that the position which man will hold in the future world is, in principle, determined by the relation in which he stands to God and his revelation, and that the allotment of that position will be made by no one else than Christ, who created the world, who continually supports it in its being and unity, who is the life and light of man always and everywhere, who appeared in the fulness of time as the saviour of the world, and who therefore knows the world through and through, and can judge it in perfect justice.   Nobody will be able to make objection to the righteousness and equity of his sentence.   Whatever may be the result of the world-history, it will be acknowledged by all willingly or unwillingly, be raised above all criticism, and be consonant with God's virtues.   Right and left from the great dividing line there remains room for such endless diversity that no single idle word will be forgotten, nor will a single good thought or noble action fall unnoted.   Nothing of any value will be lost in the future; all our works do follow us, and the kings and nations of the earth will bring together into the city of God all their glory and honor.   Above all differences, and over every variety, there will extend into the future the one holy and gracious will of God, which is the bond of the whole universe, and to which all will be subject and ancillary.   The absolute, immutable, and inviolable supremacy of that will of God is the light which special revelation holds before our soul's eye at the end of time.   For monism the present economy is as a short span of life between two eternities of death, and consciousness a lightning flash in the dark night.[73]   But for the Christian this dark world is always irradiated from above by the splendor of divine revelation, and under its guidance it moves onward towards the kingdom of light and life. Round about revelation are clouds and darkness; nevertheless righteousness and judgment are the foundation of God's throne.

NOTES

I

THE IDEA OF A PHILOSOPHY OF REVELATION

[1] H. **Winckler**, Himmels- und Weltenbild der Babylonier. Leipzig, 1903, p. 9.

[2] H. **Winckler**, Die babylonische Geisteskultur. Leipzig, 1897, p. 44.

[3] **Groen van Prinsterer**, Ongeloof en Revolutie. 1862, pp. 138 ff.

[4] Fr. **Paulsen**, Philosophia militans.[2] Berlin, 1901, pp. 31 ff. J. **Kaftan**, Der Philosoph des Protest. Berlin, 1904. Theodor **Kaftan**, Moderne Theol. des alten Glaubens. 1901, pp. 76, 102.

[5] Busken **Huet**, Het Land van Rembrandt. F. **Pijper**, Erasmus en de Nederl. Reformatie. Leiden, 1907. Paul **Wernle**, Die Renaissance des Christ. im 16 Jahrh. Tübingen, 1904.

[6] **Lezius**, Zur Charakteristik des relig. Standpunktes des Erasmus. Güterslohe, 1895. H. **Hermelink**, Die relig. Reformbestrebungen des deutschen Humanismus. Tübingen, 1907 (comp. the review of this work in Theol. Lit. Zeitung, Jan. 4, 1908). Max **Richter**, Desiderius Erasmus und seine Stellung zu Luther auf Grund ihrer Schriften. Leipzig, 1907. **Hunzinger**, Der Glaube Luthers und das religionsgeschichtliche Christentum der Gegenwart. Leipzig, 1907. Hunzinger strikingly observes that the laudation of Erasmus at the expense of Luther is in keeping with the attempt perceptible elsewhere to go back from the Christ of the Bible to the so-called historical Jesus, the Jesus of the Synoptics or the Sermon on the Mount. The line repre-

sented by Christ, Paul, Augustine, Luther, and Calvin is abandoned in favor of that represented by Jesus, Pelagius, Abelard, Erasmus, the Enlightenment.

[7] **Troeltsch**, Protest. Kirchentum und Kirche in der Neuzeit, pp. 253–458 of Die Christliche Religion, in: Die Kultur der Gegenwart. (comp. for the other side **Kattenbusch**, Theol. Rundschau, 1907, and **Herrmann**, Zeits. für Theol. und Kirche, 1907). Comp. also **Karl Sell**, Katholizismus und Protestantismus. Leipzig, 1903, pp. 56 ff. **F. J. Schmidt**, Zur Wiedergeburt des Idealismus. Leipzig, 1908, pp. 60 ff.

[8] **Lechler**, Geschichte des engl. Deismus. Stuttgart, 1841. **Troeltsch**, art. Deismus in PRE.[3]

[9] **Schelling**, Philos. der Offenbarung, Sämmtliche Werke, II, 4, p. 5.

[10] **Lechler**, op. c., p. 362.

[11] **Groen van Prinsterer**, op. c.

[12] **Haller** in Groen van Prinsterer, op. c., pp. 253 ff.

[13] Comp. the author's essay: Evolutie, in: Pro en Contra, III, 3. Baarn, 1907. **Eucken**, Geistige Strömungen der Gegenwart. Leipzig, 1904, pp. 185 ff.

[14] As regards Goethe, to whom Haeckel loves to appeal, this is clearly shown by **Vogel**, Goethes Selbstzeugnisse über seine Stellung zur Religion.[3] Leipzig, 1906. Comp. also **Frank Thilly**, The World-view of a Poet: Goethe's Philosophy, in the Hibbert Journal, April, 1908, pp. 530 ff.

[15] **Windelband**, Geschichte der neueren Philosophie. Leipzig, 1899, II, p. 311.

[16] **Bruno Wille**, Darwins Weltanschauung von ihm selbst dargestellt. Heibronn, 1906, pp. 4, 5, 16 ff., 25.

[17] **Bruno Wille**, op. c., pp. 5, 23.

[18] **L. Woltmann**, Der hist. Materialismus. Düsseldorf, 1906, p. 148. **H. Pesch**, Liberalismus, Sozialismus und christl. Gesellschaftsordnung. Freiburg, 1901, II, p. 234.

[19] **Bruno Wille**, op. c., pp. 7, 12, 14, 16, 17, 19, 23, 25.

[20] For instance by **von Hartmann**, Religions-philosophie. Leipzig, II, pp. 74 ff. **A. Drews**, Die Religion als Selbstbe-

wusstsein Gottes. Jena u. Leipzig, 1906, pp. 184 ff. J.
Reinke, Die Welt als That.[3] Berlin, 1903, pp. 292 ff.

[21] **R. J. Campbell**, The New Theology. London, 1907,
pp. 20, 31, 34, 68 ff. New Theology and Applied Religion by
R. J. Campbell, etc. London, Christian Commonwealth Co.,
pp. 12, 18, 60, 62. **Sir Oliver Lodge,** The Substance of Faith
allied with Science.[3] London, pp. 85 ff. Comp. against this
new theology among others, **Charles Gore**, The New Theology
and the Old Religion. London, 1907.

[22] **Funt**, Religion der Immanenz oder Transcendenz ? in:
Religion und Geisteskultur, 1907, pp. 287–294. **Bachmann**,
Nomen est gloriosum, ib., 1908, pp. 104–114.

[23] **Haeckel**, Der Monismus als Band zwischen Religion
und Wissenschaft.[6] Bonn, 1893. **Haeckel**, Die Welträthsel.
Bonn, 1899, pp. 381–439. **R. H. Francé**, Der heutige Stand
der darwin'schen Lehren. Leipzig, 1907, p. 17.

[24] **Troeltsch**, op. c., p. 255.

[25] **Fr. Delitzsch**, Babel und Bibel. Ein Rückblick und
Ausblick. Berlin, 1904, p. 48. Id., Zur Weiterbildung der
Religion. Stuttgart, 1908, p. 53.

[26] **Hegel**, Philos. der Religion, I, p. 120.

[27] **Gwatkin**, The Knowledge of God. Edinburgh, 1906, I,
pp. 92, 155–156, 248.

[28] **Titius**, Theol. Rundschau, Nov., 1907, p. 416. The address of **Loofs** to which Titius refers, appeared in English in
the American Journal of Theol., III, pp. 433–472, and has
been published recently also in German : Das Evangelium
der Reformation und die Gegenwart, Theol. Stud. u. Krit.,
1908, pp. 203–244. **Kattenbusch**, Die Lage der system.
Theol. in der Gegenwart, Zeits. für Theol. u. Kirche, 1905,
pp. 103–146 ff., especially pp. 128 ff.

[29] **Steinmann**, Das Bewusstsein von der vollen Wirklichkeit Gottes, Zeits. für Theol. u. Kirche, 1902, pp. 429–492.

[80] Of the many works dealing with the subject directly or
incidentally the following may be named by way of example : **Schelling**, Philosophie der Offenbarung. **Staudenmaier**,
Philos. des Christ., I, 1840. **O. Willmann**, Gesch. des Idealismus, 3 Bde, 1894–1897. **James Orr**, The Christian View of

God and the World. Edinburgh, 1893. **John Caird**, The Fundamental Ideas of Christianity, 2 vols. Glasgow, 1904. **A. M. Fairbairn**, The Philosophy of the Christian Religion.[4] London, 1905. **A. Campbell Fraser**, Philosophy of Theism.[2] Edinburgh, 1899.

[31] **Schelling**, l. c., p. 26. For the conception of revelation which it was impossible to unfold in these lectures reference may be made to the author's Gereformeerde Dogmatiek, 2d ed., I, pp. 291 ff. The present lectures elaborate in detail the fundamental ideas expressed by the author in an address on Christelijke Wereldbeschouwing, 1904.

II

REVELATION AND PHILOSOPHY

[1] **Renan**, L'avenir de la science, 1890. **Berthelot**, Science et morale, 1897. **Ladenburg**, Der Einfluss der Naturwissenschaft auf die Weltanschauung, 1903.

[2] **Haeckel**, Die Welträthsel. 1899, pp. 345 ff.

[3] **A. M. Weisz**, Die religiöse Gefahr. Freiburg, 1904, pp. 117 ff.

[4] **L. Stein**, Gedankenanarchie, in : An der Wende des Jahrhunderts, 1899, pp. 287 ff. **Ed. von Hartmann**, Religionsphilosophie, I, pp. 624 ff. **A. Drews**, Die Religion als Selbstbew. Gottes. 1906, pp. 237 ff.

[5] **Paulsen**, Einl. in die Philosophie, Vorwort. **Paulsen**, Die Zukunftsaufgaben der Philos., pp. 389 ff., in Systematische Philosophie, in : Die Kultur der Gegenwart, 1907.

[6] **Troeltsch**, Die Absolutheit des Christ. und die Religionsgeschichte. 1902, p. 56. Comp. **A. Vierkandt**, Die Stetigkeit im Kulturwandel. Leipzig, 1908, pp. 1 ff.

[7] According to the well-known saying of **Ledru-Rollin** : Je suis votre chef, il faut donc que je vous suive.

[8] In **Dilthey**, Das Wesen der Philos., p. 37, in System. Philos., in : Die Kultur der Gegenwart.

[9] **J. B. Meyer**, Philos. Zeitfragen. 1870, p. 92. Comp. further on the history of Darwinism after Darwin and its critics: **Ed. von Hartmann**, Der Darwinismus seit Darwin, in Ostwald's Annalen der Naturphilos. Leipzig, 1903, pp. 285 ff. **R. H. Francé**, Der heutige Stand der darwin'schen Fragen. Leipzig, 1907. **H. Meyer**, Der gegenwärtige Stand der Entwicklungslehre. Bonn, 1908. **A. R. Wallace**, The Present Position of Darwinism, Cont. Review, Aug., 1908.

[10] **Dennert**, Die Weltanschauung des modernen Naturforschers. Stuttgart, 1907, pp. 60 ff. **Ed. von Hartmann**, Die Weltanschauung der modernen Physik. Leipzig, 1902. **Ludwig Baur**, Der gegenwärtige Stand der Philos., in: Philos. Jahrbuch, 1907, pp. 1–21, 156–177, especially pp. 164 ff. **A. Schneider**, Der moderne deutsche Spiritualismus, Philos. Jahrbuch, 1908, pp. 339–357.

[11] **Ostwald**, Die Ueberwindung des wissensch. Materialismus. Leipzig, 1895. Id., Vorlesungen über die Naturphilos.,[8] 1905. Comp. on Ostwald: **Dennert**, op. c., pp. 222 ff. **W. von Schnehen**, Energetische Weltanschauung. Leipzig, 1908.

[12] Comp. on this tendency especially **Mach**, Populärwiss. Vorlesungen, Leipzig, 1897. Id., Erkenntnis und Irrtum., Leipzig, 1905. Also the exposition of Mach's philosophy by **Hönigswald**, Zur Kritik der machschen Philos., Berlin, 1903, and **Hell**, Ernst Machs Philosophie., Stuttgart, 1907. The following may also be consulted: **Spruyt**, Het empiriocriticisme, de jongste vorm van de wijsbegeerte der ervaring. Amsterdam, 1899. **Koster**, De ontkenning van het bestaan der materie en de moderne physiol. psychologie. Haarlem, 1904. **Jelgersma**, Modern Positivisme, Gids, Oct., 1904. **Wobbermin**, Theologie und Metaphysik. Berlin, 1901. **Schapira**, Erkenntnisstheor. Strömungen der Gegenwart. Bern, 1904.

[13] **Max Verworn**, Natur- und Weltanschauung. Leipzig, 1905. Id., Principienfragen in der Natur. Jena, 1905. Id., Die Mechanik des Geisteslebens. Leipzig, 1908, pp. 1–20. Comp. **Dennert**, op. c., pp. 130 ff. As a result of this criticism of the faculty of knowledge modern science has once more become conscious of its limitations. Not only have

Duboise-Reymond in his Sieben Welträthsel and **Balfour** in his Foundations of Belief expressed themselves to this effect, but the same views in regard to the limitations of science, and even its exclusively empirical character, are taken by **H. Poincaré**, La science et l'hypothèse; Id., La valeur de la science; **L. Poincaré**, La physique moderne; and others whose works have appeared in the Bibliothèque de philosophie scientifique under the editorship of **G. le Bon.** Comp. **Gustave Dumas**, Réflexions sur la science contemporaine, Foi et Vie, 16 Dec., 1907, pp. 752–759.

[14] **H. Cohen**, Religion und Sittlichkeit. Berlin, 1907. **P. Natorp**, Religion innerhalb der Grenzen der Humanität. Freiburg, 1894. Comp. **Ueberweg-Heinze**, Gesch. der Philos., III, 2, 1897, pp. 198 ff.

[15] **Rickert**, Der Gegenstand der Erkenntniss.[2] Tübingen, 1904. Id., Geschichtsphilosophie, pp. 51–145, of: Die Philosophie im Beginn des 20 Jahrh. Heidelberg, 1905, especially pp. 110 ff. **Heymans**, Einführung in die Metaphysik auf Grundlage der Erfahrung. Leipzig, 1905, pp. 224, 293.

[16] **Eisler**, Wörterbuch der philos. Begriffe s. v.; further: Der Monismus, dargestellt in Beiträgen seiner Vertreter. Herausgeg. v. **Arthur Drews.** I. Systematisches, II. Historisches. Jena, 1900.

[17] **Reinke**, Die Welt als That.[3] Berlin, 1903, p. 457.

[18] **Sir Oliver Lodge**, Life and Matter.[4] London, 1907. Comp. also: **Fr. Traub**, Zur Kritik des Monismus, Zeits. für Theol. u. K., May, 1908, pp. 157–180. **O. Flügel**, Monismus und Theologie. Cöthen, 1908.

[19] **L. Reinhardt**, Der Mensch zur Eiszeit in Europa. München, 1906, p. 2. **Haeckel**, Die Welträthsel. 1899, p. 6. Id., Der Kampf um den Entwicklungsgedanken. Berlin, 1905, pp. 13 ff. **L. Stein**, An der Wende des Jahrh. Freiburg, 1899, pp. 47 ff. **C. Stumpf**, Der Entwicklungsgedanke in der gegenwärtigen Philosophie, 1899.

[20] Rümelin in **de la Saussaye**, Geestelijke Stroomingen, Haarlem, 1907, p. 288, well says: " The idea of evolution must itself first be explained, before anything is explained by it," but — what cannot be explained is looked upon as

evolution. Eyes are being opened, however, to the abuse
made of the word. Comp. **Lexis**, Das Wesen der Kultur,
in: Die Kultur der Gegenwart, I. pp. 13–19. **H. Schurtz,**
Altersklassen und Männerbünde. Berlin, 1902, pp. 6 ff., 69.
Steinmetz, De studie der volkenkunde. 's Gravenhage, 1907,
pp. 30 ff.

[21] **Lodge,** Life and Matter, pp. 6, 7.

[22] **James,** Pragmatism, a New Name for Some Old Ways of
Thinking. Longmans, Green & Co., 1907, pp. 9 ff.

[23] Comp. an article by **Prof. F. J. E. Woodbridge,** Naturalism and Humanism, Hibbert Journal, 1907, pp. 1–17. **L.
Stein,** Der Sinn des Daseins. Tübingen, 1904, pp. 22 ff.

[24] **Höffding,** Philosophy of Religion. London, 1906, p. 381,
reviewed in Review of Theol. and Philos., Nov., 1907, p. 318.

[25] The idea that man's physical evolution has reached its
climax, and that henceforward it depends on him to direct
with his mind the further development and to create a new
world, occurs in many writers: **H. Schurtz,** Urgeschichte
der Kultur., 1900, Vorwort, and pp. 3 ff. **Stanley Hall,** Adolescence, 2 vols. London, 1905, I, preface. **Henry Demarest
Lloyd,** Man the Social Creator. London, 1906, p. 15. In
the last-mentioned work occur, for example, the following
statements: The laborer is the creator, he is the remaker of
man, nature, and society, p. 12. As labor is creation, by
labor men are divine and become godlike, p. 13. Every
good man (is) a creator and redeemer, p. 32. Man is a
possible God, p. 25. Man is not under the law, he creates
the law, p. 41. The creature is the creator, every creature.
Man is not *the* creator, nor the creator of all, but he is the
greatest creator we know on earth. He is the creator of
himself and society, p. 42, etc.

[26] **James,** Pragmatism, pp. 122, 127, 162, 243, 257.

[27] **James,** op. c. Comp. on the related French philosophy
of Ravaisson, Boutroux, Bergson, Le Roy, and others, an
article by **George M. Sauvage,** New Philosophy in France,
Catholic University Bulletin, April, 1906; **J. de Tonquédec,**
La notion de la vérité dans la philosophie nouvelle. Paris,
1908. **G. Rageot,** Les savants et la philosophie. Paris, 1908.

III

REVELATION AND PHILOSOPHY — *continued*

[1] **James**, Mind, 1905, p. 191.

[2] **James**, Mind, 1905, pp. 194–195.

[3] **James**, Pragmatism, pp. 52, 162 ff., 242, 264 ff., also in his article, Does Consciousness Exist? in Journal of Philosophy. New York, Sept., 1904.

[4] **Ed. von Hartmann**, Kritische Wanderungen durch die Philosophie der Gegenwart. 1890, p. 190, in: C. Willems, Die Erkenntnisslehre des modernen Idealismus. Trier, 1906, p. 13. Comp. also **Max Frischeisen-Köhler**, Die Lehre von den Sinnesqualitäten und ihre Gegner, Zeits. f. Wissensch. Philos. und Soziologie, 1906.

[5] **Paulsen**, Einl. in die Philosophie. Berlin, 1892, p. 363. **Verworn** in Dennert, Die Weltanschauung des modernen Naturforschers, p. 147.

[6] So **Helmholtz, von Hartmann**, and others, in: C. Willems, Die Erkenntnislehre des mod. Ideal, pp. 42 ff.

[7] **E. L. Fischer**, Die Grundfragen der Erkenntnisstheorie. 1887, p. 424.

[8] **Paulsen**, in Willems, op. c., p. 103.

[9] **Verworn**, Naturwissenschaft und Weltanschauung. 1904, p. 43. Comp. **Mach**. in **Hell**, Ernst Machs Philosophie. 1907, p. 23. **Heijmans**, Het Ik en het psychisch Monisme, Tijdschr. voor Wijsbegeerte, I, 3.

[10] **Stuart Mill**, in Willems, op. c., p. 79.

[11] **John McTaggart Ellis McTaggart**, Some Dogmas of Religion. London, 1906, p. 108. Over against idealism the unity and independence of the ego are upheld by **Landmann**, Die Mehrheit geistiger Persönlichkeiten in einem Individuum, 1894. **Gutberlet**, Der Kampf um die Seele. Mainz, 1903, pp. 121 ff. **Rudolf Otto**, Naturalistiche und religiöse Weltansicht. Tübingen, 1904, pp. 244 ff.

[12] Comp. **Dilthey**, Einleitung in die Geisteswissenschaften. Leipzig, 1883, pp. 322 ff. **Warfield**, Augustine's

Doctrine of Knowledge and Authority.   Princeton Theol.
Review, July and Oct., 1907.

[13] James, Pragmatism, pp. 165 ff.

[14] Mr. H. W. B. Joseph, in Mind, 1905, p. 33.

[15] Flügel, Die Probleme der Philosophie.[4] Cöthen, 1906,
pp. 114–115.

[16] Paul Kalweit, Das religiöse Apriori, Theol. Stud. u. Krit.
1908, I, pp. 139–156.

[17] Paulsen, Einl. in die Philos. 1892, p. 425.

[18] In Willems, op. c., pp. 36–47. Comp. also Bradley, Appearance and Reality,[2] London, 1906, pp. 11 ff., and further
the article by Frischeisen-Köhler, cited in note 4 above.

[19] Verworn, in Dennert, op. c., p. 140.

[20] Comp. G. E. Moore, Refutation of Idealism, Mind, N. S.
n. 48, and, in answer, C. A. Strong, Has Mr. Moore refuted
Idealism? Mind, 1905, pp. 178–189. Further, J. S. Mac-
kenzie, The New Realism and the Old Idealism. Mind,
1906, pp. 308–328.

[21] Ed. von Hartmann, in Willems, op. c., pp. 56–79.

[22] Dilthey, Einl. in die Geisteswissenschaften, pp. 26–48.

[23] James, Pragmatism, p. 257.

IV

REVELATION AND NATURE

[1] A. C. Fraser, Philosophy of Theism.   1899, pp. 24–34.

[2] Mach, Erkenntniss und Irrtum., p. 5.

[3] Ladd, The Philosophy of Religion, I, 1906, p. 11.
Gwatkin, The Knowledge of God, I, 1906.

[4] Frischeisen-Köhler, Moderne Philosophie.   Stuttgart,
1907, pp. 18–37. L. Stein, Der Sinn des Daseins, pp. 225–
239.

[5] Otto, Natural. und relig. Weltansicht, p. 44.

[6] Haeckel, Die Welträthsel, p. 209. Id., Der Kampf um
den Entwicklungsgedanken, p. 23. Comp. Otto, op. c.,
pp. 78, 112 ff., 200 ff.

[7] Ed. von Hartmann, Mechanismus und Vitalismus in der

modernen Biologie, Archiv f. syst. Philos., 1903, p. 345. Id.,
Philos. des Unbew., III. 1904, p. vi.

[8] **Ostwald**, Die Ueberwindung des wissensch. Materialismus., 1895, in Dennert, op. c., pp. 235-236.

[9] **Reinke**, Die Welt als That,[3] pp. 464 ff.

[10] **Otto**, op. c., pp. 39, 46, 47.

[11] **Alfred Dippe**, Naturphilosophie. München, 1907,
pp. 3-14.

[12] **L. Stein**, Der Sinn des Daseins, p. 24.

[13] **Haeckel**, Schöpfungsgeschichte.[5] 1874, p. 8. Comp.
Die Welträthsel, p. 15.

[14] **Haeckel**, Schöpfungsgesch., p. 28. Welträthsel, p. 18.

[15] **Lodge**, Life and Matter, p. 23.

[16] **Bradley**, Appearance and Reality, ch. IV, pp. 35 ff.

[17] **Otto**, op. c., pp. 50-57.

[18] **Lipps**, Naturwissenschaft und Weltanschauung. 1906,
p. 13.

[19] **Ed. von Hartmann**, Die Weltanschauung der modernen
Physik, pp. 195, 197 ff., 204 ff. **Dennert**, Die Weltanschauung des mod. Naturforschers, p. 143.

[20] **Fechner**, Ueber die Seelenfrage.[2] 1907, p. 214. Comp.
also **Bradley**, op. c., ch. II, pp. 25 ff.

[21] **Shentone**, The Electric Theory of Matter, in Cornhill
Magazine, quoted in The Literary World, Aug., 1907,
p. 381. Comp. also **A. J. Balfour**, Unsere heutige Weltanschauung. Einige Bemerkungen zur modernen Theorie der
Materie. Deutsch von Dr. M. Ernst. Leipzig, 1904. **M.
Shoen**, Bestaat er een oer-grondstof? Wet. Bladen, May,
1908, pp. 249-259, after an essay in Naturwiss. Wochenschrift, 2 Febr., 1908. **Reinke**, Die Natur und Wir. Berlin,
1908, p. 38.

[22] **Dippe**, Naturphilosophie, pp. 86, 89.

[23] **Rethwisch**, in Dippe, pp. 79 ff. **Reinke**, op. c., pp. 40-50.
Th. Newest, Die Gravitationslehre ein Irrtum. Wien, 1905.
For the various views on Vital Force the reader is referred
to the article by von Hartmann, quoted above in note 7, and
further to **Karl Braeunig**, Mechanismus und Vitalismus in der
Biologie des neunzehnten Jahrhunderts. Leipzig, 1907.

NOTES# NOTES 327

[24] **W. von Sohnehen,** Die Urzeugung, Glauben und Wissen. Dec., 1907, pp. 403–415.

[25] **Otto,** op. c., p. 37.

[26] **Kant,** in Eisler, Wörterbuch,[2] p. 618.

[27] **Haeckel,** Die Welträthsel, pp. 15–16.

[28] **Lodge,** Life and Matter, p. 49. **Reinke,** Die Natur und Wir, pp. 25, 26, 33.

[29] **Kleutgen,** Die Philosophie der Vorzeit,[2] II, pp. 314–335.

[30] **Von Hartmann,** Die Weltanschauung, etc., p. 203.

[31] **R. Schmid,** Das naturwiss. Glaubensbekenntnis eines Theologen. Stuttgart, 1906, p. 87.

[32] **Haeckel,** Welträthsel, pp. 117–118.

[33] **Lodge,** Life and Matter, pp. 54 ff. Comp. also **J. Froehlich,** Das Gesetz von der Erhaltung der Kraft in dem Geist des Christ. Leipzig, 1903.

[34] **Bruno Wille,** Darwins Weltanschauung, etc. Comp. Lect. I, note 16 ff.

[35] In **K. Dieterich,** Philosophie und Naturwissenschaft. Freiburg, 1885, p. 9.

[36] **Haeckel,** Welträthsel, pp. 342, 404, 405.

[37] **Haeckel,** op. c., pp. 388 ff., 439. Nat. Schöpf., pp. 156, 656. **L. Stein,** An der Wende des Jahrh., p. 51. Id., Der Sinn des Daseins, pp. 42 ff. **Dippe,** Naturphilos, p. 153. **Reinke,** Die Natur und Wir, pp. 209 ff.

[38] **Dr. W. H. Nieuwhuis,** Twee vragen des Tijds. Kampen, 1907, pp. 39, 66.

[39] **Ed. von Hartmann,** Die Weltanschauung, etc., p. 203.

[40] **Lipps,** Naturwiss. und Weltanschauung, p. 19.

[41] **Ritter,** Schets eener critische geschiedenis van het Substantiebegrip in de nieuwere wijsbegeerte. Leiden, 1906, p. 471.

[42] Natur und Christenthum, Vier Vorträge von **D. Lasson, Lütgert, Schäder, Bornhäuser.** Berlin, 1907, pp. 49 ff. **Richard Hamann,** Der Impressionismus in Leben und Kunst. Köln, 1907.

[43] **Smend,** Lehrbuch der altt. Religionsgeschichte. 1893, p. 458. **Martensen Larsen,** Die Naturwiss. in ihrem Schuldverhältnis zum Christenthum. Berlin, 1897. **Lange,** Gesch.

des Materialismus. 1882, pp. 129 ff. **Sellin**, Die alttest.
Religion und die Religionsgeschichte, pp. 28–34.

[44] **James**, The Varieties of Religious Experience. 1906,
p. 525. Id., Pluralism and Religion, Hibbert Journal, July,
1908. **Wundt**, Völkerpsych., II, 2, p. 223. **McTaggart**,
Some Dogmas of Religion, pp. 257 ff. **Rogers**, according to
Hibbert Journal, Jan., 1908, p. 445. Comp. Dr. Rashdall,
who denies to God omnipotence; Dr. Harrison, who denies
him even creation (in **McTaggart**, p. 221, note), and the so-
called "ethical modernists" in the Netherlands, who distinguish between God as nature-power and as ethical power.
Hooijkaas, God in de geschiedenis. Schiedam, 1870, p. 35.
Goethe already said : " I cannot satisfy myself in the manifold tendencies of my being with one mode of thinking : as
poet and artist I am a polytheist, but on the other hand a
pantheist as a student of nature, and one just as decisively as
the other. If I need a God for my personality as a moral
being, this also is already provided for. "

[45] In **Nieuwhuis**, op. c., p. 82.

[46] **Lange**, Gesch. des Material., p. 130.

[47] **Paul Grünberg**, Das Uebel in der Welt und Gott. Lichter-
felde, 1907. **Bruining**, Het geloof aan God en het kwaad in
de wereld. Baarn, 1907.

[48] Hibbert Journal, Oct., 1907, p. 9.

V

REVELATION AND HISTORY

[1] On these various tendencies the reader may consult : **R.
Flint**, History of the Philosophy of History in France and
Germany, I, 1893. **Rocholl**, Die Philosophie der Geschichte,
1878, 1893. **M. Giesswein**, Determin. und metaph. Geschichtsauffassung. Wien, 1905. **Fr. Oppenheimer**, Neue
Geschichtsphilosophie, Die Zukunft, Nov., 1905. **Fr. Eulenburg**, Neuere Geschichtsphilosophie, Archiv. f. Sozialwiss.
und Sozialpolitik, 1907, pp. 283–337. **Colenbrander**, He-

dendaagsche Geschiedschrijvers,Gids, May, 1907 pp. 319, 341.
P. Schweizer, Die religiöse Auffassung der Weltgeschichte.
Zürich, 1908.

[2] The appointment of Prof. M. Spahn at Strassburg in
1901 furnished a striking proof of this.

[3] **Mind**, Oct., 1907 pp. 506–534.

[4] **H. Pesch**, Liberalismus, Sozialismus und christl. Ge-
sellschaftsordnung,[2] II, 1901, pp. 283 ff. **L. Stein**, Die soziale
Frage im Lichte der Philos.[2] Stuttgart, 1903, p. 47. **R. Elsler**,
Soziologie. Leipzig, 1903, pp. 40–45.

[5] **L. Stein**, An der Wende des Jahrh., p. 50, enters a protest.

[6] **Hugo de Vries**, Afstammings- en Mutatieleer. Baarn,
1907, p. 35.

[7] In **Nieuwhuis**, Twee vragen des tijds, p. 77.

[8] **Lexis**, Das Wesen der Kultur, in Die Kultur der Gegenwart, I, pp. 13–19.

[9] **Dr. E. R. Lankester**, Natur und Mensch, Mit einer
Vorrede von Dr. K. Guenther. Leipzig, pp. xi ff., 28.

[10] **Lamprecht**, Die Kulturhist. Methode. Berlin, 1900. Id.,
Moderne Geschichtswiss., 1905. Compare on him the above
mentioned articles of **Eulenburg** and **Colenbrander**; also **H.
Pesch**, Lehrbuch der Nationaloekonomie, I, 1905, pp. 95 ff.

[11] **Dilthey**, Einl. in die Geisteswiss., pp. 39, 51.

[12] **Dilthey**, ib., p. 115.

[13] **Theob. Ziegler**, Die geistigen und sozialen Strömungen
des 19 Jahrh. Berlin, 1901, pp. 1 ff. **H. St. Chamberlain**,
Die Grundlagen des 19 Jahrh.,[4] 1903, I, pp. 26 ff.

[14] **Ranke**, Ueber die Epochen der neueren Geschichte,
1888, quoted by de la Saussaye, Geestel. Stroomingen,
pp. 301 ff. Comp. also **H. Pesch**, Der Gang der wirtschafts-
gesch. Entwicklung, Stimmen aus Maria Laach, Jan., 1903,
pp. 1–16, and Lehrbuch der Nationaloekonomie, I, pp. 107 ff.

[15] The following writers deal with the subject of laws of
history : **L. Stein**, Die soziale Frage, pp. 35–42. **Elsler**, Soziologie, p. 12. **Rümelin**, Reden und Aufsätze, 1875. **Tiele**,
Inleiding tot de godsdienstwetenschap, I,[2] pp. 193 ff. **H.
Pesch**, Lehrbuch, I, pp. 443 ff. **Dilthey**, Einl. in die Geistes-

wiss., I, 1883. **Gumplovicz**, Grundriss der Sozologie.² Wien, 1905, pp. 361 ff.

[16] **Dilthey** op. c., p. 145. **Windelband**, Geschichte und Naturwissenchaft.² Strassburg, 1900. **Rickert**, Kulturwiss. und Naturw. Tübingen, 1899. Id., Die Grenzen der naturw. Begriffsbildung. Tübingen, 1902 (cf. **Troeltsch**, Theol. Rundschau, 1903). Id., Geschichtsphilosophie, in: Die Philosophie im Beginn des 20 Jahrh., II, pp. 51–135. **Eucken**, Philosophie der Geschichte, pp. 247–280 of System. Philos. in Die Kultur der Gegenwart. **Lindner**, Geschichtsphilos. Stuttgart, 1901. **Richter**, Die Vergleichbarkeit naturwissenschaftlicher und geschichtlicher Forschungsereignisse, Deutsche Rundschau, April, 1904, pp. 114–129. **G. Heymans**, De geschiedenis als wetenschap, Versl. en Meded. der Kon. Ak. v. Wet. Afd. Lett. 1906, pp. 173–202. **Van der Wijck**, Natuur en Geschiedenis, Onze Eeuw, March, 1907, pp. 419–445.

[17] **Frischeisen-Köhler**, Moderne Philos., pp. 385 ff.

[18] **Eucken**, Philos. der Gesch., l. c. pp. 261 ff.

[19] **Marx** in **Woltmann**, Der histor. Materialismus, p. 183, comp. **Engels**, ib. p. 241.

[20] **Rickert**, Geschichtsphilos., l. c. p. 104.

[21] **Dilthey**, Einleitung, pp. 114–116, 129.

[22] **Frischeisen-Köhler**, Moderne Philos., p. 385.

[23] **Heymans**, De geschiedenis als wetenschap, l. c. p. 185.

[24] **Heymans**, ib. p. 182.

[25] In **Frischeisen-Köhler**, op. c. p. 202.

[26] **Troeltsch**, Die Absolutheit des Christ., pp. 50 ff.

[27] **Buckle** in Giesswein, Determ. und metaph. Gesch., p. 6.

[28] **Troeltsch**, op. c., pp. 23 ff. Id., Theol. Rundschau, VI. pp. 1–3.

[29] **Rickert**, Geschichtsphilos., l. c. p. 82.

[30] **Troeltsch**, op. c. Comp. **Reischle**, Hist. u. dogm. Methode der Theologie, Theol. Rundschau, 1901. **Traub**, Die religionsgesch. Methode und die syst. Theol., Zeits. für Theol. u. Kirche, 1901.

[31] **Rickert**, Geschichtsphilos., l. c. p. 131.

[32] **Eucken**, Philos d. Gesch., l. c. p. 271. In this class must

be reckoned in general all advocates of so-called Personal
Idealism. Comp. Personal Idealism, ed. by **H. C. Sturt,**
Oxford, 1902.

[33] **Rickert,** l. c. p. 121.

[34] **Dilthey,** Einl. in die Geisteswiss., pp. 123, 135 ff.
Eucken, Geistige Strömungen der Gegenwart. Leipzig, 1904,
pp. 190 ff. **Hipler,** Die christliche Geschichtsauffassung.
Köln, 1884. **Harnack.** Das Christentum und die Geschichte,
1904. **Sellin,** Die alttest. Religion, pp. 34 ff. **Fairbairn,**
The Philos. of the Christian Religion, pp. 169–185. **H. H.**
Kuyper, Het Geref. beginsel en de Kerkgeschiedenis.
Leiden, 1900.

[35] **H. Schurtz,** Völkerkunde. Leipzig und Wien, 1903, p. 5.
Steinmetz, De Studie der Volkenkunde, p. 46

[36] **Hugo de Vries,** Afstammings- en Mutatieleer, pp. 35,
36. **Schurtz,** Urgesch. der Kultur, 1900, Vorwort. **Wundt,**
Völker-psychologie, II, 1, pp. 16, 587 ff., 589, II, 2, pp. 168.
Steinthal, Zu Bibel und Religionsphilosophie. Berlin, 1890,
p. 128. **R. C. Boer,** Gids, Jan., 1907, p. 83. **Stanley Hall,**
Adolescence, I, preface, p. vii.

[37] **Eucken,** Geschichtsphilos., l. c. p. 40.

[38] **Heymans,** De geschiedenis als wetenschap, l. c. p. 191,
194. Comp. also **Emerson's** Essay on History.

[39] **Eucken,** Geistige Strömungen, p. 190.

[40] **H. H. Kuyper,** op. c. p. 19.

[41] **Dilthey,** Einleitung p. 41.

VI

REVELATION AND RELIGION

[1] **George Trumbull Ladd,** The Philosophy of Religion.
London, I, 1905, pp. 138 ff. **Gutberlet,** Der Mensch, sein
Ursprung und seine Entwicklung.[2] Paderborn, 1903,
pp. 522 ff.

[2] **Tiele,** Inl. tot de Godsdienstwet., I, pp. 141 ff.

[3] Het Vraagstuk van den Godsdienst, Ontbinding of Evo-

lutie, beantwoord door de grootste Denkers der Wereld.　Amsterdam, 1908, pp. 5, 10, 79, 80, 84, 90, 106, 115, 117, 119, 121, 197, 289, 316.

[4] Ibid., pp. 13, 21, 57, 59, 99, 212, 252, 290, 301.

[5] Ibid., pp. 21, 79.

[6] **Ladd**, op. c., I, pp. 120 ff.

[7] **Morris Jastrow**, in Tiele, Inleiding tot de Godsdienstwet., II, pp. 219.

[8] Het Vraagstuk van den Godsdienst, etc., pp. 34, 112 ff.

[9] **Dilthey**, Einl. in die Geisteswiss., pp. 170, 184, 185.

[10] **Lubbock**, Entstehung der Civilisation. Deutsche Ausgabe, 1875, p. 172.

[11] **Dilthey**, op. c. pp. 168, 172.

[12] **Oscar Hertwig**, Das biogenetische Grundgesetz, Intern. Wochenschrift f. Wissenschaft, Kunst und Technik, April 20, 1907, pp. 97, 98.

[13] **L. Stein**, Die soziale Frage, pp. 38, 63, 105, 107.

[14] **Lehmann**, Die Anfänge der Religion und die Religion der primitiven Völker, in Die Kultur der Gegenwart, I, III, p. 1.　**Troeltsch**, Die Christl. Religion, ib., p. 483.　**Tiele**, Inleiding, II, p. 183.　**Pfleiderer**, Religion und Religionen. München, 1906, p. 53.

[15] **Haeckel**, Der Kampf um den Entwickelungsgedanken, pp. 56, 70.　Haeckel is sometimes more modest and refers to his " Stammesgeschichte " as an "hypothetical structure," because the empirical records underlying it remain to a high degree defective ; comp. **H. Meyer**, Der gegenwärtige Stand der Entwickelungslehre, pp. 59, 60.

[16] **Reinke**, Die Entw. der Naturwiss. insbes. der Biologie im 19 Jahrh., 1900, pp. 19, 20.　Id., Die Natur und Wir. Berlin, 1907, pp. 151 ff.　**Branco** in **Wasmann**, Die moderne Biologie und die Entwickelungslehre,[2] 1904, pp. 302, 304.

[17] **Stanley Hall**, Adolescence, II, p. 91.　**H. Meyer**, op. c., p. 71.　**Lankester**, Natur und Mensch, p. 24.　**Dr. H. C. Stratz**, Wij stammen *niet* van de apen af.　Baarn, 1907, p. 23.

[18] **Wasmann**, op. c., p. 295.

[19] **Prof. Dr. C. Ph. Sluiter**, Het Experiment in Dienst der Morphologie.　Amsterdam, 1907.

[20] Oscar Hertwig, Das biogenetische Grundgesetz nach dem heutigen Stand der Biologie, Intern. Wochenschrift, April 13 and 20, 1907, p. 93. Most botanists, zoölogists, and palæontologists are at present believers in polyphyletic development. H. Meyer, Der gegenw. Stand der Entwickelungslehre, pp. 50 ff. Reinke, Die Natur und Wir, pp. 126 ff., 139 ff. Wasmann, Der Kampf um das Entwickelungsproblem in Berlin. Freiburg, 1907.

[21] Stanley Hall, Adolescence, I, pp. 35, 45, 49. Stratz, op. c., p. 17.

[22] Gutberlet, Der Mensch, sein Ursprung und seine Entwickelung.[2] Paderborn, 1903.

[23] Stanley Hall, Adolescence, I, p. 107; II, p. 67.

[24] Ib. I, p. 55.

[25] Ib. II, p. 568.

[26] Ib. I, p. 241.

[27] Fr. Ratzel, Völkerkunde, 3 Bde. Leipzig, 1885, I, p. 5.

[28] Schneider, Die Naturvölker, 2 Bde., 1885, 1886. Gutberlet, op. c., pp. 380 ff., 412 ff. 474 ff. Froberger, Die Schöpfungsgesch. der Menschheit in der voraussetzungslosen Völkerpsychologie. Trier, 1903.

[29] Steinmetz, De Studie der Volkenkunde, p. 31.

[30] Wundt, Völkerpsychologie, II, 2, 1906, p. 150.

[31] Steinmetz, op. c., p. 41.

[32] Orr, God's Image in Man. London, 1906, pp. 163 ff.

[33] Steinmetz, op. c., pp. 32 ff. Fr. Ratzel, op. c., I, p. 10. H. J. Koenen, Het Recht in den Kring van het Gezin. Rotterdam, 1900, pp. 65, 69.

[34] Stanley Hall, Adolescence, II, pp. 649–650, 685, 713 ff., 726 ff.

[35] Korte Beschouwingen over Bloei en Verval der Natiën, Wetensch. Bladen, July, 1904, pp. 117–128.

[36] Zöckler, Die Lehre vom Urstand des Menschen. Gütersloh, 1879, pp. 140 ff. Orr, God's Image in Man, p. 301.

[37] H. Schurtz, Völkerkunde, 1903, p. 25. Steinmetz, op. c., p. 49. Orr, op. c., p. 186. Zöckler, op. c. 135.

[38] Fr. Ratzel, Völkerkunde, p. I, p. 14.

[39] Ibid.

[40] **Steinmetz**, pp. 45, 54.

[41] **Dilthey**, Einleitung, pp. 38, 39.

[42] **Wundt**, Völkerpsychologie, II, p. 428.

[43] **Gutberlet**, Der Mensch.

[44] **L. Stein**, Der Sinn des Daseins, pp. 220–239.

[45] **G. Ratzenhofer**, Die soziologische Erkenntniss. Leipzig, 1898, p. 125. Comp. **L. Stein**, op. c., p. 226.

[46] In **L. Stein**, op. c., pp. 227 ff.

[47] **Dr. Joseph Müller**, Das sexuelle Leben der Naturvölker.[8] Leipzig, 1906.

[48] **Schmoller**, Grundriss der allgem. Volkswirtschaftslehre. Leipzig, 1901, I, p. 122; II, p. 654.

[49] **Steinmetz**, op. c., p. 54.

[50] **Wundt**, Völkerpsychologie, II, 1. Leipzig, 1905, pp. 64, 85, 335. II, 2, p. 165. Id., Vorlesungen über die Menschen und Tierseele,[4] 1906, p. 17. **Fr. Ratzel**, Völkerkunde, I, p. 13. **Gwatkin**, The Knowledge of God, I, pp. 253 ff. **Reinke**, Die Natur und Wir. 1908, p. 84.

[51] **Wundt**, Völkerpsychologie, II, 2, p. 165. **Gutberlet**, Der Mensch., pp. 398 ff.

[52] **Troeltsch**, Die Christ. Religion, in Die Kultur der Gegenwart, p. 483.

[53] **Schroeder** in Beiträge zur Weiterentw. der Christl. Religion, 1905, p. 8. **Tiele**, Inleiding, II, pp. 108, 202, 204. **H. de Vries**, Afstammings- en Mutatieleer, p. 36.

[54] **Garvie**, art. Revelation, in Hasting's Dictionary of the Bible.

[55] Comp. the author's address: Christelijke Wetenschap, 1904, pp. 73 ff. **Bertholet**, Religion und Geisteskultur, II, pp. 1 ff.

[56] **Flournoy**, Les Principes de la Psychologie religieuse. Genève, 1903, pp. 8, 9. **James**, The Varieties of Religious Experience, pp. 26, 27.

[57] Comp. the author's Psychologie der Religie. Versl. en Meded. der Kon. Ak. v. Wet., Afd. Lett., 1907, pp. 1–32.

[58] **Troeltsch**, op. c., p. 481.

[59] **Tiele**, Inleiding, I, p. 61; II, pp. 66, 110, 214, 215.

[60] **Dilthey**, Einl. in die Geisteswiss., pp. 167 ff.

[61] **Tiele,** Inleiding, II, pp. 64 ff.

[62] Ibid., p. 65.

[63] Ibid.

[64] **Pierson,** Gods Wondermacht en ons Geestelijk Leven. 1867, p. 42. **W. Sanday,** The Life of Christ in Recent Research. Oxford, 1907, pp. 204 ff. The Nature of Prayer, by the Rev. **Lyman Abbott, Moncure D. Conway,** the Rev. Dr. **W. R. Huntingdon,** North American Review, Nov., 1907, pp. 337–348.

[65] **Ch. de la Saussaye,** Lehrbuch der Religionsgeschichte, I,[8] 1905, p. 6.

[66] **Bethe,** Mythus, Sage, Märchen. Leipzig, 1905, pp. 43, 44.

[67] **R. C. Boer,** Heldensage en Mythologie, Gids, Jan., 1907, p. 84. Comp. also **Steinthal,** Zu Bibel und Religionsphilos., pp. 127, 150. **Dilthey,** Einl., pp. 169, 171, 174 ff., 178. **Wundt,** Völkerpsych., II, pp. 551 ff. De historische achtergrond der Europeesche sprookjeswereld, Wet. Bladen, July, 1908, pp. 1–16, after an article by **A. S. Herbert,** in The Nineteenth Century, Febr., 1908.

[68] **J. G. Frazer,** The Golden Bough. Comp. **Ladd,** I, pp. 144 ff.

[69] **Preuss,** Der Ursprung der Religion und Kunst, Globus Bd. 86, 87, p. 249.

[70] **Tiele,** Inl., II, 120. **Ladd,** I, pp. 103, 144. **Gwatkin,** The Knowledge of God, I, pp. 249, 252, 263.

[71] **Jeremias,** Die Panbabylonisten. Leipzig, 1907, p. 17.

[72] **Bethe,** op. c., p. 40.

[73] **Dilthey,** Einl., pp. 178 ff.

VII

REVELATION AND CHRISTIANITY

[1] **Clemens Alex.,** Stromata, I, 5; VI, 8.

[2] **Augustinus,** de Civ., VIII, 9–12; de Doctr. Chr., II, p. 40. Retract., I, 3.

[3] **Lactantius,** Inst., VII, 7, 22.

[4] **Willmann,** Geschichte des Idealismus, I, 1894, pp. 14 ff.; II, pp. 23 ff. **Mausbach,** Christentum und Weltmoral.[2] Munster, 1905, pp. 9 ff.

[5] **Willmann,** Gesch. des Ideal., III, pp. 763 ff.

[6] **A. Stöckl,** Lehrbuch der Philos., I, 1887, pp. 406 ff.

[7] **Schurtz,** Urgeschichte der Kultur, pp. 298 ff. **Ulrich Wendt,** Die Technik als Kulturmacht. Berlin, 1906.

[8] **Schurtz,** op. c., p. 441. **S. Müller,** Urgeschichte Europas, Grundzüge einer prähist. Archaeologie. Strassburg, 1905, p. 40. **J. Guibert,** Les origines.⁴ Paris, 1905, p. 348. **C. W. Vollgraff,** Over den oorsprong onzer Europeesche beschaving. Gids, Dec., 1905.

[9] **S. Müller,** op. c., p. 19.

[10] Ibid., p. 21.

[11] Ibid., p. 22.

[12] Ibid., p. 24.

[13] Ibid., p. 3. Comp. also pp. 25, 26, 28, 29.

[14] **L. Reinhardt,** Der Mensch zur Eiszeit in Europa. 1906, p. 249.

[15] **Holwerda,** in Ch. de la Saussaye, Lehrbuch der Religionsgeschichte, II,³ p. 245.

[16] **S. Müller,** op. c. pp. 49–52.

[17] Ibid. pp. 30 ff.

[18] **Willmann,** Gesch. des Ideal., I, pp. 2 ff.

[19] **Dilthey,** Einl., pp. 184 ff. **Karl Joël,** Der Ursprung der Naturphilosophie aus dem Geiste der Mystik. Basel, 1903. **Willmann,** Gesch. des Ideal., I, pp. 1 ff., 33 ff., 142 ff. **R. H. Woltjer,** Het mystiekreligieuse Element in de Grieksche Philologie. Leiden, 1905.

[20] **D. Gath Whitley,** What was the Primitive Condition of Man? The Princeton Theol. Review, Oct., 1906, pp. 513–534.

[21] **O. Weber,** Theologie und Assyriologie im Streite um Babel und Bibel. 1904, p. 17. Comp. **Tiele,** Inl., II, p. 220. **Winckler,** Religionsgesch. und gesch. Orient. Leipzig, 1906, p. 9. Id., Die Babylon. Geisteskultur. Leipzig, 1907, pp. 18 ff.

[22] **H. H. Kuyper,** Evolutie of Revelatie, Amsterdam, 1903, and the literature there quoted. **Felix Stähelin,** Probleme der Israël., Geschichte. Basel, 1907.

[23] **Steinmetz,** De Studie der Volkenkunde, pp. 36, 37, 39.

[24] **Richthofen,** in **Jeremias,** Die Panbabylonisten. Leipzig, 1907, p. 15.

[25] **Winkler**, Religionsgesch. und gesch., Orient, pp. 7, 8, 9, 17, 33. Id., Die Weltanschauung des alten Orients, p. 4. Id., Die Babyl. Geisteskultur, pp. 6, 47, 48.

[26] **A. Bastian**, Der Völkergedanke im Aufbau einer Wissenschaft vom Menschen. Leipzig, 1881. Cf. **Gumplovicz** Grundriss der Soziologie, pp. 27 ff.

[27] As regards language comp., **Fritz Mauthner**, Die Sprache. Frankfurt a. M., pp. 45 ff.

[28] **Wundt**, Völkerpsych., II, 1, p. 570.

[29] **Wundt**, op. c., II, pp. 343, 571.

[30] **G. F. Wright**, Scientific Confirmations of Old Testament History, Oberlin, 1906.

[31] **Wundt**, op. c., pp. 342, 570.

[32] **Jeremias**, Die Panbabylonisten., pp. 15, 16.

[33] See note 44 of Lecture IV.

[34] **Andrew Lang**, Magic and Religion, p. 224, in Ladd, I, p. 153. **Waitz**, Anthropologie der Naturvölker. 1860, II, pp. 168 ff. **C. von Orelli**, Allg. Religionsgesch., pp. 39, 745, 775 ff. Id., Die Eigenart der bibl. Religion. 1906, pp. 11, 12. **Schroeder**, in Beiträge zur Weiterentw. der Chr. Rel. 1905, pp. 1 ff. **Jeremias**, Monoth. Strömungen innerhalb der Babylon. Religion., 1904. **Baentsch**, Monoth. Strömungen und der Monoth. Israëls., 1907. **Gloatz**, Die vermutlichen Religionsanfänge und der Monoth., Religion und Geisteskultur, 1907, pp. 137–143. **Söderblom**, Die Allväter der Primitiven, ib., 1907, pp. 315–322. **Lehmann**, in : Die Kultur der Gegenwart I, III, p. 26.

[35] **James**, Pragmatism, pp. 165, 169, 170, 171, 181 ff.

[36] **Willmann**, Gesch. des Ideal., I., pp. 119 ff.

[37] **Jeremias**, Monoth. Strömungen innerhalb der Babyl. Religion, 1904, p. 8.

[38] **O. Weber**, Theol. und Assyriologie, 1904, p. 4.

[39] Gen. 14 : 18–20, 20 : 3 ff., 21 : 22 ff., 23 : 6, 24 : 50, 26 : 19, 40 : 8, etc. Comp. also **Dr. M. Peisker**, Die Beziehungen der Nicht-Israëliten zu Jahve, nach der Anschauung der altt. Quellen. Giessen, 1907.

[40] Joz. 24 : 2, 14, 15; Deut. 26 : 5, etc.

[41] **Ed. König**, Schlaglichter auf dem Babel-Bibelstreit. Beweis des Glaubens, 1905, pp. 3–23.

[42] **Biesterveld**, De jongste Methode voor de Verklaring van het Nieuwe Testament, 1905.

[43] **Willmann**, Gesch. des Ideal., II., pp. 12 ff., 20 ff.

[44] **Giesebrecht**, Die Geschichtlichkeit des Sinaibundes. Königsberg, 1900. **Lotz**, Der Bund vom Sinai., Neue Kirchl. Zeits., 1901.

[45] Jer. 51: 7, Comp. **Fr. Delizsch**, Mehr Licht. 1907, p. 45.

[46] **Köberle**, Oriental. Mythologie und Bibl. Religion, Neue Kirchl. Zeits., 1906, pp. 838–859. **Ed. König**, Altorient. Weltanschauung und Altes Test. Berlin, 1905.

VIII

REVELATION AND RELIGIOUS EXPERIENCE

[1] Comp., e. g., **Otto Pautz**, Mohammeds Lehre von der Offenbarung. Leipzig, 1898.

[2] **Frederic W. H. Myers**, Human Personality and its Survival of Bodily Death. Ed. and abridged by his son, L. H. Myers, 1907, p. 2.

[3] Ibid., p. 3.

[4] **Kant** gave to his Allgemeine Naturgeschichte und Theorie des Himmels, 1755, the sub-title of Versuch von der Verfassung und dem mechanischen Ursprung des ganzen Weltgebäudes nach Newtonschen Grundsätzen abgehandelt.

[5] **Troeltsch**, Die Absolutheit des Christ. und die Religionsgesch., 1902. **Bernoulli**, Die wissenschaftliche und die kirchliche Methode in der Theologie. Freiburg, 1897. **Gross.** Glaube, Theologie und Kirche. Tübingen, 1902. **Rade**, Zeits. fur Theol. und Kirche, 1900, pp. 80 ff.; 1901, pp. 429 ff.

[6] **G.** Berguer, L'Application de la Methode scientifique à la Théologie. Genève, 1903.

[7] **Ritschl**, Rechtf. und Versöhnung, II,[2] p. 12.

[8] **Bachmann**, Zur Würdigung des religiösen Erlebens, Neue Kirchl. Zeits., Dec.; 1907, pp. 907–931.

[9] **Schleiermacher, Ritschl, Herrmann, Harnack, Schian**, one and all, connect Christian experience in some way or other

with the Person of Christ and the revelation given us by God in him.

[10] **Bachmann**, l. c.

[11] **Mulert**, Zeits. f. Theol. und Kirche., Jan., 1907, pp. 63, 436.

[12] **James**, The Varieties of Religious Experience, p. 506.

[18] **Troeltsch**, Psychologie und Erkenntnisstheorie in der Religionswissenschaft. Tübingen, 1905. **Scheel**, Zeits. f. Theol. u. K., 1907, pp. 149-150, 305-307. Id., Die moderne Religionspsych., ib. 1908, pp. 1-38.

[14] **G. A. Coe**, The Spiritual Life, 1903, pp. 23-27.

[15] **E. D. Starbuck**, The Psychology of Religion, 1901, pp. 143-153.

[16] **Starbuck**, pp. 28 ff. **Coe**, pp. 29, 40 ff. **Stanley Hall**, Adolescence, I, pp. 411 ff.; II, pp. 95 ff.; 288 ff.

[17] **James**, Varieties, pp. 178 ff., 195, 196, 201 ff. **Starbuck**, op. c., pp. 101-117. **Alfred Binet**, Les Altérations de la Personalité.[2] Paris, 1902.

[18] **James**, Varieties, pp. 3, 6, 29, 30, 486. **Flournoy**, Les principes de la psych. relig. 1903, pp. 16, 17. **Murisier**, Les maladies du sentiment religieux.[2] Paris, 1903, préface, p. viii.

[19] **James**, op. c., pp. 135, 163, 325, 430.

[20] **James**, op. c., pp. 333, 374, 487, 506, 507.

[21] **James**, op. c., pp. 122, 131-133, 525, 526 Comp. Lecture IV, note 44.

[22] **Schian**, Der Einfluss der Individualität auf Glaubensgesinnung und Glaubensgestaltung, Zeits. für Theol. und Kirche, 1897, pp. 513 ff. Id., Glaube und Individualität, id. 1898, pp. 170-194.

[23] **Pfister**, Das Elend unserer wissensch. Glaubenslehre, Schweizer. theol. Zeits., 1905, pp. 209 ff. **Häberlin**, Ist die Theologie eine Wissenschaft ? ib. 1906, pp. 17 ff.

[24] **Herrmann**, Christ. Protest. Dogmatik, pp. 583-632 of Die Christl. Religion, in Die Kultur der Gegenwart. Id., Die Lage und Aufgabe der evang. Dogm. in der Gegenwart, Zeits. für Theol. und Kirche, 1907, pp. 315, 351. Id., Die Altorthodoxie und unser Verständniss der Religion, ib. Jan.,

1908, pp. 74–77. Comp. **C. Wistar Hodge**, The Idea of Dogmatic Theology, The Princeton Theol. Review, Jan., 1908.

[25] Comp. **Walther**, Eine neue Theorie über das Wesen der Religion, Religion und Geisteskultur, 1907, 3, pp. 201–217. **Bruining**, Over de Methode van onze Dogmatiek, Teylers Theol. Tijdschr., 1902, 2, pp. 175 ff.

[26] By way of example we name : **F. J. Schmidt**, Zur Wiedergeburt des Idealismus. Leipzig, 1908. **Dorner**, Die Bedeutung der spekulativen Theologie für die Gegenwart, Die Studierstube, 1907, pp. 193–207. **McTaggart**, Some Dogmas of Religion, pp. 1–12.

[27] **C. Stumpf**, Die Wiedergeburt der Philosophie. Leipzig, 1908, especially pp. 23 ff.

[28] **Max Dessoir**, Das Doppel-Ich. Leipzig, 1896, p. 80.

[29] **Höffer**, Grundlehren der Psychologie.[2] Wien, 1905, p. 108.

[30] **Coe**, The Spiritual Life, p. 93.

[31] **Max Dessoir**, op. c., p. 77.

[32] **Möbius**, Die Hoffnungslosigkeit aller Psychologie. Halle, 1907, p. 56.

[33] **Schmidt**, Zur Wiedergeburt des Idealismus, p. 96.

[34] Comp. the preëxistenceism of **McTaggart**, Some Dogmas of Religion, pp. 112 ff. **Myers**, Human Personality, p. 26.

[35] **Bennett**, La société Anglo-américaine pour les recherches psychiques. Trad. de M. Sage. Paris, 1904.

[36] **Myers**, Human Personality, p. 16.

[37] As to the dangers for body and soul comp. **Zeehandelaar**, Het spiritistisch Gevaar, Gids, Aug., 1907. **Traub**, in **Kalb**, Kirchen und Sekten der Gegenwart. Stuttgart, 1905, pp. 437 ff., 448, 460. **Coe**, The Spiritual Life, pp. 169 ff. **Joseph Hamilton**, The Spirit World, 1906, p. 264.

[38] **Traub** in **Kalb**, op. c., p. 449 ff.

[39] **Myers**, Human Personality, pp. 1 ff., 8, 24, 340 ff.

[40] **Traub**, l. c. 449 ff.

[41] **Harnack**, Die Aufgabe der theol. Fakultäten und die allgemeine Religionsgesch., 1901.

[42] **J. Kaftan**, Die Wahrheit der christl. Religion. Basel, 1888, pp. 266 ff., 318, 319.

[43] **Troeltsch**, Der Begriff des Glaubens, Religion und Geisteskultur, 1907, 3, pp. 191–221.

[44] **G. Vos**, Christian Faith and the Truthfulness of Bible
History, The Princeton Theol. Review, July, 1906, pp. 289–
305. **Troeltsch**, Glaube und Geschichte, Religion und Geisteskultur, 1908, pp. 29–39. **R. Eucken**, Hauptprobleme der
Religionsphilos. der Gegenwart.[2] Berlin, 1907, p. 38 : Religion und Geschichte.

[45] E. g. **Ed. von Hartmann**, Die Krisis des Christenthums
in der modernen Theologie. Berlin, 1880, pp. 1 ff.

[46] **W. von Schnehen**, Der moderne Jesuskultus. Frank-
fort a. M., 1906. **O. Pfleiderer**, Der moderne Jesuskultus,
Protest. Monatshefte, 1906, No. 5.

[47] **Henry W. Clark**, The Philosophy of Christian Experience. Edinburgh, 1905, pp. 75 ff.

[48] Comp. the well-known saying of Emerson : "The less we
have to do with our sins the better," and further, **Ph. Vivian**,
The Churches and Modern Thought,[2] 1907, pp. 208 ff. ; **F. R.
Tennant**, The Origin and Propagation of Sin.[2] Cambridge,
1906. **W. R. Inge**, Personal Idealism and Mysticism, 1907,
p. 171. **Lodge**, The Substance of Faith,[3] pp. 46 ff. Comp.
John M. Edwards, The Vanishing Sense of Sin, Presb. and
Ref. Review, Oct., 1899, pp. 606–616.

[49] Thus **Lubbock, Lombroso, Bagehot**. Comp. **Wynaendts
Francken**, Sociale Vertoogen. Haarlem, 1907, pp. 245 ff.

[50] **Corre** in **R. P. Mees**, Wetenschappelijke Karakterkennis.
's Gravenh., 1907, p. 63.

[51] In **James**, Varieties, p. 63.

[52] **Stanley Hall**, Adol., II, p. 72.

[53] **Henry Scott Holland**, Vital Values, pp. 107–110.

[54] **Höfler**, Grundlehren der Psychologie.[2] 1905, p. 108.

[55] **Joh. Herzog**, Der Begriff der Bekehrung. Giessen, 1903,
pp. 21 ff. **Jacques de la Combe**, Les nouveau nés de l'Esprit.
Paris, 1905, pp. 133 ff.

[56] **John W. Diggle**, Short Studies in Holiness. London,
1900, pp. 47 ff.

[57] **Starbuck**, Psychol. of Religion, pp. 85, 108, 158.

[58] **James**, Varieties, pp. 78–126, 127–165.

[59] Joh. **Herzog**, op. c., p. 103.

[60] Ibid., pp. 99 ff.

[61] **James**, Varieties, pp. 196 ff., 242–270. **Coe**, The Spiritual Life, p. 144.

[62] **James**, op. c., pp. 178 ff., 201, 203.

[63] **James**, op. c., pp. 78 ff.

[64] **James**, op. c. pp. 162, 374, 377, 487.

[65] Heidelberg Catechism, questions 88–90. Comp. **Gennrich**, Die Lehre von der Wiedergeburt, die Christl. Zentrallehre in dogmengesch. u. religionsgesch. Beleuchtung. Leipzig, 1907.

[66] John W. **Diggle**, op. c., pp. 25 ff.

[67] **Stanley Hall**, Adolescence II, p. 86.

[68] **James**, Varieties, p. 163.

[69] See above, note 61.

[70] **James**, Varieties, pp. 230 ff., 270, 501, 520 ff.

[71] **James**, op. c., pp. 433, 513–525.

[72] The operation of a supernatural factor in the subliminal consciousness is denied by **Peirce**, **Jastrow**, **Stanley Hall** (Adol., I, preface, II, p. 43), over against **Myers** and **James**.

[73] **Forsyth**, The Distinctive Thing in Christian Experience, Hibbert Journal, April, 1908, pp. 481 ff.

[74] **Sabatier**, Les Religions d'Autorité et la Religion de l'Esprit. Paris, 1904.

[75] **Seeberg**, Grundwahrheiten der Chr. Religion. Leipzig, 1903, pp. 11–37.

IX

REVELATION AND CULTURE

[1] In Joh. **Herzog**, Der Begriff der Bekehrung, p. 19.

[2] **Harnack**, Mission und Ausbreitung des Christentums in den ersten drei Jahrhunderten,[2] I, pp. 185–197. **Sell**, Katholiz. und Protest. Leipzig, 1908, pp. 24, 103 ff.

[3] **Harnack**, Das Mönchtum, seine Ideale und seine Geschichte.[2] Giessen, 1886. **Zöckler**, Askese und Mönchtum. Frankfurt a. M., 1897.

[4] **P. Höveler,** Prof. **A. Harnack** und die katholische Askese. Düsseldorf, 1902.

[5] **E. g.** The True History of Joshua Davidson, Communist. 1873 (2 ed.: The Life of Joshua Davidson, by E. Lynn Linton, 1889). **Sheldon,** In his Steps : or "What Would Jesus Do?" Chicago, 1897, Rev. ed. 1899. Comp. also **Hall Caine,** The Christian, and **Marie Corelli,** The Master-Christian.

[6] **Tolstoi,** Worin besteht mein Glaube ? 1885.

[7] **Weinel,** Jesus im neunzehnten Jahrh. Tübingen, 1903. **Schweitzer,** Von Reimarus zu Wrede. Tübingen, 1906. **W. Sanday,** The Life of Christ in Recent Research. Oxford, 1907.

[8] **W. Baldensperger,** Das Selbstbewusstsein Jesu im Lichte der messian. Hoffnungen seiner Zeit I.[3] Strassburg, 1903. **J. Weiss,** Die Predigt Jesu vom Reiche Gottes.[2] Göttingen, 1900.

[9] The literature which deals with Jesus in this spirit is increasing daily; witness such works as the following : **Kalthoff,** Das Christusproblem, Grundlinien zu einer Sozialtheologie.[2] Leipzig, 1903. **Pfleiderer,** Das Christusbild des urchristl. Glaubens in religionsgesch. Beleuchtung. Berlin, 1903. **Paul Wernle,** Die Anfänge unserer Religion,[2] 1904. **W. B. Smith,** Der vorchristl. Jesus nebst weiteren Vorstudien zur Entstehungsgesch. des Urchrist. Mit einem Vorwort von P. W. Schmiedel. Giessen, 1906. **Th. J. Plange,** Christus ein Inder ? Stuttgart, 1907. **Dr. de Loosten,** Jesus Christus vom Standpunkte des Psychiaters. Bamberg, 1905. **E. Rasmussen,** Jesus, eine vergleichende psychopathol. Studie. Leipzig, 1905. **Binet-Sangle,** La Folie de Jésus. Paris, 1908. **Arthur Heulhard,** Le mensonge Chrétien (Jésus-Christ n'a pas existé), I. Le Charpentier. Paris, 1908. **Bolland,** Het Leven en Sterven van Jezus Christus, 1907.

[10] Thus among others **Mill** On Liberty, chap. 2. **Theob. Ziegler,** Gesch. der christl. Ethik, I, pp. 62 ff. **Paulsen,** System der Ethik, pp. 50 ff. **Strauss,** Der alte und der neue Glaube.[2] 1872, pp. 57 ff. **Ed. von Hartmann,** Das Christentum des N. Testam. 1905. Vorwort, etc.

[11] **Nitzsch,** Die Weltanschauung Fr. Nietzsche's, Zeits. für Theol. und Kirche. 1905, pp. 344360.

[12] **Lexis**, Das Wesen der Kultur, in Die Kultur der Gegenwart I. **Eucken**, Geistige Strömungen, 1904, pp. 226 ff.

[13] Compare the contrasts drawn by **Forsyth** between the Reformation and the "Enlightenment," Hibbert Journal, April, 1908, pp. 482 ff.

[14] Comp. the Pensées of **Pascal**.

[15] **Haeckel**, Welträthsel, p. 439, and above, Lect. I.

[16] Comp. Lectures: I, note 2; VI, note 7; VII, note 19.

[17] **Portig**, Religion und Kunst in ihrem gegenseitigen Verhältniss. Iserlohn, 1879.

[18] **Eisler**, Kritische Einführung in die Philosophie. Berlin, 1905, p. 297.

[19] **Ernst Linde**, Religion und Kunst. Tübingen, 1905.

[20] **Gutberlet**, Ethik und Religion. **Kneib**, Die Jenseitsmoral, pp. 239 ff.

[21] **Eisler**, Krit. Einführung, p. 297.

[22] Ibid. p. 302.

[23] Ibid. p. 292. **Stange**, Der heteronome Character der christlichen Ethik, Neue Kirchl. Zeits. June, 1908, pp. 454–473.

[24] Ibid. pp. 312 ff., 324, 330 ff., 334.

[25] Comp. Lecture I, note 27; Lecture VI, note 60.

[26] **A. Ehrhard** Kathol. Christentum und moderne Kultur. Mainz, 1906. **E W. Mayer**, Christentum und Kultur. Berlin, 1905.

X

REVELATION AND THE FUTURE

[1] **Carneri**, Der moderne Mensch., Volksausgabe. Stuttgart, p. xi.

[2] **H. D. Lloyd**, Man the Social Creator. London, 1908, p. 3.

[3] **Ellen Key**, Das Jahrhundert des Kindes. Berlin, 1902, p. 358.

[4] **Lloyd**, op. c., pp. 12, 13.

[5] **Jeruzalem**, Gedanken und Denker. 1905, pp. 133–148.

[6] **L. Stein**, Der Sinn des Daseins. 1904, p. 15.

[7] **Proudhon**, Philosophie du Progrès. Bruxelles, 1853, pp. 20, 24, 25.

[8] **Stanley Hall**, Adol., I, pp. 131.

[9] **Proudhon**, op. c., pp. 25, 19, 156.

[10] **G. Portig**, Das Weltgesetz des kleinsten Kraftanwandes in den Reichen der Natur. 1903–1904.

[11] **E. Key**, Das Jahrh. des Kindes., pp. 322, 3–5.

[12] In **Fr. Galton**, Probability, the Foundation of Eugenics. The Herbert Spencer Lecture Delivered on June 5, 1907, p. 10.

[13] **E. Key**, op. c., p. 2. **Stanley Hall**, Adol., II, p. 123.

[14] **Galton**, op. c., **Stanley Hall**, Adol., II, p. 722. **Lankester**, Natur und Mensch, pp. 44, 49. **Ludwig Wilser**, Rassentheorien. Stuttgart, 1908. **Wynaendts Franken**, Sociale Vertoogen. Haarlem, 1907, pp. 1–46. **H. Treub**, Verspreide Opstellen. Haarlem, 1904. **Nijhoff**, De Noodzakelijkheid van geneeskundig Onderzoek vóór het Huwelijk. Rotterdam, 1908.

[15] **Stanley Hall**, Adol., II, pp. 561 ff. **Ellen Key**, op. c., p. 86, 253. **Louise Stratenus**, Het Kind., pp. 128, 336.

[16] **Stanley Hall**, op. c., I, p. ix; II, p. 55.

[17] **Stanley Hall**, op. c., I, p. viii; II, pp. 62, 69.

[18] **Ellen Key**, p. 293. **Stanley Hall**, I, pp. 168 ff.

[19] **Ellen Key**, pp. 110 ff. 181. **Louise Stratenus**, Het Kind., p. 103. **Stanley Hall**, II, p. 497. **Lodge**, Literary World, Aug., 1907, p. 380;

[20] **Stanley Hall**, I, pp. 131 ff., 170 ff. II, pp. 40 ff., 58 ff., 204 ff.

[21] **Stanley Hall**, II, pp. 153 ff. **Lankester**, Natur und Mensch, pp. 56, 66. **Mach**, Popular-wissensch. Vorlesungen. Leipzig, 1896 (last lecture). **Lehmann-Hohenberg**, Naturwissenschaft und Bibel. Jena, 1904, pp. 5, 45, 55, etc.

[22] The Socialistic literature is sufficiently well-known. Comp. only **H. D. Lloyd**, op. c. **H. G. Wells**, New Worlds for Old. London, 1908. **R. J. Campbell**, Christianity and the Social Order. London, 1907. A series of articles on The New Socialism, an Impartial Inquiry, in the British Weekly, 1908.

[23] **Woltmann**, Der histor. Materialismus, pp. 418–430. **Weisengrün**, Das Ende des Marxismus.[2] Leipzig, 1899. **Ed.**

Bernstein, Wie ist wissensch. Socialismus möglich? Berlin, 1901.

[24] **Paul Kleinert,** Die Profeten Israëls in sozialer Beziehung. Leipzig, 1905, p. 27.

[25] **Bebel,** Die Frau, 16e Aufl. 1892, pp. 263 ff.

[26] **Gumplovicz,** Grundriss der Soziologie,[2] p. 361.

[27] **L. Stein,** An der Wende des Jahrh., p. 332. Id., Der Sinn des Daseins, pp. 149 ff.

[28] **Metschnikoff,** Beiträge zu einer optimistischen Weltauffassung. Deutsch von Michalsky. München, 1908.

[29] **Stanley Hall,** Adol., I, pp. viii, xviii.

[30] **James,** Pragmatism, pp. 243 ff.

[31] Comp. also **Proudhon,** Philos. du Progrès, p. 65. **H. D. Lloyd,** op. c. p. 12.

[32] Comp. **Paul Kalweit,** Religion und Philos. Idealismus, Religion und Geisteskultur, II, 1908, pp. 44–60.

[33] **Paulsen,** Ethik, in Die Kultur der Gegenwart, System. Philos., p. 309. **Haering,** Das Christliche Leben,[2] 1907, pp. 104 ff. **Külpe,** Einl. in die Philos.[4] 1907, p.332. **Külpe,** here declares : ''No immanent definition of the supreme good can possess more than relative character; the positing of a transcendental goal alone (which as such is inaccessible to scientific ethics) satisfies the idea of an ultimate, supreme, absolute value.'' Comp. also **C. Fraser,** Our Final Venture, Hibbert Journal, Jan., 1907, and **G. F. Barbour,** Progress and Reality, Hibbert Journal, Oct., 1907.

[34] **Lankester,** Natur und Mensch, p. 26.

[35] **Gust. Le Bon,** Psychologie du Socialisme. Paris, 1902. **Ed. Dolléans,** Le Caractère religieux du Socialisme. Paris, 1906. **Diepenhorst,** Naast het Kruis de roode Vaan., Amst., p.46.

[36] **Lloyd,** op. c. pp. 6 ff. **Stanley Hall,** Adol., I, pp. 546 ff. ; II, p. 123.

[37] **Bruno Wille,** Darwins Lebensanschauung, p. 6.

[38] **Stanley Hall,** Adol., I, p. viii ; II, pp. 63–64.

[39] Comp. **Jos. Royce,** Immortality, Hibbert Journal, July, 1907. **Sir Oliver Lodge,** The Immortality of the Soul, ib., Jan., April, 1908. **Eucken,** The Problem of Immortality, ib., July, Jan., 1908.

[40] For example, **William Crookes, Alfred Wallace, Sir Oliver Lodge, Fred. W. H. Myers** in England, **Fechner, Zöllner, Carl du Prel** in Germany, **Hartogh Heys van Zouteveen** in Holland.

[41] For example, **McTaggart,** Some Dogmas of Religion, pp. 112 ff.

[42] Comp. **W. Bruhn,** Theosophie und Theologie. Glückstadt, 1907.

[43] **Schelling,** Philos. der Offenbarung, p. 365. **Liebmann,** Analysis der Wirklichkeit, pp. 398 ff.

[44] **Bruno-Wille,** Darwins Lebensanschauung, p. 6. **Ed. von Hartmann,** Die Weltanschauung der modernen Physik, p. 33. **Otto,** Natur und relig. Weltansicht, p. 47. **J. Ude,** Monist. oder Teleolog. Weltanschauung. Graz, 1907. **J. C. Snijders,** De Ondergang der Wereld, Tijdspiegel, Oct., 1907. **Fridtjof Nansen,** Hibbert Journal, July, 1908, pp. 748 ff.

[45] **Höffdign** in **Paul Kalweit,** Religion und Geisteskultur, 1908 pp. 44 ff.; in **Lodge,** Hibbert Journal, April, 1908, p. 565, and **Barbour,** ib., Oct., 1907, pp. 59 ff. **Münsterberg** in **Royce,** ib., July, 1907, pp. 724 ff.

[46] About Schopenhauer's Nirvana comp. **J. de Jager,** De Beteekenis van Schopenhauers Pessimisme, Gids, Nov. 1907.

[47] **J. Kaftan,** Aus der Werkstätte des Uebermenschen, Deutsche Rundschau., Oct. and Nov., 1905. **George S. Patton,** Beyond Good and Evil, The Princeton Theol. Review, July, 1908, pp. 392–436, especially pp. 430 ff. On the idea of an endless return of things, comp. **Zeller,** Die Philos. der Griechen,[3] III, pp. 154 ff. Further, **Gumplovicz,** Soziologie, pp. 158, 166 ff., 348 ff. **Arrhenius,** Die Vorstellung vom Weltgebäude im Wandel der Zeiten. Das Werden der Welten, 1907.

[48] Comp. also **Ostwald,** Biologie en Chemie, Wet. Bladen, Dec. 1904, pp. 420–443.

[49] **Ostwald,** Naturphilos., Syst. Philos. in Die Kultur der Gegegenwart, pp. 170–171.

[50] Thus, in agreement with **Huxley, Romanes, James,** also **Siebeck,** Der Fortschritt der Menschheit, in Zur Religionsphilosophie. Tübingen, 1907.

[52] **Hieron. Lorm,** Der grundlose Optimismus, in **Jeruzalem,**

Gedanken und Denker, pp. 156–163. **L. Stein,** An der Wende
des Jahrh., p. 54. Der Sinn des Daseins, p. 76. Comp. an
address by **Dr. D. G. Jelgersma** on, Is de Geschiedenis der
Philosophie meer dan eene Geschiedenis van menschelijke
Dwalingen? Handelsblad, Oct. 33, 1907. Also **Topinard** in
Philip Vivian. The Churches and Modern Thought. London,
1907, pp. 266 ff.

[53] **Prof. H. van Embden** expressed himself to this effect in a
discussion with Prof. Aengenent, Handelsblad, Nov. 28, 1907.

[54] **James,** Varieties, pp. 136 ff.

[55] **Joh. Jüngst,** Kultus- und Geschichts-religion (Pelagian-
ismus und Augustinismus). Ein Beitr. zur relig. Psych. und
Volkskunde. Giessen, 1901.

[56] **Berthelot,** Science et Morale. Paris, 1897. **Ladenburg,**
Der Einfluss der Naturwiss. auf die Weltanschauung, 1903.

[57] Comp. Lect. VI. note 33.

[58] E. g. **Max Weber,** Die Protestantische Ethik und der
"Geist" des Kapitalismus, Archiv. f. Sozialwiss. und Sozialpolitik, XX pp. 1 ff. XXI pp. 1 ff. He concludes his important survey with the question whether culture is to
issue in this, that men become "professionals without spirit,
pleasure-seekers without heart; non-entities of this sort
pride themselves on having mounted to a previously un-
attained stage of culture."

[59] **Paulsen,** Parteipolitik und Moral. Dresden, 1900. **Valck-
enaer Kips,** Tijdspiegel, March, 1908.

[60] **Dr. D. van Embden,** Darwinisme en Democratie. Maatsch.
Vooruitgang en de Hulp aan het Zwakke. 's Gravenhage,1901.

[61] **J. St. Loe Strachey,** Problems and Perils of Socialism.
London, 1908. Comp. Handelsblad, April 12, 1901, Avond-
blad 2, on an essay by **R. Ehrenberg,** Over het Ontstaan en
de Beteekenis van groote Vermogens, and **Ammon,** Die Gesellschaftsordnung und ihre natürlichen Grundlagen, 1895–1900.

[62] **Van Deyssel,** Prozastukken, 1895, pp. 43 ff., 277 ff. **Karl
Bleibtreu,** Die Vertreter des Jahrh. Berlin, 1904, II,
pp. 260–303. **W. His,** Medizin und Ueberkultur. Leipzig, 1908.
Gérard, Civilization in Danger, Hibbert Journal, July, 1908.

[63] **Steinmetz,** De Rassenquaestie, Gids, Jan. 1907.

[64] **L. Stein,** An der Wende des Jahrh., pp. 348 ff.

[65] **Steinmetz,** Die Philosophie des Krieges. Leipzig, 1907.

[66] Thus also **Ruskin,** who declared that he had always observed that all great nations acquired their power of resistance and mental vigor in war, that war has instructed, peace has deceived them; war has schooled them, peace led them astray, in a word that war has made and peace has unmade them.

[67] **Gumplovicz,** Soziologie pp. 158–166 ff., 348.

[68] Ibid. pp. 350, 352, 354. **A. J. Balfour,** Decadence. Cambridge, 1908, p. 42.

[69] **Balfour,** op. c., p. 48.

[70] **C. Frazer,** Hibbert Journal, Jan., 1907, p. 242.

[71] **C. Frazer,** Philos. of Theism., p. 277. **McTaggart,** Some Dogmas of Religion, p. 114.

[72] **Kant** judged an " Ausgleichung" between virtue and happiness necessary hereafter, and **Paulsen** is of the same opinion, Ethik, in Die Kultur der Gegenwart, System. Philos., pp. 304 ff. Comp. also a paper, with discussion, on Eschatological Expectations in the meeting of Modern Theologians, April 28, 29, 1908.

[73] **Poincaré,** La Valeur de la Science. Paris, 1905, p. 276. Comp. **J. Woltjer,** De Zekerheid der Wetenschap. Amsterdam, 1907.